PROMISE ME
YOU'LL SING
MUD!

PROMISE ME YOU'LL SING *MUD*!

The Autobiography of
IAN WALLACE

JOHN CALDER
LONDON

First published in Great Britain 1975
by John Calder (Publishers) Ltd
18 Brewer Street, London W1R 4AS

ISBN 0 7145 3500 1

Typeset in 11/12 point Baskerville by Gloucester Typesetting Co. Ltd.

Printed in Great Britain by Whitstable Litho, Straker Brothers Ltd.,
Millstrood Road, Whitstable, Kent.

Contents

List of Illustrations

PROMISE ME
YOU'LL SING
MUD!

Dedication

To Pat, Rosie and John who never tempted me to abandon it, to Sarah De Souza for giving it a good start by taking dictation and laughing at the jokes, to David Money for listening to it all, and finally to my Mother for realising my ultimate destination very early on and helping my Father to bow to the inevitable.

If you want to know who we are

(The Mikado)

There was a long silence while my father considered the news I'd just broken to him as gently as I could.

'Well,' he said at last, 'I suppose that's that. If you'd gone to the Bar I could have helped you. If you'd thought of business I could have helped you a great deal, but if you're determined to go on the stage, you'll have to paddle your own canoe.'

Then his face lit up with the sort of smile that had become a rarity since his impending retirement had begun to worry him. It was 1945 and he was seventy-seven. All through the war he had gone, six days a week, to his office in Aldersgate Street in the City of London, often climbing over piles of rubble and fire-hoses to get there. During the 1940 Blitz his offices, along with the Westminster Bank next door and Aldersgate Street Station, now called Barbican, eventually became a miraculously preserved island site completely surrounded by devastation. He seemed quite indifferent to the danger and totally absorbed in his job. His firm made anti-gas clothing, shells and bombs, a tremendous contrast to their peace-time products. From being a sales manager he had become a sort of liaison officer with government departments, staying at his post long after the normal retiring age. Now the war was over and the strain had begun to show. Forgetfulness, irritability over trifles and an obsessive interest in his health were signs that at last he'd surrendered to old age. Then came the day when he was told rather brusquely to fix a date to hand over to his successor. It

9

was unfortunate that I chose this moment to add to his problems; but there's never a good time for bad news.

Like all fathers with an only son, his ambitions for me were high. A successful career as a barrister was to be the springboard from which I would leap into the political arena. My education had been suitable and expensive; now all that lay between me and the glittering prizes of politics and the law were a few dinners at the Inner Temple, two stiff exams and about ten years of back-breaking slog at the wages of an unskilled labourer, all of which I would have to tackle bearing the trifling handicap of an honours degree—third class. He must have been disappointed that I had now scratched from that particular race but he never showed it; yet a similar bomb-shell, delivered to his own father at the same stage in life, would undoubtedly have triggered off an explosion of righteous indignation with a fit of apoplexy definitely on the cards.

Grandfather died long before I was born. My father seldom mentioned him, though he once volunteered that the old man's death at the age of ninety-two was brought on by taking a cold bath in a fit of pique. Evidently my grandmother hadn't heated the water as it wasn't his usual night. Grandfather hotly maintained that it was and decided to prove his stamina by having one anyway. My father's comment on the outcome was

'Serve the old devil right.'

'The old devil' was a Scottish hand-loom weaver. He was born and lived his entire life in Kirkcaldy, a town famous for linoleum and the pleasant odour of boiling linseed oil, which stands on the shores of the Firth of Forth in the kingdom of Fife. His quick temper and intimidating black beard so impressed his employers that they made him foreman of the linen factory where he worked. Using the same assets, he brought up his seven children according to his own strict interpretation of the Christian Faith. His hobby was writing hell-fire sermons with which he regaled his large family—frequently. Over and above they all had to attend the kirk three times every Sunday, and it's a fair bet that there were evening prayers on weekdays into the bargain. Predictably, this stern regime left its mark. Jessie, the eldest, never married and dutifully looked after her parents until they died. She took a fairly grim view of life. As a child I once heard her describe the local picture house as the devil's den. Charlotte married a minister and Robert became a lay preacher. On the other hand my father, whose name was John, never entered a church, except for weddings and funerals, for the last twenty-five years of his life in order, as he explained to me, to put the average right. For my money he was as good a Christian as anyone. I wish I'd met his mother. My father said she was an angel and he wasn't prone to exaggeration.

In 1881 young John Wallace decided the time had come to get a job. He was thirteen years of age. One morning he knocked on every door in the street where he lived starting with Kidd the baker. He was out of luck until right at the far end he came to the offices of Michael Nairn & Company, one of two great rival linoleum works in the town; they started him as office boy at half a crown a week; he stayed for sixty-five years. Long before that time was up he had become an elder statesman of the linoleum industry: not bad going in a family business—when you're not one of the family. His talent was for selling, but he wasn't the fast-talking, back-slapping, sheer force-of-personality type of operator. His gimmick was a transparent honesty that shone from his firm and distinguished features, which were enhanced by a shock of wiry coal-black hair and large bushy eye-brows. In repose his expression had a touch of severity, not lessened by his thick-lensed pince-nez, the legacy of a bad attack of measles in childhood. His striking appearance gained him the nickname 'Lion-face'. People trusted my father, and he usually knew when it was wise to return the compliment.

At the beginning of the century he became Nairn's Newcastle agent. The circle of friends he made on Tyneside set great store by musical evenings in which everyone was expected to take part. Though completely tone deaf, he purchased two popular songs of the period, 'The Trumpeter' and a nautical ballad entitled 'Three For Jack', and gamely embarked on a course of singing lessons with the best teacher in the city. Two months later his unfortunate instructor committed suicide. The reasons that led the poor man to take his life were, of course, nothing to do with my father. However, the melancholy event, and the ribald comments it inevitably drew from his friends, enabled him to withdraw, permanently, from the musical scene.

He often recalled the Sunday evening he came on a Salvation Army street corner service being taken in the pouring rain by a member, who had perhaps seen the light after a life of sin. As my father approached he heard the preacher announce to the small, saturated congregation in rich 'geordie' tones:

'Dearly beloved, owing to the inclement weathergh we'll joost sing three verses of 'Oly, 'Oly, 'Oly and then we'll all boogergh off.'

I never asked him why he didn't marry till he was forty-five. We were never quite on those terms of intimacy. There was a hint of it in his reaction to my engagement.

'A young man should wait until he's earning two thousand a year,' he observed, 'otherwise he's heading for trouble.'

He certainly took his own advice. Still single in his early forties, he became manager of Nairn's Glasgow warehouse and based himself at a hotel in what must then have been a solidly respectable if somewhat dingy neighbourhood mid-way between the delights of Sauchiehall Street and the sluggish, misty River Clyde. Most of his fellow guests were commercial travellers and touring actors—an uninspiring prospect but for the presence of Jimmy Mathieson, another successful business man of similar age who shared my father's interest in golf. They decided to join forces and find more congenial surroundings for the summer months. Kilmacolm, a pleasant Renfrewshire village seventeen miles west of the city, which had once been a serious rival to Balmoral when Queen Victoria was seeking a Scottish retreat, was their choice. The Hydropathic—built when Victorian Scotland was infected by the European craze for hotels offering water cures—was exactly what they wanted. It boasted a steam room, a cold plunge and an ex-army physical training instructor who, each morning, directed a powerful hose at the diaphragms of the male residents to tone them up for a day in the office. But it was the nearby golf course and the excellent cuisine that principally attracted them. The fact that Kilmacolm was, and is, dry was the one thing that made their choice something of a surprise.

My grandmother died after a long illness in the summer of 1912. On the evening after the funeral my father stepped out of the horse-bus that carried guests from Kilmacolm station up the steep hill through the Hydro grounds to the big, rambling grey-stone edifice on the summit. He was grief-stricken and exhausted by the journey back from Fife; mistaking the dark haired young woman in the entrance hall for the book-keeper, he asked her if at such a late hour she could get him a hot drink.

The young woman, who was not the book-keeper, was touched at his woebegone appearance:

'I believe my father has a bottle of whisky in his room; would that be any good?'

Seemingly it was for they were married a year later.

Her name was May Temple, and she was on holiday with her younger sister Peggy and their father James, a widower. James Graham Temple was a respected Glasgow journalist whose father had covered the Franco–Prussian War for a Scottish newspaper and represented the British Press when Napoleon III surrendered his sword after the Battle of Sedan. My mother still has his passport and an old pistol picked up on the battlefield. James's speciality as a young man was reporting important political meetings. In those days newspapers carried verbatim accounts of all the principal speeches, and the job of taking them down in shorthand in a crowded hall, distracted by cheers and heckling, was a demanding and nerve-wracking business. Many of the speakers were inaudible, though it was usual for the more considerate, or more publicity-conscious among them to let their notes flutter from the platform in the direction of the press-table. After a meeting the copy had to be rushed by horsecab to the nearest telegraph office. Journalists have always been slaves to a deadline; most seem to revel in the sense of urgency; not grandad. He hated the constant anxiety and retired without regret in his early fifties. Years later he told me that he still had nightmares in which his pencil broke at a critical moment. To the day of his death in his ninety-third year he carried at least two in his pocket, each sharpened at both ends.

Slightly below medium height, he was stout and dignified. The large Roman nose and white moustache were impressive; but it was his eyes that I remember best. To talk to him was to be the object of a shrewd piercing stare. His conversation was a series of questions, and those dark brown gimlet eyes missed nothing. The reporter in him never died, yet he almost certainly missed his vocation. Journalism hadn't much use for his fine light baritone voice or amusing comedy patter; but fortunately his press assignments were often theatrical. He interviewed Henry Irving and was on terms of friendship with Harry

Lauder. On more than one occasion when they met by chance in the streets of Glasgow, grandad was steered by the great comedian into the comparative seclusion of a close-mouth,* to be regaled with an unaccompanied rendering of the latest Lauder song and then asked his opinion. This was a compliment to them both, for Sir Harry must have possessed the concentration of an Indian fakir to perform solo without embarrassment in the face of grandad's unwinking gaze. Perhaps the leap from a miner's cottage to the music hall that Lauder made was easier than crossing the ocean of family disapproval that lay between grandad's solid middle-class background and the stage door. As a young man he took one look at the angry waves and decided against embarkation.

Both May and Peggy inherited the talent that he forsook. My mother was the undoubted star of every school production and a good public speaker. Aunty Peggy was a gifted singer and pianist. Such accomplishments were regarded in middle-class Edwardian Glasgow as useful social assets for young ladies— unthinkable as the basis for a professional career. I'm sure my mother never thought of going on the boards. Aunty not only thought about it, she went; alas, not for long.

Soon after the outbreak of the 1914 war my father, too old and short-sighted for military service, was appointed managing director of Nairn's London office, but he had by no means shaken the dust of Scotland from his feet. A debating society in Kirkcaldy, which he joined as a young man had kindled a life-long interest in politics, and in 1918 he was returned as Liberal member of parliament for Dunfermline District of Burghs, a constituency only thirteen miles from his birthplace.

Poverty and early struggles are often the secure foundation of success in life. They were never a part of mine. Perhaps my arrival on the scene in July 1919, six years after my parent's union, was a little overdue; but right from the outset I made my presence felt. Tipping the scale at ten pounds dead, I made certain that I was not only the first, but the last of the line.

* The draughty stone-walled hallway of a tenement building.

Ten, twenty, thirty, forty, fifty years ago!

(My Old Shako)

It's impossible to research one's childhood. One remembers things or one doesn't. Mine was happy and spent in a detached house—with a garden the size of a tennis court—in that part of London described by estate agents—and no one else—as the Northern Heights. We were one notch too low in the social scale for me to be dominated by a nanny, but our household, like the others round about, included a cook-general and a house parlourmaid. I lived in a female world, for my father's double career of business and politics occupied all day, half the night and at weekends he re-charged his batteries on the golf course. I only saw this remote, benevolent figure at breakfast time, when one of my earliest entertainments was to watch him fastening his spats in front of the dining room fire with a button-hook, an exercise involving heavy breathing and mild expletives.

The parlourmaid, fair and, according to my mother, man-mad, was called Gwen; Elsie, the cook, was dark and gipsy-like. Most afternoons they took me for a walk on which we invariably met either Frank or George, two moustachioed members of the local constabulary, who somehow always managed to coincide their beat with our walk; maybe it was the other way round. I couldn't understand my mother's lack of enthusiasm when I told her that once again we had met Frank—or George. This intelligence would be greeted with a snort, and the word 'flighty' would be whispered, but never explained.

My favourite route was along Highgate's Archway Road

with its small, crowded shops and the red 'General' buses grinding up the hill from Holloway, carrying advertisements on the side for 'Bovril', guaranteed to prevent 'that sinking feeling', or shows like *Hit The Deck* and *One Dam Thing After Another*. Northbound lorries reached the summit so slowly that small boys pursued them, jumped on the tail-boards and risked death as they leaped off near the police station, where the road levels and the lumbering giants began to gather speed. Best, though, were the funerals, endless processions of them, horse-drawn and sombre, making for one of the numerous cemeteries in the district at a measured trot; my mother taught me always to raise my hat to the hearse;

'Respect the dead,' I would murmur, doffing my woolly bonnet. She came to regret this lesson in courtesy; my elastic head-gear was intended to correct a tendency I had to sticking-out ears, and she, or whoever was with me, only managed to get them tucked in again when yet another cortège hove into sight.

I had the good fortune to be a pre-plastic-age child, when toys lasted for years and could frequently be repaired. The first possession I remember was a 'Pip & Squeak Annual' for the year 1924. Pip, Squeak & Wilfred were a dog, a female penguin and a rabbit, whose adventures I eagerly followed in the *Daily Mirror*', a staunch supporter at that time of the Conservative Party. Pip and Squeak both spoke English—in little balloons above their heads; Wilfred communicated by sounds like 'nunc' and 'ick'. For a year or two he became a national hero when the *Daily Mirror* organised a society for all the children who liked these cartoon pets. It was called 'The Gugnuncs', and members were given a round enamel brooch with a white, long-eared Wilfred on a blue background. There was the famous Gugnuncs' rally at the Albert Hall attended by 6,000 of us. The highlight came when the *Daily Mirror's* Uncle Dick shouted out the first part of our password at the top of his voice,

'Ick, Ick Pah Boo!'

This was the moment we had been waiting for.

'GOO, GOO PAH NUNC!' we yelled back, and then burst into spontaneous applause. I have absolutely no other recollection of what took place on that stirring afternoon.

16

I'd hate you to think that this sheltered, comfortable existence was completely insulated from the sterner aspects of life. Not so. Even before I was born I was no stranger to theatrical dressing-rooms, and if you think they are all like the ones you see in old Hollywood movies, with padded settees, full-length mirrors and tables groaning with magnums of champagne, piles of telegrams and bouquets—well, maybe there are a few like that, but most bear as much relation to that extravagant fantasy as a five star hotel to a bed-sitting room. How did I experience these rigours so early? It was like this.

My mother's sister Peggy came south to study singing and piano at the Royal College of Music towards the end of the first war, and emerged from that establishment with glowing reports indicating a career on the concert platform as a light soprano. Unfortunately, she also had a considerable talent for mimicry. Aunty Peggy could imitate famous singers of her day with accuracy and wit. If she had confined herself to taking off prima donnas, all might have been well; but included in her list of impressions were the surprising names of John McCormack, the famous Irish tenor, and Harry Lauder.

News of such an unusual comic turn soon reached the grapevine of the variety stage. Instead of persevering with the songs of Fauré and Debussy, she soon found herself giving an audition to Mr. Oswald Stoll, the owner in those days of a chain of music halls. Stoll was impressed, so impressed that he offered her a contract on the spot. She was to appear at the London Coliseum presenting her vocal impressions of famous singing stars while accompanying herself at the piano. The salary was £20 per week, an enormous sum for a beginner. He was very surprised to learn that she had never appeared professionally in any theatre, and decided to break her in with a week at Chiswick Empire and another at Shepherds Bush Pavilion before tackling the vast auditorium in St. Martin's Lane. Every night my mother, many months pregnant, struggled across London to keep her company in the dressing room. Half way through the second week at Shepherds Bush, it became obvious that aunty would never make the Coliseum. Her act was well received, but the strain of imitating Harry Lauder and the rest twice nightly in a large theatre with no microphone was quite beyond her. An acute attack of laryngitis brought to an end her brief career on the halls.

A few years later when broadcasting began at Savoy Hill, she applied for an audition, thinking that the microphone would not require her to push the voice so hard. Once more she made a good impression and was told to go away and add to her repertoire of imitations. This time the laryngitis attacked her as she studied, and though her voice returned with rest, she never again attempted a professional career of any kind. For some reason, singing without trying to make the audience laugh never appealed to her. I'm afraid it's a family failing.

Keeping poor aunty company in the music halls gave my mother a taste for that kind of entertainment, and, when I was about five, she began to take me to matinees at the Coliseum. I saw the brilliant sunset of a great tradition, as unaware of its significance as the pigeons outside in Trafalgar Square. Grock, the musical clown, Layton & Johnson, The Houston Sisters, Nervo & Knox, Naughton & Gold, Norman Long—'A Song A Smile And A Piano', Billy Bennett—'Almost A Gentleman', plus a regiment of jugglers, uni-cyclists, acrobats and magicians appeared regularly to my infinite delight, each turn preceded by a suitable burst of music from the pit orchestra, and a number in red electric light bulbs twinkling across the dark auditorium from two gilt, glass-fronted boxes mounted on the columns of the proscenium arch either side of the stage. These were the last of the pre-microphone acts and I could catch every word, sung or spoken. For a little boy the chief delights were the slow-motion wrestling act of Nervo & Knox and the humorous monologues of Billy Bennett. Dressed in badly fitting tails, red cummerbund, black tie, sporting a waxed black moustache and a quiff, he would advance truculently to the footlights and announce:

'I went for me holidays to the Cascara Mountains. Very healthy place the Cascara Mountains. They had to shoot an old man to start a cemetery.'

A surprising number of these acts performed over the years in that famous and prosperous theatre in front of a faded back-cloth depicting the Embankment near Westminster Bridge with two or three globe-shaped street lamps in the foreground. Even as a child I felt it wasn't quite good enough.

18

Round about my fifth birthday my mother led me by the hand to the green front door of Byron House, a co-educational kindergarten school in Highgate Village, which has now passed into history. It was a cheerful place, claiming among its former pupils Sir John Betjeman, who lived with his family and a teddy-bear called Archibald halfway down nearby West Hill. The entirely female staff were women of character and personality. I imagined they were all well over eighty, yet only the other day I saw one of them still moving briskly through Highgate Village under her own steam. The headmistress was Miss Katherine Legge, a statuesque, well-corseted lady, whose hair-style, clothes and impassive expression would have made her a capable understudy for the late Queen Mary.

Once a week in winter, the boys were taken to Kenwood, a nearby open space, for a game of football under the supervision of Mr. Wilson, who mysteriously appeared for this one responsibility, puffing a curly pipe and tucking his trousers into his socks before starting play with a blast on a police-whistle, which was liable to produce Frank—or George—at the double from Hampstead Lane. The field we played on was, to say the least, uneven. From one touch-line to the other it fell away at an angle of 20°, and from goal to goal, a suitably short distance for nippers, there was also a steepish gradient. On my first time out, Mr. Wilson assumed that I knew the rules and told me to play at right back. Ours was the stronger of the two teams, and, for most of the afternoon, I stood watching play at the far end. Clearly the object of the game was to kick the ball between the posts, so when, finally, there was a break-away, and the ball was kicked up the field towards me, I decided that it would be much easier to turn round and kick it between the two posts behind me. There was only the goalie to beat and he wasn't paying attention. I scored. To my surprise, the captain of our side was very upset. He ran over, seized me by the arm and gave me my orders for the rest of the game.

'Stand at the side and do nothing!' he muttered through teeth clenched with rage. At the side stood the only spectator—my mother.

'Well done!' she cried, and slapped me on the back.

My theatrical debut at Byron House was equally disastrous. As the only extrovert in a shy class, I was entrusted with the title role in *King Alfred and the Cakes*, a historical play to entertain parents and friends on the summer open-day. The first scene found the king, disguised as a wandering minstrel, lying under a table in the tent of Guthrum, his enemy, who was feasting with his henchmen as they made plans for the forthcoming battle. Then, having heard enough, the disguised king was to leap out of his hiding-place as if he was just entering the tent (a difficult move to execute convincingly) and offer to entertain the company.

The costume provided for this scene was simple. A pair of champagne bottle straws on my legs, fastened in criss-cross Anglo-Saxon fashion with brown tape, were topped off with a hessian cloak. That was all. As the performance was to be in the garden, my mother, concerned about some sort of under-garment in case the afternoon was windy, hit on the happy idea of making me wear the tartan trews from my kilt. The Wallace tartan is a fairly riotous mixture of red, black and yellow.

Crouched under the table, I heard Guthrum getting into his stride. When my cue came I tightened my grip on my cardboard lyre and sprang to my feet. I hadn't noticed that one of the legs of Guthrum's chair was standing on a corner of my cloak.

'Hail to thee, Guthrum!' I cried, 'Wouldst thou hear a song?' There was no reply. The poor chap was lying flat on his back with his chair on top of him. My cloak, ripped from my back, was lying on the lawn. The combination of tartan trews, champagne straws and a cardboard lyre stopped the show. I don't remember if we ever got it started again.

My appearance in any theatricals until I was about thirteen was something of a lottery, for I was a martyr to colds which, to use the doctor's phrase, always 'slipped into bronchitis'. When, with heavy jocularity, he produced his stethoscope and announced that he wanted to listen to my 'box of whistles', he was only stating the truth. For at least forty-eight hours of these frequent attacks I lay, propped up on pillows, wheezing and fighting for breath.

A day or two before I was to play 'Bottom' in *Midsummer Night's Dream*, the ominous sound of coughing could be heard from my bedroom. For once my breathing remained normal, and my mother phoned the school to ask if I could appear at the risk of infecting the other performers. Miss Legg replied that at such short notice she had no alternative. Long before the end, the audience were in no doubt about what was the matter with me. 'Bottom' is a strenuous part and the more I exerted myself the more I whooped. Fortunately, in our severely abridged version of the play, I wore the ass's head most of the time—and kept my germs to myself.

I must have been about eight when a shadow fell across my childhood. During one of my father's many absences in Scotland for political meetings, my mother steeled herself for a domestic ordeal of grave proportions, the installation of a parquet floor in the drawing room. At first sight this might sound a gross exaggeration. I assure you I am in earnest. My mother belongs to that large number of intensely house-proud Scotswomen who view the arrival of workmen, however careful and inoffensive, with dread and foreboding. There is in the minds of these ladies a certainty that some disaster will befall the carpets or the furniture or the paintwork—probably all three, and the only tradesmen with whom they feel at ease are those who have served them for many years without so much as breaking the cup containing their 'elevenses'. But such riff-raff as parquet floor installers were not only total strangers, but were proposing to fit hundreds of individual pieces of wood on top of coats of freshly boiled glue! Small wonder that for a whole week she stood sentry over the gas-rings and bubbling pots in the midst of her beloved drawing room. When the job was completed without the feared conflagration, and not even a spot of glue out of place, she retired upstairs, satisfied and exhausted, to have a bath.

She was more tired than she realised. The languors of sleep overtook her in the warm water; when she woke it was stone cold. The following day she complained of a chill, stayed in bed and dared anyone to send for the doctor. By the evening she was delirious. Gwen and Elsie, as frightened as I was, put me to bed in my father's room and climbed in beside me—it was a double bed—as we listened to what sounded like snatches of a political speech, constantly interrupted by a harsh barking cough. My mother was always a splendid electioneer; now she was fighting the fiercest campaign of her life and no one had lifted a finger all day to help her. The maids conversed in dramatic whispers and the telephone stood unused on the bed table. Finally, they plucked up the courage to disobey my mother's orders by ringing for the doctor and my father. To prevent her hearing the voices through the wall, we muffled our cries for help by taking the instrument under the bedclothes.

For two weeks she was nursed day and night by two starched nightingales from a London hospital. Our doctor, a bearded Aberdonian, who wore a jewelled ring round his tie, given him by a grateful patient, began to call two and three times a day. His black Renault with a bonnet like an enormous parson's nose stood like a symbol of approaching doom at the front gate. I wandered, aimless and frightened, round the house, never allowed into the sick-room and undeceived by the attempts of the grown-ups to talk to me brightly of other things. The word 'crisis' was used a great deal. One day my father, who was no better at concealing his anxiety than the maids, told me that he was sending for a very famous doctor, who would know how to make mummy better. In an emergency my father never did anything by halves; within a couple of hours the royal physician, no less, was climbing the stairs, the agitated day nightingale at his heels. Lord Dawson of Penn, a tall, spare man arrayed in frock coat and leaving a black silk topper on the hall table, was not long in starting the treatment. The room where my mother lay had been kept at the temperature of the reptile house in a zoo by means of tightly shut windows and a blazing coal fire.

'Open the windows!' he cried, 'And give her air. How can she fight without oxygen?'

The crisis was surmounted and she became one of the comparative few in those days to survive a severe attack of double pneumonia. Recovery depended on two things, skilful nursing and the patient's fighting spirit. My mother had both.

A few days later the silk topper was back. This time he came down the stairs with my father, both of them positively jaunty.

'You won't need me again, Mr. Wallace,' said the great man, 'and you won't get my final prescription at the chemist. Give her oysters and champagne. You, boy, go and see your mother for two minutes, no more.'

I suppose I expected her to look her normal self, and was unprepared for the thin face with cheeks the colour of clay, or the feeble smile. Only the voice, weak but familiar, was reassuring. Her convalescence was long and dogged with complications. Eventually she was well enough to go to a hotel in Eastbourne, returning a month later unbelievably better. It was then that the doctor, never the most optimistic member of his profession, recommended a regular afternoon nap. My mother treated this suggestion with contempt.

'I abhor people who rest in the afternoon' she declared. She still does.

Looking back on one's school-days is the view through the wrong end of a telescope. There is an impression of great distance, yet some of the figures remain sharply in focus. I can see very clearly the Reverend A. R. K. Wells, headmaster of Heathmount Preparatory School, Hampstead, ex naval chaplain and old Etonian. He was tall, aristocratic, pipe-smoking, his bald egg-shaped head surrounded by a fringe of grizzled white curls.

'Boys,' he informed my parents, 'should be treated like the miserable little worms they are.' Fortunately this policy was only implemented occasionally. I became a day-boy, bowling across Hampstead Heath in the new-found splendour of the family limousine, an Austin 20 with disc wheels, driven by Mackenzie, our Scottish ex-serviceman chauffeur, who became a friend and ally for the rest of my childhood, regaling me with stories of service under General Allenby and confessing to a passion for light classical music with a particular fondness for the overture to *Zampa*.

But almost from the day I entered the asphalted playground, with white goals and wickets painted on the brick walls, the phrase 'Common Entrance Examination for the Public Schools' seemed to obsess every adult in the place. Our bible was a large book in dark green hard-back covers, which contained the Common Entrance papers for the previous few years. Round and round these trial courses we were galloped until we became as familiar with them as three-year-old colts with Newmarket Heath. In fairness we also had the benefit of good teachers. Wells retained one naval tradition. Every Sunday the Gymnasium was rigged as a chapel, and he ensured our fairly regular attendance at the 'voluntary' service with the bribe of an annual choir treat. For this an open-topped double-decker London bus like those used to rush troops to the front in World War I, was hired to rush us, laughing and singing, to Twickenham. The seats on the top deck were as hard as park benches, each equipped with a small tarpaulin to protect passengers from the rain. A motor-launch took us some miles up the river for a picnic, where we demolished ham rolls by the half dozen, doughnuts oozing jam, and buckets of lemonade made from a powder that produced a liquid of vivid green and a flavour far removed from the more expensive Kia-Ora.

Another look through the telescope reveals the school bursar, a retired brigadier, tall, gaunt and stooping, who constantly enjoined us to tell the truth and keep our bowels open. His large, beaky nose, its purple veins like a map of the Nile delta, was always moist in winter, and he added mustard to everything, even boiled cod. In summer he would bowl at us in the nets, his long thin legs clearly delineated by his ancient white flannels, shrunken and yellowed by a lifetime of regimental matches in India. Two stiff paces to the wicket and the old arm creaked above his bald head, then, in the last second, there was a downward thrust, a grunt of pain, and the ball was upon us with deceptive speed, whirring with the spin. None of us had the answer to his leg breaks and googlies, while his delight at our discomfiture was child-like and unaffected.

Wells sold out to a developer soon after I left, and the school decamped to Hertfordshire, where it still flourishes. I've never quite forgiven him for depriving me, as I drive into town, of a glimpse of the old house near the top of Heath Street on the right hand side going down. It's difficult, looking at the pleasing blocks of flats that stand there now, to visualize just where the window was that I broke with a tennis ball during a game of play-ground cricket, followed by the dash indoors to own up and apologize (by the Wells code this halved any punishment), and the shocked standstill that ended my headlong progress into the room, where the tennis ball lay amongst the broken glass on the carpet, to see Mrs. Wells, completely bald, making a vain effort to reach the wig on the dressing-table. I hadn't knocked. We stood staring at each other for a moment.

'Well, young man, now you know. Have a good look and then go and tell the others. We'll put the window on the bill.'

It wasn't all roses. There were plenty of opportunities for bullying in a community of small boys thrown together forty

24

years ago at a private school, just as, no doubt, there are today. The slightest false move and one could be an object of ridicule leading to violence. It was important to conform, particularly over one's clothes, and it was even wise to see that one's parents didn't pass through the school gates unless they were correctly attired for whatever function they had come to attend. To be good at games was the one eccentricity that was acceptable, provided the athlete treated his success with suitable self-deprecation.

To have as one's sole accomplishment a capacity for singing was downright dangerous; that was simply a form of 'showing off', the ultimate sin. Luckily for me, Mr. Wells was a bit of a 'show-off' himself, and organized an annual Christmas entertainment when I briefly came into my own. My farewell performance was as 'Uncle John' in *Dick Whittington*, a character not normally found in that pantomime, but 'written in' to accomodate a plump boy soprano, otherwise uncastable. As well as playing 'Uncle John' I also sang 'Cherry Ripe', arranged by Liza Lehmann, in the wings in the original key, with the cadenza at the end, which I suppose was quite a feat, while a much smaller boy, dressed in rags and clutching a bunch of 'prop' cherries, mouthed it silently on the stage. He mouthed it very well and got a good applause, which caused a slight coolness between my parents and his in the interval. But even if one's school-fellows were prepared to applaud and pat one on the back, one was still expected to respond with some fatuous insincerity like:

'Oh I say, really? I thought I was absolutely rotten.'

When I was a lad

(H.M.S. Pinafore)

Charterhouse, after I had adjusted myself to the miseries of washing in cold water, lessons at seven-thirty a.m. and the change in status from a prep school admiral to a public school powder-monkey, suited me down to the ground. The air on the hill above Godalming blew away the wheezes from my chest, and I soon began to enjoy the faintly monastic flavour of life outside school hours spent away from home with boys my own age. And that life revolved round one of the eleven boarding houses into which the school was divided. Mine was called Gownboys, an echo of the days when there had been a house devoted to scholars. In 1933 we were a mixed bag like the other ten, which were named after the original housemasters appointed as the school steadily expanded after moving from Smithfield to Godalming in 1872. Gownboys is part of the original building, a late-Victorian ecclesiastical-looking complex, poking out of the trees a mile or two to the left of the Guildford by-pass, if one is foolhardy enough to take one's eyes off the road about half a mile beyond the Hog's Back turning. The names of those former housemasters have added to them the suffix 'ites'. Hence, Pageites was after the famous Dr. T. E. Page, a redoubtable classical scholar, whose tall, venerable figure, always dressed in suits of near white, made from a huge bale of shaggy Donegal, that he had bought many years previously, and which he rightly prophesied would survive him unfinished, was still to be seen on Saturdays watching cricket matches on the beautiful first

27

eleven ground during my first summer term, when he was eighty-three or thereabouts.

He knew my father slightly—they were both members of the Reform Club—and one such Saturday I felt a tap on the shoulder and heard a deep rumbling voice far above me say:

'There you are, boy, and let me know if you get bullied. Promised your father I'd look you up.'

He quickly pushed a parcel into my hands and shambled away before I'd managed to thank him. It was a large punnet of fresh raspberries from his garden.

Inter-house competition was keen, and the housemaster a more important figure for the sixty or seventy boys in his care than anyone else, including the Head. Ours was more or less a permanent invalid for the whole time I was there. His suits of shapeless grey tweed had been made when he was physically more robust, for his pale, pointed face peered out from the folds of his jacket like a tortoise from its shell. He remained mostly in his study, the windows shut, the air heavy with pipe smoke and a rug spread over his knees, even in July. Yet Ivor Gibson, known, inevitably, as 'Gibbo', was in command, and the discipline he achieved, mostly in absentia, was remarkable. His methods were subtle; for instance, he would never accuse a boy of lying; instead he would observe in his nasal tones 'Are you, perhaps, being economical with the truth?'

We were proud of our ailing housemaster; he was seldom able to walk further than from his study to the dining hall for prayers, yet he followed the fortunes of his boys playing football or cricket on the remotest field, driving his ancient Austin 16 saloon along footpaths and through narrow gaps between trees to get there. As far as we were concerned, he was the equal of all the able-bodied housemasters, and we took pride in the fact that several of them had been known to enter his hermetically sealed sanctuary in search of advice. His knowledge of house affairs and our personal idiocies constantly impressed and disconcerted us. It was rumoured that he had a network of spies. Years later I asked him about it.

'No need for spies,' he chuckled, 'boys are so transparent.'

House discipline was administered by monitors or other senior boys. Part of it was based on our old friend sartorial conformity. A list of absurd rules was printed on the house notice-board and had to be strictly observed. For the first year, all three buttons of one's black jacket had to remain done up all the time. After a year one could put one's hands in one's trouser pockets, but they had to enter from behind, so as not to sweep back the lower part of the jacket. These regulations, devised by a previous generation of boys, made it possible to tell at a glance the seniority of one's fellows. The final privilege was to sweep back an unbottoned jacket, revealing a long, black cable-stitch jumper with holes in the sides, through which one could reach one's trouser pockets without hitching it up. One waited four years for that!

Corporal punishment existed, but scarcely flourished. It was administered by the head monitor, after evening prayers, for certain crimes known as 'beating offences', and the approval of the house master had to be obtained in advance. The instruments used were known as 'bum sticks', delivered as required in bundles of half a dozen by a mildly sinister character known as the School Sergeant. They were about four feet long, as thick as walking sticks, yet the victim could expect little sympathy from his friends unless one 'bum stick' at least had broken at the point of contact. One knelt on a bench, one's body stretched across a refectory table, hands grasping the far side. The head monitor measured out his short run like a bowler, and, as he returned to his mark between each stroke, there was time to speculate on whether it would be four or six. For some reason it was never five. Unadventurous by nature, I was only beaten once, for a spectacular, unintentional offence. A large fire extinguisher stood outside the door of our dormitory. One evening a friend of mine noticed signs of corrosion and expressed doubts about the efficiency of its plunger. I disagreed with him, but conceded that it would require a pretty sharp blow to set it off.

'It would never work if you just tapped it like this,' I declared.

A powerful jet of chemical spurted from the nozzle, dashed itself against the fuse box above the door, shattered its little glass window and put out every light in the house. I only got four for that, with none broken; nevertheless, I attracted some sympathy at the customary bruise inspection in the changing room next day, because the head monitor, one of the best bats in the school, had landed them all on the same spot.

Undoubtedly it was a degrading practice, with unhealthy

29

sexual implications, but none of us seemed to think so at the time. Certainly, there was no relation between this and 'The Cat', even allowing for our tender years. A flogging in a strange environment, long after the offence, by a complete stranger, representing to the prisoner a revengeful society, can hardly be compared with a situation where your executioner bade you a cheery good night, and restored you to the passage, where your friends had been gleefully counting the strokes.

Chapel services, games and corps were all compulsory at pre-war public schools. Of these corps was universally unpopular. Once a week we struggled into khaki and emerged on parade looking like miniature tommies from World War I, our puttees always in danger of unwinding, our cumbersome webbing belts and haversacks never quite fitting, the smaller among us staggering under the weight of our Lee Enfield rifles. Arms drill, tactics and marching were our staple fare, though we did occasionally fix bayonets to liven it up a bit. Once a term, on a day when it invariably rained, we had a 'Field Day'. In our haversacks were a ground sheet and a paper bag containing a ham sandwich, a piece of cherry cake, an apple and a small bar of Cadbury's chocolate. Our ammunition pouches bulging with six blank cartridges, we sallied forth in buses to some lightly wooded Surrey heath to fight a mock battle. Young masters dressed as second lieutenants, reinforced by a few regulars from Aldershot, bounded at us from behind trees and screamed 'Bang, bang, bang, you're all dead!' One hadn't the remotest idea what one was supposed to be doing, but at least one could then fire one's blanks happily into the air, eat ones' rations and find a sheltered spot to wait for the bus. It was hardly the preparation for dealing with Panzer divisions, but we might have given a few lightly armed Fuzzy-wuzzys a run for their money.

Though an indifferent performer at all games, I enjoyed them with an optimistic certainty that one day I would improve. Each house fielded enough cricket and football teams to provide every boy with at least a couple of afternoon's play a week. For a highly intelligent and physically unco-ordinated minority, those endless games in the lowest elevens must have been a humiliating waste of time. For me they invariably produced the 'Walter Mitty' syndrome. I was always going to score a hundred or take

seven for eighteen, and though our game was only one of half a dozen proceeding simultaneously on the huge field, as I walked to the crease it was Wallace, unexpectedly chosen to play for England, about to take his first ball in the tense atmosphere of a Lord's Test. Seeking my forte I tried everything, batting, wicket-keeping, bowling (over and round the wicket), while in winter I played in every position from goal-keeper to centre-forward for my lowly team with equal pleasure and unsuccess. Had games been only for the élite, none of these enjoyable experiences, lacking only a sense of achievement, would have come my way. I did once score a century, though you will not find it in any of the record books. The opposite side had no bowlers worthy of the name, and the opening batsmen, Wallace and another, scored freely without loss until our captain declared. Only then was it discovered that Wallace had made ninety-nine. In this class of cricket it was the work of a moment to reverse the declaration and persuade our opponents to take the field for one more ball, a deliberate long hop, which I dispatched for the necessary single. This generous gesture was not made to feed my self-esteem. Every boy, friend or foe alike, knew that there was a reward of a large strawberry ice with syrup and cream for anyone scoring a century, and nobody cared to stand between another fellow and such a delectable treat for the sake of one miserable run. Alas, when the circumstances were explained to the house captain, he ruled that the original declaration must stand, and that ninety-nine not out just failed to qualify for the prize. Who dares to say that public schools are not an adequate preparation for life?

The many hours we were obliged to spend in Chapel were nothing like so wearisome for me as for many of the others simply because I've always enjoyed singing and gained some spiritual inspiration in the process.

Dr. Thomas Fielden, the musical director at Charterhouse, possessed energy and enthusiasm, qualities which frequently inspire ridicule and embarrassment in the young. He often produced both, but a mixture of insensitivity and moral courage helped him to achieve minor miracles like interesting a largely unmusical sixth form in the structure of a Beethoven symphony, or persuading over six hundred boys to take a real pride in singing hymns and psalms in Chapel.

31

I met him my first evening at Charterhouse. Within two hours of our arrival, he gathered up all the new boys and auditioned us for the choir. My fairly powerful treble made even this home-sick and slightly tearful crew roar with laughter. He silenced them with a glance.

'What's your name?'

'Wallace, sir.'

'Wallace, eh? Are you a Scot?'

'Yes, sir.'

'Well, Wallace, pay no attention. Always remember the old Scotch saying. "They say. What say they? Let them say!" '

It could have been his motto.

Although I had been singing since early childhood, I was no musician. I had a succession of piano teachers, starting with a lady at Byron House with an Eton crop and a hoarse baritone voice, who rapped me over the knuckles with a ruler for wrong notes. None of them succeeded in extracting from me anything beyond the most elementary of pieces. My repertoire of songs, too, was not aimed at a discriminating audience: 'Ee By Gum', 'Never Have a Bath Till You Need One', 'Wagon Wheels', 'Play to me Gipsy', 'He Played His Ukelele as the Ship Went Down' and 'Lullaby in Blue' comprised an entertainment I was prepared to give at the slightest encouragement, accompanying myself on a banjolele. I had mastered four or five simple chords on this demanding instrument whilst convalescing from whoop-ing cough. Greatly to his credit, Fielden never showed any sign of distaste for these songs, but was determined to bring a wider selection to my notice. This was a labour of love, for I didn't learn an instrument with him, and he had no responsibility for me except as a member of the choir. When my voice slipped down to baritone (I was lucky enough to avoid a period of squeaky croaking), he taught me an aria from Mendelssohn's *Elijah* and made me sing it in Chapel after evensong one Sunday in front of the whole congregation. It was called 'It Is Enough'. It was a valuable, alarming experience, which marked the beginning—and the end—of my career in oratorio.

My five years at Charterhouse were equally divided between two headmasters, Frank Fletcher and Robert Birley. More con-trasting figures it would be difficult to imagine. When Sir Frank Fletcher, on his last Saturday in office, stepped into the small car, which Claude Wright, the head of the school had presented on our behalf, and drove it slowly away through lines of cheering boys on a golden summer evening, (Sir Carol Reed couldn't have staged it better), it was likely that the departure of this spare, stooping, puckish-featured old man with an awesome reputation for discipline, would signal a change of direction by the Governing Body when choosing his successor. Fletcher was a great headmaster in the classic mould, aloof and treating the boys with a half smiling disdain. He had been appointed when the school was at a low ebb, and he left it fourth in the league table, the best anyone could hope to do unless Eton, Harrow and Winchester were burnt to the ground.

He had a grim sense of humour. Once a group of boys, myself included, persuaded him to allow us to present a revue in the School Hall, much of it written by Richard Stone, the theatrical agent. Music was provided by The Charterhouse Dance Band, and the conductor, resplendent in tails, white tie, and even white gloves was Ronald Millar, whose dramatic adaptations of C. P. Snow's novels have been so successful on the London stage in recent years. I appeared in a series of comic sketches, one of which required me, for some reason long forgotten, to sing 'Many Brave Hearts are Asleep in the Deep, so Beware!' The entertainment was entitled *All Alight at Scholars' Court*, and the news that the headmaster proposed to attend was received with some misgiving. There was nothing in it risqué or insulting to the staff—but we just had a feeling that one whose idea of an enjoyable theatrical evening was *The Frogs* of Aristophanes would scarcely appreciate our amateurish attempts to recreate the atmosphere of the London Palladium in a neo-gothic hall on the top of Frith Hill.

At the end he left without a word, long before the vociferous, excited applause had subsided—a bad sign. However, it filtered back that he had said later:

'It was not so much an entertainment as a bacchanalian rite. Not unenjoyable, but it must never, never happen again.'

I was confronted with his successor at 7.30 a.m. on the first Monday morning of the following term, and in his study what's more! Not for some heinous crime, committed during the night and requiring instant punishment, but because, in going over the curriculum, he had noticed that four of us in a history set would have, *faute de mieux*, to endure the identical maths syllabus that we had already covered the previous term. He, therefore, decided to enliven our existence with a little Carthaginian history. This shy mountain of a man took us across the Alps with Hannibal's elephants, and even in the half light of early morning, rubbing the sleep from the corner of one's eye, it was impossible not to share his enthusiasm for this remarkable feat of arms.

Birley was in his early thirties, which made him one of the youngest headmasters ever appointed to a public school. It took him a little while to settle down. We sensed that a hanging judge had been replaced by an unconfident young magistrate, and there was at least one early attempt to undermine his authority. At his first Calling Over, which was the school's name for a review of the term's work given by the headmaster in front of all the boys and staff just before the holidays, he faced unmistakable signs of a challenge to his powers of discipline. As he started to speak he was nervous, and his unease was scarcely improved by the sound of laughter and chatter in the hall, which under Fletcher's eye would have been as silent as a mortuary. For a few moments the proceedings threatened to get out of hand, and it looked as if he would have to call in one of the subordinate disciplinarians that surrounded him to restore order; indeed several of them were growing red in the face and twitching restively at their M.A. gowns. It undoubtedly happened because of the acute contrast between the old and the new, and the new had a number of disadvantages. He was tall and rather clumsy in his movements, he had fair curly hair, a pink and white complexion, and when angry he would stare straight ahead with narrowed eyes, all of which briefly earned him the nickname 'Piglet'. Worst of all he had come from Eton. Unexpectedly, the potential riot subsided as quickly as it had begun without any threats or intervention from the rest of the staff; for Birley had never lost control of the situation. It was painfully obvious that he was embarrassed, but he managed to convey that the embarrassment was not for himself, but for us.

He was a dedicated teacher, who had to overcome considerable shyness in getting to know over six hundred boys. Where Fletcher was as unapproachable as Pooh Bah, Birley, once the ice was broken, would converse animatedly on any subject a boy was likely to raise, and displayed a warmth and kindness of personality as unexpected as it was disarming. I must be only one of many of my generation, who have the privilege of enjoying his friendship to this day. His talent for educational organisation has since become legendary, and he first exercised it bringing this enclave of tradition up to date—imperceptibly and by stealth.

My school holidays were as conservative as the family's politics. At Easter my father could never spare any time, but my mother would bear me off to some southern watering place like Eastbourne, Bexhill or Frinton-on-Sea, where we once found ourselves sharing sole occupation of The Beach Hotel with Gladys Cooper and her husband, Philip Merivale. With typical British phlegm we never exchanged a single word.

This was the hotel where Ribbentrop once stayed before the war when he was German Ambassador to the court of St. James. During his visit, some of the younger visitors had discovered that the automatic lift had a faulty circuit, and by pressing the buttons on different floors with careful timing it was possible to keep the unfortunate passengers going up and down almost indefinitely without their managing to stop long enough to open the doors and get out. As Ribbentrop and his government were already unpopular in England, they decided to give the Nazi ambassador a long ride. He emerged late for dinner and not in the least amused. It may have been a coincidence that the only building in Frinton to be razed to the ground by German bombs was The Beach Hotel, but some local residents have other ideas. I hasten to add that I wasn't there when the ambassador was literally sent up; I wish I had been.

Only once did we vary this Easter pilgrimage of golf, bathing and listening to a military band on the prom; that was when, greatly daring, my mother and I boarded the Golden Arrow for gay Paree. We did the Louvre, Napoleon's Tomb, the Eiffel Tower and l'Église du Sacré Coeur. We wandered round Versailles and Fontainebleau and sailed down the Seine past the Renault works, where hundreds of strikers sat with their legs almost dangling in the water and jeered as we floated by.

But for all my mother's Scots presbyterian upbringing, she has a broad mind. The climax of our trip was a visit to the

35

Folies Bergere, which, even in the thirties, employed nudes, who moved. Sitting with one's mother at such a spectacle, one has to assume the same air of detachment as Lord Longford at a strip club, but I have a vivid memory of the comedian of the show encountering a well built young lady clad in a G string. He raised his hat and indicated in mime that he wished to measure her height with his silver knobbed cane. He placed it at her toes, then carefully raised the ferrule to where the silver knob had been, which meant that the silver nob. . . . On our way back my mother suddenly caught my arm:

'This taxi isn't taking us the way we came!'

She was absolutely right. Were we *en route* for some sleazy thieves' kitchen? Would our bodies, stripped of valuables, be dragged from the river in the morning? It was something of an anti-climax when we arrived safely at our hotel, where the driver pointed out that the one-way system made it impossible to return the same way as we'd gone, and though the fare was, admittedly, four times what we had paid going, this was only because it was now after midnight. At first my mother would have none of it. But after an altercation in which the hotel night porter backed up the taxi driver, and we were threatened with a call to the gendarmerie, she was forced to pay up, *sans pourboire*, of course. Still she had the last word; including both men in a withering glance, she delivered a final salvo of which Nelson would have been proud.

'Une chose est tres certaine,' she cried, 'Vous n'aidez pas l'Entente Cordiale!'

For the month of August we invariably went to Scotland. My mother and I would set off in the Austin 20 limousine with a mountain of luggage strapped on the grid—no such things as boots existed then—and the inside of the car packed to suffocation with golf clubs, tennis racquets, fishing tackle, the budgerigar cage, hand luggage, picnic baskets and a splendid variety of travelling rugs from tartan to sheepskin. The uniformed Mackenzie always insisted on an early start; we were usually on the road by 6 a.m. reaching the George Hotel at Stamford for a bacon and egg breakfast.

'Welcome to Stamford' announced a sign each year, 'And linger awhile amid its ancient charm.'

36

We never did. By this time the heavy lorries were starting to congest the old A1 and we were lucky to reach the Crown & Mitre at Carlisle by early evening.

Next day we would make for Kilmacolm, where grandad and aunty Peggy lived at the aforementioned Hydro. We usually spent a few days there whilst my mother and her sister talked endlessly of friends and relations, and grandad puffed at his pipe, occasionally making an observation, which was destined—nine times out of ten—to be hotly contradicted by one or both of his two daughters.

At the time of one of these visits he was under severe pressure from his doctor to lose weight. Short and very stout, he'd suffered all his life from weak ankles. They were now being asked to carry rather more than 15 stone, and protested in the only way they could—puffing themselves up and letting out sharp yelps of pain. Grandad loved his grub, and though the doctor ordered a stringent diet, which my aunt was determined to enforce, the patient had no intention of collaborating. It was arranged that every other day he would wear the same clothes and walk down to the local chemist to be weighed. The 'diet' had the most unusual effect. As each week passed grandad always weighed less on Wednesday than he had on Monday, and less on Saturday than he had on Wednesday. Then, unaccountably, his weight on Monday would soar dramatically. It was many weeks before aunty discovered in his bedroom the pound weights that he had bought in order to handicap himself like a steeplechaser through the week.

In the end he was saved by another weakness, a blood vessel. One night he had a prodigious nosebleed, which, far from alarming the doctor, drew from him the comment 'Don't try to stop it, Mr. Temple, it'll give you another ten years of life.' He was wrong. It gave him another twenty.

For years the rest of our summer holiday was spent at St. Andrews, where we would be joined by my father, who preferred an L.N.E.R. sleeper to the Austin. He and my mother played golf most mornings and bridge in the evening. This was his only real break in the year and I didn't grudge him his adult pursuits, though it meant that I never saw a great deal of him at any time in my life. Mackenzie and I were left to our own devices for part of most days. He was an excellent companion. We

37

played golf on the Jubilee Course, which is the least distinguished of the four to be found at that Fife mecca, and in those days it was very undistinguished indeed. Golf was a new experience for Mackenzie but, in the manner of all old soldiers, he turned his hand to it, and we hacked cheerfully round. I think it cost us 6*d*. a day each. The only time he had ever come across the game in the army had been when a sergeant-major called for volunteer caddies for an officers' match.

'Wot's golf, Sarn' major?' one of the soldiers had enquired.

'Golf, my lad,' replied the sergeant major, 'is 'ockey at the 'alt!'

I much preferred it when we discovered a village further north, Spey Bay in Morayshire, with just a small family hotel, a sporty golf course with fairways of cropped heather, the fast flowing Spey dashing into the sea, and the Cullen Bin rising at the far end of the bay, as if its only job in life was to give some balance and contrast to the view from my bedroom window.

I've already confessed to being a victim of the Walter Mitty syndrome. At Spey Bay, one never-to-be-forgotten morning, Walter had nothing on either me or Mackenzie. I played golf with the Prime Minister and Mackenzie drove him to the match. To explain why, at the age of fifteen, I had this exhilarating experience, it's necessary to skim rapidly over my father's political career.

He was first elected to Parliament as a Coalition Liberal in 1918. He made his mark and might well have abandoned business for politics had he not lost his seat at the following election by a couple of hundred votes, and failed to win it back at the one after that by a couple of thousand. He'd had enough. His constituency, Dunfermline, seemed to be rapidly becoming safe for Labour, and he didn't try to look for another. In the 1931 crisis election he was persuaded to return, this time as a National Liberal, and he was in with a majority of nearly five thousand.

The Prime Minister of that National Government was, of course, Ramsay Macdonald, who for reasons of patriotism agreed to head a coalition of the middle and right, destroying in the process his party's electoral chances for the next twenty years.

The Macdonald family home was at Lossiemouth, which lay only a few miles west of Spey Bay. In his earlier pacifist days the golf club there had refused Ramsay membership. When the committee decided that Macdonald the Premier was another matter, and invited him to join, he proudly declined. My father had no close political ties with him, but he didn't share in the general criticism of his policies, and found him congenial company. Knowing his fondness for the game of golf, he decided in August 1934 to ask him for a round at Spey Bay. The invitation was gratefully accepted. He would be over the next morning in his official car, a stately black Hillman barouche, which looked impressive but broke down on the way. Mackenzie and the Austin were dispatched to the rescue.

My father had decided on a four ball match, he and I against the Prime Minister and aunty Peggy, who was a good player, but, like her nephew, a compulsive giggler. As we arrived on the first tee there was a stampede of caddies to gain the honour of carrying the great man's clubs. All but one were young boys, sons of local fishermen.

The exception was a man of indeterminate age, mentally deficient, his face tanned a deep mahogany, from which stared expressionless blue eyes marred by a slight squint. Though the morning was hot and sunny, he wore a heavy dark brown serge suit with the sleeves turned inside out so that his bronzed forearms were visible, and the upper arms were encased in a double thickness of cloth with the lining on the outside. Scattering the small boys like chaff, he won the race for the precious bag, seizing it from the startled private detective as if it were the Standard on the Braes of Mar. My father tried to wave him aside, until Ramsay, elegant in tweed knickerbockers and a cap to match, insisted that he should be allowed to carry on. The caddie was delighted at his good fortune, but when he bent down to tee up the Prime Ministerial ball, it was clear that his eyesight was likely to prove unequal to the task. At every tee he put the peg into the ground at a slight angle, and when he put the ball on top, it fell off. Puzzled, he would try again with the same result. He resisted all our attempts to help, while the Prime Minister observed the interminable pantomime through his thick horn-rimmed glasses without comment. Aunty and I shook with silent mirth, not daring to let our eyes meet. My father, who inclined towards irritability, muttered inaudibly not trusting himself to speak aloud.

39

Round about the fourteenth, the caddie achieved a seemingly impossible feat of ball balancing. The tee was at an even steeper angle than ever before, yet, incredibly, the ball stayed on top of it. He straightened up with a triumphant, toothless grin and Ramsay took up his stance. He addressed this miniature Leaning Tower of Pisa for a long time, eventually beginning his slow back stroke. He had just reached the top when the ball finally bowed to the law of gravity and fell the inch and a half to the ground. Aunty and I yelled with laughter. My father, crimson with outrage, barked at me:

'For God's sake shut up and tee up the Prime Minister's ball.'

I rushed forward to do his bidding, so did aunty, so did the caddie. We collided heavily, falling in a heap at the Premier's feet. Fortunately, my father saw the funny side; if Ramsay did, he gave no sign. He helped us all up with grave courtesy, and, as none of us was capable of doing anything except giggle hysterically, he teed up his own ball and, as the pros say, knocked it down the middle.

The Ship of State seemed to be in safe hands.

All the time I was at Charterhouse it never crossed my mind that I would be able to do anything else in life except pursue the legal career that my father had mapped out. I had no feeling for it, but any suggestion to him that I might go on the stage was always met with the counter suggestion that theatricals would be a splendid hobby, not a reliable source of income. Few actors would quarrel with that judgement! Aunty Peggy advanced another objection.

'I liked the people I met on the halls,' she would say. 'But they were all very common—not your sort at all.'

My mother was more sympathetic, contenting herself with injunctions to finish my education and acquire other strings to my bow.

In 1935 my father was knighted for political and public services, an honour that gave him and his many friends great delight. It's only at such a time that a boy realizes the extent of his father's popularity, and the event strengthened, for the time being, my resolve to follow a similar path. Tommy Fielden, however, had other ideas. He was determined that I should try for a choral scholarship at King's College, Cambridge. Gibbo was dead against it:

'Do you really want to spend Christmas singing carols in that chapel? Do you want your life at university to be one long choir practice? Is your father so hard up that he can't pay the fees at Trinity Hall?'

I knew the answers to all those questions; if I'd given them, that would have been the end of it. Instead I shrugged and left him. I was young, had never been to Cambridge, fancied the trip, and anyway Fielden had already sent in my name.

The evening before the examination I developed a cold. Gibbo was delighted.

'Good luck and I hope you don't get it,' was his parting shot.

He needn't have worried. So certain was Tommy Fielden that I'd 'knock 'em cold' with my solo, I don't think he'd bothered to read the other requirements of the examiners. In charge of the proceedings was the organist of Kings College, the late Boris Ord.

'Good morning, I'd like to begin by testing your intervals.'

'My what?'

'Your intervals.'

'Oh.'

'Sing me a diminished fourth.'

'I don't know what that is.'

'I beg your pardon?'

'I said I don't know what that is.' It was perfectly true.

'I see. Well, perhaps you'd be kind enough to read this.' He handed me a hideously difficult piece of music. Nearly every bar had a change of tempo and the key signature was five sharps.

'I don't think I can.'

'Try.' I tried. My slightly colded voice swooped uncertainly and then died into an embarrassed silence.

'Yes, I see what you mean.'

'Would you like to hear my solo?'

'If you wish, though I think I should warn you that you have absolutely no chance of a choral scholarship.'

'Yes . . . well . . . even so I think I'd like to.'

'Of course. What is it?'

'It is "Enough."'

Unfortunately it wasn't.

Later, I took the history scholarship paper for Trinity Hall,

41

never came within a mile of any award, completely misunderstood the subject of the essay paper, but evidently satisfied the examiners, for in the autumn term 1938 I took up residence on P staircase with a nice view of the Cam from the lavatory window.

Gaudeamus igitur

(Student song of the middle ages)

I can't honestly say that I look back on Cambridge with anything approaching affection or nostalgia. When I got there it only had a year or two of the old life to run and maybe that had something to do with it. Charterhouse had been a closely knit community where I revelled in the companionship, and the last year there had been the most enjoyable of my first eighteen. I had become, over the years, a sort of licensed jester because of my regular appearance in school plays and house entertainments, which were always the subject of criticism and ribaldry among my contemporaries.

'Not again, Wallace, what are you going to be this time? Joan of Arc?'

But most of it was good natured, and I had one unusual asset. I was the perfect subject to be on the receiving end of practical jokes. If all the trophies the house had won were built in a pyramid in a dark passage with a trip-wire hopefully rigged a couple of yards short of them, I would obligingly take the correct number of unwitting steps to be spread-eagled at the exact spot where, when one flung one's hands forward for support, they demolished the pyramid, rending the air with a good imitation of a bull in a silversmiths.

If my bed were dismantled, then delicately balanced, so that the two ends would collapse and the middle crash to the floor as I got in, I would provide, without any foreknowledge, a far more satisfactory result. The bed would unaccountably remain in one piece until my regular breathing made the others lying in the dark, hugging themselves with anticipation, begin to wonder if the whole plot had misfired. That was the moment when a heavy crash and a startled cry would give everyone but me a great deal of pleasure. One night it didn't collapse for a solid hour, long after the conspirators had given up hope and gone to sleep. I got the blame for waking them up, but then a jester's life inevitably invites a few kicks.

Now, sitting in my college room, which was just like the first act of *Charley's Aunt*, a cheerful fire burning in the grate, my brand new gown hanging behind the door, a pile of advertisements from tailors, book-sellers, college societies, political clubs and religious bodies lying on the table, I felt excited, emancipated and almost unbearably lonely. I was no longer hunting in a pack, I was on my own, which was an essential part of the whole damned character-forming exercise. The pamphlets lying on my table were only a tiny fraction of the activities available in Cambridge to a freshman like me. Unfortunately, none of them interested me.

My fellow law students were a pleasant crowd, but I had little in common with them. Some were the sons of lawyers, who talked in the jargon already, and knew exactly where they were going. Several were Indians, all extremely intelligent, for whom a good degree could mean high office in their native land. I saw little of any of them outside lectures and the study periods, known as supervisions.

The other freshmen reading subjects like medicine and natural sciences tended to keep to themselves, as did the athletes. The college only had the atmosphere of school when, each evening, we dined in Hall. It was a mellow, candle-lit occasion with good conversation, but afterwards everyone drifted away to work or join one of the myriad of pursuits that interested them. Time after time I returned alone to my rooms, longing for company and disinclined to open my law books. I soon realized that my heart wasn't in it.

I couldn't blame my teachers. Dr. Ellis Lewis, a red haired Welshman was acknowledged to be a brilliant exponent of the Law of Real Property, to say nothing of Contract and Tort. I liked him enormously, still do, yet I scarcely understood a word he said. When in supervisions one of the Indians would ask a question, I was not always certain what was being asked,

44

let alone the answer. Dr. Whalley Tooker, our mentor for International Law, took a group of us in his rooms at a college some distance from Trinity Hall. I was invariably late. He was unfailingly courteous, possibly realizing, that had I attended at his rooms twelve hours a day instead of two hours a week, my only chance of getting to the Hague would still have been on a package-deal holiday.

Cecil Turner, a celebrated and much loved bursar of Trinity Hall, who took us for Roman and Criminal Law had marginally more success. Resembling an elderly, dried-up, family solicitor, he soon displayed a crackling sense of humour and a twinkling eye. Whether he was describing card-sharpers on a race train to Newmarket or the manumission of Roman slaves, it was a down to earth account of ordinary mortals wrestling with the everyday problems of turning an honest—or dishonest—penny. I felt that if I had any future as a barrister, it would be in the limited, but fascinating field of burglary, murder and rape.

Though Trinity Hall was known as a 'Law College', it also had a reputation for prowess on the river. If I had little stomach for solving abstruse legal problems, maybe I would fare better skimming at speed over the water with seven other carefully drilled oarsmen and a skilful cox. Walter Mitty was at work again. I put my name down for a place in the rugger boat. I didn't play rugger, but it was the name of the lowliest crew, and an alibi to protect the reputation of those who rowed seriously.

'I say, Nigel, your boat club had a pretty ghastly crew out this afternoon, eh?'

'No, no, no, my dear chap. That's the *rugger* boat; nothing to do with us at all.'

It was certainly something to do with me. I'd never been in a racing boat in my life, Charterhouse didn't go in for that sort of thing. My fellow oarsmen, who turned up on the appointed afternoon, exhibited the signs of suppressed excitement that marked them as Walter Mittys too; soon we would be prepared for the question that always cropped up in those days at parties when one admitted to being an undergraduate at Oxbridge.

'I say are you going to be in the Boat Race?'

'No . . . but I do row a bit.'

45

Before letting us embark, there was a short training period sitting in a simulator on the bank, manipulating an oar with holes in the blade which allowed it to pass through the water with some semblance of the real thing. All too soon we were stepping into one of those long narrow jobs, associated for generations with the calm stentorian tones of John Snagge. On the tow-path was a more experienced member of the boat club, equipped with a bicycle and a megaphone. The cox suggested we practice a few starts. On a word of command we dug our oars lustily into the water as we slid back on our seats. The boat leapt forward.

'Well done!' yelled the young man on the bicycle, his voice sounding curiously tinny through the megaphone.

'In—out! In—out! Remember, when I say stop rowing, stop at once! In—out!'

Undoubtedly we had beginners' luck. Our rhythm was astonishing and the boat gathered speed.

'In—out! Don't dig so deep, Wallace, loosen up, you're as stiff as a board! In—out!'

We hissed through the water. Out the tail of my eye, trees, people and boat houses flashed past on the bank; our coach pedalled faster and faster. The moment of truth arrived with dramatic suddeness. I dug too deep. The momentum of the boat snatched the oar from my grasp. I fell off my sliding seat flat on my back, while the oar flailed rapidly backwards and forwards, as if in the hands of an invisible demon. Every time I attempted to sit up and regain control, it gave me a sickening thump in the solar plexus. The order to stop rowing from the bank never came. Cycling one-handed, while shouting over your shoulder to a boat crew, requires luck as well as judgment. Our coach had experienced an acute shortage of one or the other, and had disappeared with megaphone and bicycle into a hawthorn bush. Shortly afterwards I handed in my resignation and applied for membership of the college association football club. They were glad to see me. They only had ten members before I arrived.

But there was still a vacuum in my life. I described how it was filled in a parody on a famous ditty from *HMS Pinafore* written more than twenty years later for a cabaret appearance at— a legal function.

'When I was a lad my father said
'You'll be a lawyer born and bred,
You'll go to Cambridge, Trinity Hall,
Until to the Bar you get your call.'
I listened to professors preach on Tort,
My attention, alas, was seldom caught.
I struggled with the Law of Property,
But I also joined The Footlights and the A.D.C.*

I studied some cases, chapter and verse,
Like the late Mr. Owens in his hearse,
Who collided with a lorry driven by some fool,
Who was emptying the dustbins up in Liverpool.
Another that gave my spirits cheer
Was the snail in the bottle of ginger beer;
But the Indian students took it seriously
And compared it with Regina versus Komarjee.

My tutor said 'You've managed to pass.
You're top of the section marked 'Third Class''. '
The Indians all with joy did burst,
For every single one had got a loverlee furrst.
But a man like me of lowly ilk
Was most unlikely to take silk.
So I put to use, as you can see,
What they taught me at The Footlights and the A.D.C.'

The A.D.C. with its own theatre and cosy clubroom in Park
Street soon became my regular haunt. I made some sort of
impact in the Christmas pantomime *Dick Trumpington and his
Cat'*, playing a wicked squire, Baron Bottisham of Beef. The
dame was played by the president, Wallas Eaton, and it was
from him that I got my first inkling of the demands and self
sacrifice exacted by a theatrical career.

During the pantomime week I was lunching in the clubroom
one day and mentioned, by way of conversation, that I was
keeping goal for Trinity Hall in a Cup match on Friday
afternoon.

'You're what?' cried a scandalized Wallas.

* The Amateur Dramatic Club.

47

I repeated the information.

'Do you realize', he was labouring under some emotion, 'that we have sold every seat for that night and both shows on Saturday?'

'Yes,' I replied, 'Isn't it splendid?'

'It will be even more splendid if you break a leg, or sprain an ankle and can't appear. You know perfectly well you've no understudy, and we desperately need the money to keep the club going next year. I can't stop you, of course.'

Perhaps that was the moment when I relized that I would eventually land up on the stage. I nerved myself for a difficult interview with the captain of football.

The theatrical scene in the university was greatly influenced in those days by two dons from Kings College, the fair and inscrutable George Rylands, still known to his intimates as Dadie, and the late Donald Beves, a falstaffian figure, balding and sporting a semi-military moustache that gave him the look of a senior member of the CID off duty. He was reputed to be the best amateur actor in England.

Dadie ran the prestigious Marlowe Society which presented an annual spring production at the Arts Theatre of a play by Shakespeare, or one of his contemporaries. To be invited to take part in one of these productions was a signal honour. Dadie was deeply concerned with the speaking of the lines, and could be more biting in his comments when displeased than any other director I've ever worked for since. He was, and is, no amateur, with a number of successful West End productions and some remarkable recordings of the whole of Shakespeare's plays to his credit. Though there was honour in appearing in a Marlowe production, there was precious little glory, for they were anonymous. The programme listed the dramatis personae, but not the personae who were playing them. The spring production in 1939 was *Macbeth*. I was invited to play Banquo.

This was the time when monkeying about with Shakespeare was first becoming fashionable. Dadie decided to bring the date of the tragedy forward to the time of the 1745 Rebellion. The costumes had previously been used for the René Clair film, *The Ghost Goes West*, starring Robert Donat. Whether the chance to get these romantic costumes from another period on the cheap set Dadie on this course, or whether it was just good fortune that they were available to enhance this anachronistic *coup de theatre*, I don't know; if asked, Dadie would only volunteer a mandarin smile.

He had also commissioned, or had thrust on him, some incidental music, which was played by enthusiastic under-graduates on instruments of the period and earlier. Sackbuts, lutes and early wood-wind instruments abounded in the small orchestra pit on the first night.

It had been arranged that the National Anthem would be played before the performance, but somehow this had not been made clear to the stage manager. As the sackbuts and lutes struck up, sounding like Esterhazy's musicians on a bad night, he failed to recognize the tune, thought it was the opening music, and put the curtain up on the three witches. With Hitler on the rampage, Munich in the recent past and a strong sense of patriotism alive in Britain, the witches did the only thing possible. They stood to attention round the cauldron.

The stage manager could be forgiven. I've only heard one less recognizable version of the anthem in my life. It was played at the Edinburgh Festival by the musicians of the Kabuki Theatre of Japan.

If the evening had begun inauspiciously, there was worse to follow. King Duncan's arrival at Dunsinane Castle to accept Macbeth's grisly hospitality was followed by a procession of servitors, bearing the necessary utensils to wash the old monarchs feet. One of the survivors, Hugh Popham by name, carried a towel draped over his arm. For the second time a gale of laughter swept the theatre. Whether by accident or design it bore the legend in large red lettering 'L.N.E.R. LAVATORY'.

The next morning I eagerly opened the *Cambridge Daily News*. *The Times* and The *Daily Telegraph*, discarded on the breakfast table, didn't seem to have noticed Banquo at all; this was my last hope of a mention. Ah yes, here we are;

'The actor [that was something] who played the part of Banquo has physical attributes such, that although he gave a conscientious and painstaking performance, he appeared to be miscast.'

Nobody could have called me fat in those days; well covered, perhaps, but there's nothing in *Macbeth* to indicate that Banquo

49

had a poor appetite. So what physical attributes was he talking about? I was too proud to write and ask him, but he was probably right. When managements are casting a tragedy, my name is not one that seems to spring readily to mind.

Donald Beves, whose subject was modern languages and who had never been known to say more in praise of a French essay than *pas mal*, was nevertheless a great encourager. He gathered round him people who shared his interests with the efficiency of a magnet. His collection of antique glass was impressive, and not all of it was displayed in cabinets. Once at a party in his rooms an inebriated guest pointed to his glass.

'Gorgeous, Donald.'

'Yes, they are rather nice, worth about fifty quid each.'

After a first night in Cambridge there was either a Donald party or one given by his close friend Camille or 'Pop' Prior. And unlike theatrical parties anywhere else, Donald, vast and urbane, or 'Pop', diminutive and shrewd, would mingle praise with highly articulate criticism, all the more telling because it was delivered in a quiet and kindly voice in some secluded corner of the room.

It was, of course, absolutely the right car for Donald, but it was something of a surprise to see him one day climbing into a Bentley. Dons couldn't afford them. He noticed me looking past him at the noble and well polished barouche.

'Oh that! Yes, well, that's the one great extravagance of my life; but then one never regrets extravagances. It's the economies you regret.'

I hope such as Donald and Dadie still figure on the university scene, though I doubt it. The art of living as they understood it was good conversation, the theatre, music, wine, beautiful possessions, and they were prepared to welcome and advise anyone who expressed an interest in these extra-curricular subjects. To give the undergraduate population such advice today, without being accused of paternal or, at the very least, avuncular activities, intended to seduce the young with the symbols of the hated middle-class bourgeois culture, would be pretty difficult. I'd like to think that one or two such thinly disguised establishment figures of the present day are giving it a try.

The A.D.C. was not my only refuge. At least once or twice a

week I mounted my Sunbeam with its oil-bath gear-case and pedalled swiftly along King's Parade, one of the few thoroughfares in England with a cycle density to rival the motor-car, turned right down Silver Street, and headed for one of the most evocative sounding addresses imaginable: The Old Oast House, Malting Lane. It was the home of W. S. Drew, a friend of Tommy Fielden, who had a high reputation as a teacher of singing and wrote a famous book on the subject;* Tommy's introduction to him had been an invaluable leaving present.

He lived with his wife Sybil, who taught fencing, and two daughters with beautiful eyes and painted finger and toe-nails, the elder no more than ten, who called their father Billy. He was a small man, who had been a considerable athlete in his undergraduate days, and spoke about singing as an athletic pursuit, which, of course, it is.

'You wouldn't box out of your weight if you had any sense; so don't sing out of it either. That's the way to wreck your voice.'

I went to him expecting to be given long lists of scales and exercises to practise. Instead he told me that I had a good natural voice, which I produced reasonably well, and the thing to do was enjoy my singing.

'You can work at it when you're older if you want; you're only 19, so sing for pleasure.'

He gave me a list of noted classical songs that were well within my range.

'Take care of the middle of the voice,' he would say, 'and the ends'll take care of themselves.' But he could be a martinet over interpretation.

'Never sing a song until you have spoken the words several times, and know exactly what they mean.' It sounds elementary —until you catch an established singer at a concert with poor diction, or so hell bent on making a beautiful sound that he's forgotten to punctuate.

One day he introduced me to Schubert's 'Death and the Maiden'—one of the shortest songs ever written. For the first few bars the terrified girl pleads with the spectre-like figure of Death to spare her. Then in sepulchral tones Death commands her to give him her hand. Reading the words aloud, one automatically

* *Singing The Art & The Craft.* O.U.P.

changes the tone of one's voice to portray the two characters, and so I learnt one of the great secrets of singing, the use of vocal colour, without the long techincal rigmarole that usually introduces this subject. Vocal colour is simply altering one's tone of voice, while singing, to express different emotions or shades of meaning. It presents technical difficulties, and doing it successfully, with skill and subtlety, is one of the most important assets a singer can possess. One other piece of advice from Billy, perhaps less necessary now than then:

'Never be afraid of vulgarity; it's only the second rate artist, who's scared of it.'

It was a casual remark, on a crowded Northern Line Underground train between Tottenham Court Road and Leicester Square, that made the only Cambridge Long Vacation I was to have unforgettable. John Ehrman, who had gone up to Trinity to read history, and was my direct contemporary in Gownboys, had taken me to a film. Jammed tight in the swaying rush-hour train on our way home he yelled in my ear.

'There's going to be a war. Let's go to America next month. We may never have another chance.'

Later he outlined his plan. We would get over as cheaply as possible and buy a second-hand car. We would head for The Adirondaks and New England. We would get to the grass roots and find out what sort of people the Americans really were. At the end we would sell the car, perhaps at a profit, and return home. John is now one of the outstanding historians of his generation, and he was really looking forward to the consequences of such an enterprising sensible way of spending a holiday. Unfortunately for him it didn't turn out that way.

When I asked my father for passage money to America, he took it calmly. We set off towards the end of June 1939 in the *S.S. Caledonia*, an Anchor Line Boat, that plied between Glasgow and New York for the modest tourist return fare of £46. He realized, too, that war was imminent and that his only son might as well have some fun while the going was good. He also gave me £100 in travellers' cheques and wrote a letter to an American friend telling him that we were coming over, and should we land up in gaol, we would appreciate the name of a good lawyer.

My father's friend was called Al; and Al was a millionaire.

He was at least six feet four and weighed around 230 pounds. I had met him once or twice when he and his soft-spoken, dark haired wife Francie, who came from the deep south, had been in London on business trips—Al was in linoleum in America, but, unlike my father, who was managing director of Nairn's London office, he was president of his company, and looked every inch the part. Al never stooped. He stared challengingly at the world through his horn-rimmed glasses, and his stentorian voice communicated his thoughts loud and clear—though rather slowly—so that even when he was only commenting on the weather, it sounded like a State of the Union Message.

Caledonia docked in New York after nine days at sea, John and I stared delightedly at the sets of every movie we'd seen: sky-scrapers, the Statue of Liberty, yellow cabs and dockers smoking cigars. Unexpectedly a steward handed me a letter marked 'URGENT!'.

'My dear Ian,

As the Governor of North Carolina said to the Governor of South Carolina: "It's a long time between the drinks". As soon as you and your friend have checked into your hotel, call my office and I will have Edward pick you up and bring you right out here . . . '

There was a good deal more about any son of John Wallace being very welcome this side of the Atlantic and the importance of making the most of a vacation trip to this great country. I handed it to John.

'I smell danger,' he said with a wry smile. As far as his plans were concerned, he was one hundred per cent correct.

Strange adventure!

(The Yeomen of the Guard)

I 'phoned Al's office from our hotel. A secretary said he was in conference and that Edward would call for us at two-thirty.

'Who's Edward?' said John.

''I haven't the faintest idea—maybe he's a relation; what about going up the Empire State building before lunch?'

Edward was dead on time. He wore a well-cut grey uniform and flung open the door of a Cadillac limousine, so enormous that an usherette with a torch would have been a help in finding the back seat. He was coal-black, doggedly cheerful, an excellent driver, and he treated us, then and subsequently, like a couple of wayward nephews. Indeed, his out and out paternalism towards us—and his employer on occasions—would have confused the whole civil rights movement.

Al was still in conference when we arrived but Edward, who clearly enjoyed a special status, pushed us through the door of the conference room and gestured to the boss that he had accomplished his mission, failed to catch his eye, sighed loudly, pointed to two empty chairs and departed.

Once again I had the impression of a scene from a film unfolding in real life. Al was seated at a desk mounted on a dais at the far end of the long, narrow room with his executives facing him in rows like the audience at a small theatre. The walls were panelled to shoulder height and from there to the ceiling the cream emulsion was relieved by photographs of deceased captains of industry, new factories, maps of sales territories and the odd graph. On the floor at each end of his desk stood a large

55

brass spittoon, and they were not there for ornamentation. Indeed during the next half-hour they were in constant use, for Al was experiencing some difficulty with the fraying end of his cigar. The left-hand spittoon was the subject of high-level precision attack—usually at the end of a long sentence. He would run his tongue in a slow circle round his teeth, gathering up any stray shreds of Corona-Corona, take a sighting glance over his left shoulder and 'phut!'—a new sales target was fixed for the State of California. The right-hand cuspidor was only in action once or twice, when he swooped down unexpectedly to within a foot of it and expectorated violently to emphasize his disgust at some evidence of inefficiency.

'We just don't tolerate that kinda thing in this organization—phut!'

From all over the room came cries of:

'You said it, Mr. Hawkes!'

'Yes, siree!'

'Zowie!'

'Yer goddam right, sir!' and

'Attaboy, Al!'

Suddenly it was over, and the men in the dark-blue suits hurried out to take up the absorbing task of selling floor-cloth from Oregon to Florida, doubtless inspired by Al's rhetoric—and impeccable aim.

'What are your plans, fellas?'

We outlined our modest scheme. Al waved it aside.

'Hey listen! Ya gotta wunnerful opportoonity to see our great country and I'm darned if ya're gonna miss it! Ya made a great start goin' up the Empire State an hour after ya docked—jest the kinda thing I'd expect from a son of John Wallace.'

John Ehrman gave me a baleful look.

'Tell ya what I'm gonna do, Ian. I'm gonna pay yer rail fare right round the United States and Canada. Ya travel West with Francie and my niece, then ya come back on your own.'

Suddenly he seemed to notice John for the first time and frowned.

'I guess I can't pay for you as well, young fella—I'm not made of money, ya know. D'ja figure yer pop would fix it?'

'Yes, I think so.'

'Fine. We'll get a cable off right now. Incidentally, Ian, ya pay your own hotel bills—O.K.?'

'O.K. sir.'

'Now go find Edward and tell him ya're gonna go right back to your hotel, check out, and be my guests at Upper Mountain Avenue. See ya for dinner huh?'

*   *   *

'I feel terrible about this,' I said to John as we packed up at the hotel. 'I've let your father in for a hell of a lot of money, and your plan has just been abandoned without us having a moment to discuss it.'

'Never mind—it'll probably be fun,' he replied consolingly.

His father gallantly agreed to pay his fare, so a day or two later we returned to the conference room for a briefing on our trip. We found Al in a buoyant frame of mind:

'I sure hope this is gonna be memorable—jest wish I could come right along—wait till ya see the Grand Canyon, fellas— one of the most impressive sights in the world. D'ja know how I feel when I see it?'

There was a pause while his eyes misted with emotion.

'I feel—small.' He took off his glasses, wiped them with his handkerchief, blew his nose and continued more briskly,

'I have alerted a senior executive of this company to meet ya at each main centre on your route. He has orders to show ya every goddam thing of importance in his territory before ya pass on through. Incidentally, Ian, though ya're responsible for your hotel bills, I've made the reservations so ya've nothin' to worry about. One thing's for sure—a month from now ya'll have seen more of the United States than ninety-five per cent of the population ever will.'

'Just one question, sir.'

'Go right ahead, Ian.'

'When we're in Washington, sir, I believe it's possible for visitors to meet the President—could you arrange it?'

Al's face reddened, his fists clenched, his neck muscles bulged.

'No frienda mine shakes hands with that goddam son of a bitch—jest don't mention his name again willya? Ya know how he gotten himself re-elected? I'll tell ya—nobody shoots Santa Claus.'

Not only was Al a Republican, but Roosevelt's landslide victory

57

in 1936 on the success of his 'New Deal' policy had deprived him of the chance of a promised ambassadorship. I had touched a tender spot.

* * *

'It's going to be even worse than I thought,' muttered John as we studied the itinerary outside.

The trip was in two parts. The first journey was a long one to Chicago, thereafter in quick succession came Banff, Lake Louise, Vancouver, Victoria, Seattle, Portland, San Francisco, a few days in Pasadena and Los Angeles, then on to the Grand Canyon, Williams, Albuquerque, Washington, and back to New York. The time allotted was approximately three weeks, and every journey was to be by train. Part two was scarcely less exacting—but I'm getting a little ahead of myself.

Francie was a dear. The many years in New York hadn't eradicated the soft drawl of her voice. She loved Al dearly but confessed on one occasion that when, as a young bride, she'd got up and done a solo dance at a party, he hadn't approved. 'I jest knoo that from then awn I'd do better to sit quiet,' she told us in the train with a twinkling smile that made it clear she regarded being in the background as no hardship. The niece was eighteen—all puppy-fat and clichés, and shared with her aunt a distaste for sight-seeing. This left John and me to face the tender mercies of Al's representatives on our own.

The Chicago man took us to see the Cubs play the Cincinnatti Reds—and—having once got the hang of it—this life-long Arsenal fan found himself on his feet yelling with the rest. After the game our host became more and more impatient with the traffic congestion outside the baseball stadium. Unexpectedly he announced to the driver of the car in front, who couldn't possibly have heard him,

'Well, buddy boy, if you ain't gonna go *I* sure am.'

With superb aggression and indifference to yelling traffic cops, he swung out of line, mounted the sidewalk with his near-side wheels, continued thus for a good quarter of a mile, and then roared up a deserted one-way street in the wrong direction. I quietly revised my opinion, formed at the spittoon session, that Al only employed yes-men.

It was in Chicago that we got out first shock—the hotel bill.

58

When Al arranged Francie's trip West, he had, as a matter of course, reserved her a suite in the best hotels *en route*, to be shared with her niece. But millionaires have some difficulty in estimating the gulf between their income and other people's. Al was no exception. He'd booked John and me similar accommodation in the same hotels—at a similar price. The only snag was that we were paying for it.

Two nights in Chicago made an alarming hole in our travellers' cheques. We looked at the next hostelries on the schedule and shuddered—the Banff Springs Hotel and Chateau Lake Louise. Both command views of magnificent country—but they're not country pubs.

We held a council of war in the train and made a plan, taking advantage of the fact that Francie and the niece—I can't remember her name but it was something like Toots—had so much baggage that we always needed two cabs from the railroad centre to the hotel. This gave us an opportunity to explain our plight rapidly to the driver of our cab, and ask him to pick a quarrel with us over the fare on arrival at the hotel. Not one cab driver let us down all the way to California.

'Hey, doc!'

'Excuse me, Mrs. Hawkes. I think our cab driver looks upset. You and Toots check in and we'll meet you for dinner.'

'Hey, doc. I said *two* dollars forty—whadda ya tryin' to do to me huh? Do ya want me to call that cop?'

'Please go on in, Toots, John and I will straighten this out and see you later.'

As soon as they'd gone upstairs we would approach the desk clerk.

'Good evening, gentlemen, and welcome to Banff Springs. You have a reservation?'

'Er—yes—arranged by Mr. Albert Hawkes.'

'Yes, *sir*!'

'Is it—a suite?'

'Naturally sir, only the best for friends of Mr. Hawkes.'

'Naturally. You—er—haven't, by any chance, some rather cheap little attic or a shed in the garden?' Within a few days we could reduce the average desk clerk to tears. Every one of them eventually played ball, the reservations were modified and bills that would have been horrifying become merely frightening.

The only meal we could afford was breakfast, and we used all kinds of excuses to avoid lunch or dinner with Francie and Toots—even on trains—surreptitiously buying a hot dog or a hamburger when the hunger pangs became over-insistent. It's an odd sensation to be starving in a five star hotel. We never divulged our secret but I'm sure Francie knew. She began inviting us to have meals as her guest, and on those blessed occasions all our pride went out of the window, our feigned illness that kept us from the restaurant miraculously disappeared, and she smilingly egged us on as we ordered the sort of meal a cattle rancher would have devoured after twelve hours in the saddle—if he'd been able to afford it. But as the trip unfolded, we began to dread our encounter with Al's representatives, who carried out their guide duties with superficial charm and ruthless efficiency. In the train we were cosseted and clucked over by coloured sleeping car conductors.

'Now sah—ef you jes tek a liddle stroll along to dat club car an' reelaax fo' ten o' fifteen minutes, I'll mek you bed so soft an' snug you won't stir fo' eight 'owers.'

Then in the morning we would step off the train down the ladder—always wondering why America never got around to building railway platforms—to be confronted with a beaming, mechanical smile, a blue suit, a straw boater, and a briefcase that always contained a copy of the schedule—pronounced 'skedyul'. We had barely time to do our taxi-bilking act, followed by the cheaper-room-fast-talk, before he'd be pacing the lobby, impatient to be off. On several occasions I fell asleep in the sight-seeing car, and in Washington—near the end of the first trip—our guide got a surprise.

'Well, fellas,' he said at the rail-road centre, 'we'd best git goin'. We gotta cover a helluva lot of ground.'

'Will you please take us to the post office?'

'Sorry, fellas, it ain't on Mr. Hawkes' list and Jesus, it's some list!'

'We're not going anywhere else till we've been in the post office.'

'Now, look, boys. I don' wanna be tough . . .'

'Nor do we; but we left England a month ago and "c/o GPO Washington" is the first post restante address we gave.'

There were lots of letters for us both; we read them rudely

60

and unashamedly as the car passed by the White House and Capitol Hill, Al's man gamely persevering with the running commentary. We did see the Museum of the F.B.I. and I recall being impressed by Dillinger's straw-hat, punctured by bullet holes and Al Capone's armoured car.

If this seems an ungrateful account of Al's extreme generosity, which I still appreciate over thirty years later—it must be remembered that before we reached Washington we had viewed the stock-yards of the middle-west, the Canadian Rockies from end to end, the majesty of British Columbia, the Golden Gate, to say nothing of two World Fairs, a concert at the Hollywood Bowl, film making in Hollywood, the Grand Canyon, and a hot gospel meeting at Aimée Semple Macpherson's Temple. It was all the experience of a lifetime, impossible to digest at a sitting.

Our visit to the Temple ended prematurely. After an unpromising beginning when it was announced that Aimée had a cold and wouldn't be appearing, a paper collection was taken to provide her 'Mom' with a fur coat for their forthcoming crusade to Europe. Then a jolly, plump young man in a cream linen suit bounded on to the platform.

'Hallelujah, folks! I feel pretty good in my soul tonight, so I'm gonna sing you a little song. Brother George, would you oblige? Thank you, Key of G. One! two! three!

> "This ole world will never hold me.
> Any moment I'll be gone,
> For I've had ma consecration (right hand up)
> And I've got ma wedding garment on."

All together now!'

It was about then that John and I were thrown out. We weren't laughing audibly but, admittedly, the whole row of seats was shaking with the effort of trying to stifle our hilarity.

At Pasadena we said goodbye to Francie. She was going to stay for a few weeks with her married daughter Louise, who placed a guest house and swimming pool at the disposal of John and myself for our short stay. I was greatly impressed one evening when she casually mentioned that she was an old friend of Bette Davies—

'She's awful nice, not at all like those bitches she plays on the screen.'

We fell for Louise because she was a giggler—like us. At the end of three days blissful rest from tourism she bade me an affectionate farewell.

'Goodbye, you great fool,' she called as the train pulled out. We were headed for the scenic highlight of the trip—the Grand Canyon.

Though my memory of some things that happened thirty-years ago is fairly clear, it's not equal to the statistics of that vast gorge in Arizona, which, according to my encyclopaedia, is six thousand feet deep, over two hundred miles long and at the widest part measures eighteen miles from rim to rim. The general effect is like looking down on a stretch of yellow clay that has been dried and cracked by the sun and then magnified about fifty times, so that the clay between the cracks becomes mountains and plateaus with a few trees and a fair number of bushes to soften slightly the starkness of this light brown back drop for a film about dinosaurs.

Earnest sightseers hired ponies and picked their way to the bottom. Others took an expensive flip in a light plane, which flew down into the depths of the canyon. We, with very little time or money at our disposal, just stood and stared; then sat with our legs dangling over the edge. Al was right. It certainly does make you feel small—and hot. It was 104° in the shade—enough to set the restaurant where we dined on fire, but not before we'd paid the bill.

The rail-head for the Canyon, if they still have a railway, is a place called Williams. After our sweltering day and the evening train journey back to Williams, we found that we had to wait there till two a.m. for the sleeper to Washington. As we sat on our cases in the moonlight John pulled his tattered copy of the 'skedyul' from his pocket.

'God, look at this!'

'What?'

'It's now one forty-five a.m. and we're supposed to stop for an hour at seven to see the Indian reservation at Albuquerque.'

'Bugger the Indians,' I said. 'I'm going to sleep till we're an hour from Washington.'

They had to rouse us both shortly before the train docked.

Al must have had a pang of remorse about his anti-Roosevelt outburst (how dangerous it would be today for an American president to greet foreign tourists) because he'd arranged a powerful counter-attraction to end our day in Washington—a visit to the British Embassy to meet the Ambassador. The fact that His Excellency was away on a fishing trip was just bad luck. Instead, we had a short and embarrassing conversation with the first secretary, an exquisitely polite Old Etonian in a chalk-striped double-breasted grey-flannel suit, who tried not to notice the really terrible trousers I was wearing. I had inadvertently left three out of the four pairs I had brought from England in Pasadena, and the dark blue linen survivors hadn't recovered from the dust and sweat of Arizona. Worst of all, I had no jacket that matched them.

'Tell me something about your trip,' he said without enthusiasm. I recited the place names.

'Mm, pretty comprehensive, I'd say. How long has it taken?'

'Something under three weeks.'

'Three weeks!' He looked at us now with genuine concern. 'Well, I must say you both look remarkably fit. I dare say you could use a gin and tonic.'

*   *   *

Dinner with Al on the evening of our return to his home in New Jersey was a rather formal, candle-lit affair just for the three of us, served by his stout, coloured cook-housekeeper with whom he kept up a running battle of banter and repartee from the iced melon right to the coffee. Then, lighting a cigar, he leaned back in his chair and said:

'I can't tell you how glad I am ya enjoyed your trip, boys. Now I'd jest like ta hear all about it.'

John, with a nod, appointed me as spokesman. I suppose I talked solidly for about twenty minutes. When I'd finished there was a long pause.

'Yeah. Now tell me, Ian, you've seen the World's Fair in New York and the one in San Francisco—so you're one up on me. What have I missed?'

I didn't think he'd missed a great deal, but I rambled on about San Francisco being an expression of American culture whereas New York was angled on her industrial achievements.

'Atta boy! That's exactly what my people out there tell me. Now, what didya think of the water front at San Francisco?'

'Most impressive, sir'—the previous month had placed a severe strain on our superlatives.

'I'll bet ya never saw an Aquarium like that before.'

'An Aquarium? I don't think we actually saw that, sir.'

'What!' he yelled—the candle flames bent over forty-five degrees and the housekeeper came in at the run.

'I lay out all that goddam dough and ya miss the finest Fish Theayter in the world!'

I glanced across the table at John who was staring at the remains of a passion-fruit and carefully avoiding my eye.

Eventually Al regained his composure, and we managed pass marks for California and the Grand Canyon. Then came the one I'd feared ever since he'd lit the cigar.

'Whaddya think of the Injuns at Albuquerque, Ian?'

'Very impress . . . er splendid.'

'Yeah. Those souvenirs they sell ya—kinda fascinatin' huh?'

'Fascinating.'

'Ya bought some, of course.'

'Of course.'

'Such as what?'

'Oh, er, totem poles and leather goods.'

'Did ya, by God. I'd like to see 'em after dinner.'

John went a rather nasty shade of mottled purple.

'I'm very sorry, sir, that won't be possible, I'm afraid.'

'Why the hell not?'

'Well, by the time we got to Albuquerque we had so much extra baggage, that I gave those Indians five dollars to mail the whole lot straight home to London.'

Al looked at us both for a full ten seconds before replying.

'That was kinda smart,' he said. The investigation was over.

*   *   *

John had by this time decided not to accompany me on the whole of the second trip. It suited his family's plans better for him to catch a faster boat to Southampton, which was near their home, than to land up days later in Glasgow. Before setting off we had a day or two in New York, which included two expeditions under Edward's supervision, one to see Ginger Rogers in *Bachelor Mother* at the Radio City Music Hall, the other to climb up the inside of the Statue of Liberty. Edward was in his element, buying us ice-creams and seeing us across the road like eight year olds.

After we had 'done' Buffalo, Niagara, Toronto and Montreal, we parted at Quebec, John boarding *The Empress of Britain*, I climbing the steps of yet another sleeping-car bound this time for Boston.

Al's Boston man was quite different from the others. He stood at the bottom of the steps large, jacketless, bald, mournful, his head cocked on one side and slightly turned away, like so many people who are deaf in one ear. He had no briefcase—only the 'skedyul' clutched in the left hand.

'Hi ya, Ian,' he beamed. All the others had stuck to Mr. Wallace. 'I'm Fred Mulziger.*'

'Hi, Fred.' I was really getting the hang of the language.

'I got here a skedyul of all the places of interest in Boston that I'm supposed to show ya by nightfall. Boston, Ian, is a very cultural city. Ya *could* say it's lousy with culture.'

'I suppose you could.'

'Gee, it's hot.' It certainly was, even at eight o'clock in the morning. Boston in early August is no place for Eskimos. Fred was now looking so mournful that I expected him to burst into tears. Instead he smiled—it was a sly, conspiratorial grin.

'I gotta great idea! Why don't we tear this up and go play golf?'

Looking back on that terrible game in the steaming heat with borrowed clubs, size eleven shoes (I take nines) and a pair of forty-five-inch-waist trousers flapping round my ankles, I wish we'd seen the sights. We played a four-ball aggregate, which meant holing out whatever your score. At several holes I went into double figures, and on these occasions Fred's deafness was particularly trying.

'How many did ya shoot there, Ian?'

'Thirteen.'

'I can't hear ya.'

'Thirteen.'

'Speak up fella.'

'THIRTEEN.'

'Gosh darn it. That'll cost us another fifty cents.'

* Not his real name.

And another twenty golfers on the crowded Country Club course wondered who that clown was with Fred. At least nobody laughed. Golf is a serious game and anyone who scores that high on a Saturday morning at Boston, St. Andrews, or Sandy Lodge is either a better player off his game, or shouldn't be there at all. They gave me the benefit of the doubt.

In the afternoon Fred and his conscience decided we should take a quick trip round the sights; we never left the car—it never stopped. The only place in the city we went inside, apart from Fred's home, was a fish restaurant where he took me for a shore dinner in the evening. He ordered mine: Crab-meat cocktail, clam chowder, steamed clams (a bowlful), fried lobster with onions and french fried potatoes, a chocolate ice, a glass of iced beer, and a ten cent cigar.

Afterwards we went to his flat to spend the rest of the evening till it was time for me to get on the sleeper back to New York. His plump, blonde wife, who had not accompanied us to dinner, made some coffee and, sitting herself beside me on the sofa, patted my arm and said:

'This is what I've been waiting for all day.' Fred had disappeared. I moved six inches in the opposite direction.

'I've been saying to myself "Ian will give us all the inside story on Wally and David." '

Americans at that time didn't seem to appreciate that their newspapers had kept them far better informed about the Abdication Crisis than our own. I was about to tell her this when I noticed that my wrists were sweating. Then I saw myself in a mirror on the opposite wall. I looked like one of the disciples in a green stained-glass window of The Last Supper. During the next hour I wondered more than once if I'd just had mine. I dashed from the room and by sheer luck opened the right door. I remained in there for a very long time.

It never occurred to Fred or his wife to send for a doctor. You've got to be very ill in America before that particular sales resistance breaks down. I was determined to catch my train even though I was so weak—and empty—that Fred and the porter had to help me into the sleeping berth. My last sight of Fred was leaning over me looking mournful again.

'Better in the morning, huh?' His head was cocked to catch my reply.

66

'Huuuh,' was all I could manage.

*　*　*

I was a little better in the morning and reported my return to Al
in his office. He looked at me over his glasses.

'Ian, yer lookin' kinda rough.'

'Yes sir, I think it was something I ate last night.'

'What didya have?' I told him.

'What about the orange juice?'

'No orange juice, sir.'

'Well, the lemon juice.'

'No lemon juice, sir.'

'Well, for Christ's sake, the grapefruit juice!'

'No sir.'

'Jesus, a meal like that without the nootralising effect of
citric acid! What did he have?'

'A fillet steak—medium rare.'

Al exchanged glances with his personal assistant who was
hovering near the desk.

'Sulkes—get on the 'phone to Boston and fire Mulziger. This
boy's big and strong, but it might have been a customer!'

It took me a good five minutes to get Fred's punishment
reduced to being told by his boss over the 'phone not to be such
a bloody idiotic son of a bitch in future.

That night, my last in America, Al took me for a final visit to
the World's Fair. He'd found out by careful cross-questioning
that on our previous visit John and I had missed what was in his
opinion the great event of the show—the General Motors
exhibit. We'd been more interested in the nude show and the
high spot for me had been the Inkspots singing 'If I didn't Care'.
To tell the truth we hadn't even noticed the General Motors
exhibit—but Al wasn't going to let me go home without adding
this thrilling experience to my already bulging cornucopia.

It was a warm August night and he had chosen an open-air
restaurant in a quiet corner where the clamour of the exhibition
was muted. The strains of 'Deep Purple' could be heard from a
nearby panatrope. I hadn't eaten all day.

'Ian, ya still look kinda rough. I guess ya ought to go careful.
Waiter! Bring this young man a plate of stooed lamb and a
large scotch on the rocks.'

The wash-room in the restaurant was presided over by an enormous coloured man in a white coat. Naturally my first two visits didn't call for any comment, but when I emerged from being 'glued to the mahogany' for the third time in twenty minutes, he put a huge arm round my shoulders and observed.

'Boy, you'se been eat'n clams.'

By this time Al realized that his cautious diet was not having the desired effect.

'Ian, I guess we'd better make this an early night. We'll jest take a look at that General Motors exhibit and then go home.'

At that moment the first and, thank God, not the last large scotch on the rocks of my life began to get the upper hand of the stewed lamb.

'I'm afraid, Mr. Hawkes, I . . . I don't seem to be able to stand up.'

That was the moment when I discovered why Al was a millionaire and, in retrospect, why Americans were first to the moon.

'Waiter!' he shouted. 'Have you any wheelchairs in this restaurant?'

'Yes sir.'

Al wheeled me towards the General Motors exhibit. I never actually saw it. I passed out as we went through the entrance.

*   *   *

I was miraculously better next morning—the day I was leaving. So much so that I decided to end my American trip as I had begun it, by going up the Empire State Building. When I emerged at the eighty-second floor there was a great deal more activity than five weeks before. A man with a microphone was standing on a stage surrounded by a crowd. As I joined them he called out:

'Is there anyone here from outside the United States?' A forest of hands went up, including mine.

'Where are you from?' he shouted in my general direction.

'Glasgow,' I lied. It worked. He had ignored everyone who said London.

'Come up here, young man.'

I needed no second bidding. In my amateur days I was a compulsive performer at the slightest provocation.

'Good morning everybody. This is W.H.N. presenting *Microphone in the Sky*, a programme of interesting travellers from all over the globe.'

The first traveller really was interesting. He was an airman called Corrigan, who had taken off in his single-engined aircraft to fly solo to California, misread his compass and ended up in Ireland. Then it was my turn. After the usual questions the interviewer looked at his watch then pulled a card out of his pocket.

'And now we come to the prize winning question for our interesting traveller sent in by one of our listeners. This week's winning entry is all the way from Wisconsin and here it comes: What is your hobby?'

'Singing,' I said, my heart putting on a spurt.

'Singing. We-e-ll why don't you boo, boo, boo a little for us?'

I sang 'The Rose of Tralee' unaccompanied.

'Say, I don't know why you go back to Scotland. Why not stay and we'll get a sponsor for you.'

I can't say the idea grabbed me. I thanked him and went for a farewell lunch with Al, which lasted dangerously close to sailing time.

'I ain't comin' to the boat, Ian. They always make me cry. So long, fella, remember me to your dear father and mother.'

My thanks seemed very inadequate. As Edward headed for the docks I said to Mark Sulkes, Al's assistant, who was seeing me off:

'Can we stop at a branch of the Chase National Bank? I want to cash a Travellers' Cheque for the boat.'

'You'll miss it if we do.'

'There's one!' I shouted. 'It'll only take a minute.' Edward screeched to a halt. Mark and I ran into the small branch of the bank. The single cashier put his hands up.

'It's not a raid, buddy,' said Mark. 'We just wanna cash a cheque, fast.'

'Go somewhere's else then,' snarled the angry clerk. 'Scarin' folks like that!'

'Mark, could you lend me fifty dollars till I get home?'

'Sure.' He got it back—after the war. We cut the boat so fine that the gangway had gone. I left America literally walking a plank. I've never been back.

Alla gloria militar!

When war was declared three weeks later I tried to join the navy. What bent my steps towards a recruiting office for the Silent Service is a mystery; perhaps two nine-day trips across the Atlantic, tourist class, had gone to my head. If I'd known then that S.S. *Caledonia* which took John Ehrman and me to New York would, in less than a year, be torpedoed and sunk by a German submarine eighty miles west of the island of Barra, I might have had second thoughts. Anyway the navy, awash with volunteers, turned me down flat. The army, too, was unable to take any more recruits for the time being; there was nowhere and nobody to train them, so undergraduates were told to return to their universities and complete their courses. By then, we were told, more training establishments would be ready. I never bothered the R.A.F., having always regarded the aeroplane as an unlikely and dangerous form of transport, only to be used as a last resort.

It was a strange anti-climacteric winter. The Faculty of Law at Cambridge decided to give a degree on the strength of two years' work instead of three, knocking the Tripos, Parts I and II into one examination. Though this was done as a concession to a generation of students who were about to fight for their country, I found it harder than ever to get to grips with my law books. The pace of tutorials quickened beyond my capacity to take them in and it was obvious that much was having to be left out. To say the least, it wasn't a favourable moment to sit down and study a subject that I knew in my bones would never

71

provide me with a career, war or no war. Even if it could have done, the day when I would don a barrister's wig seemed so remote and unlikely as to be hardly worth the effort. Not many of us believed that this war would be 'over by Christmas'. As 1940 progressed, we knew that if it were, we were unlikely to be on the winning side.

The A.D.C. set about providing a touring revue to entertain evacuated mothers and villagers isolated by the black-out or petrol rationing. It was entitled *Blackout Revels* and, awful as it must have been, provided some amusement for a great many people. The sketches were pinched from pre-war revues. Donald McWhinney, now a B.B.C. drama producer, played the piano, while I and Anthony Hampton, who recently became chairman of a consortium of tool manufacturers in Sheffield, and is a former Master-Cutler, sang songs like 'Touch and Go', 'You Can't Black Out The Moon' and 'Are You Havin' Any Fun?' We had a certain amount I must confess.

The Footlights collaborated with us on several occasions, offering the services of a fresh-faced, rosy-cheeked, clean-shaven lad, Jimmy Edwards by name, who was waiting to go into the R.A.F. and was always good for a short sketch in which he portrayed a comic U-boat captain. There weren't too many of those knocking about the Atlantic.

I had applied for the artillery and, to improve the chance of getting a commission, joined the Senior Training Corps, the university equivalent of the O.T.C. In peace time the theory was that if you got Certificate A at school and Certificate B at university, you would get a pip on your shoulder very soon after a war was declared. The S.T.C. gunnery lectures seemed much more relevant to the months ahead than the ones on contract or conveyancing. They were also slightly easier to understand.

When the results of the Law Tripos I and II were announced, I was not surprised to learn that I had got a third, though quite taken aback when 'Tel', our nickname for Dr. Ellis Lewis, told me that he had fought with the examiners for an hour in an unsuccessful attempt to get me placed bottom of the seconds instead of top of the thirds. He seemed deeply upset at his failure, for he was a dedicated teacher, whose loyalty and commitment to his pupils was absolute. I felt I'd let him down, though I don't think he was under any illusion about my ultimate destination. He must have known the weakness of my legal hand—even if it did include one undoubted ace.

When I was born, my father made an early move to further the career he so earnestly hoped I would pursue. He persuaded a House of Commons friend, Sir John Gordon Hewart, the Solicitor-General, to be my godfather. In that particular role he was not a notable success, never remembering me for a single birthday or Christmas throughout my childhood, nor evincing the slightest interest in my religious up-bringing; but then he had more important matters on his mind. In 1922 he became Lord Chief Justice of England—a position he held until ill-health forced resignation upon him in the late summer of 1940.

Occasionally in my youth we visited him before lunch on Sunday at his gracious house in Totteridge. He was small, round and pale, with an expression of sardonic malevolence sometimes observable in the faces of shrewd Lancastrians—he hailed from Bury. His eyes were flinty, his mouth small and pursed. He'd have been excellent casting for the Caterpillar in *Alice in Wonderland.* My father would never have asked him outright to help me in my legal career, not that I ever progressed far enough along the road to be in the sphere of influence of such an exalted figure. He once suggested, with a certain reluctance, that I might care to be his marshall* the next time he went on circuit. I didn't press the point. I felt he'd have been embarrassed if I had.

There are many good stories told about Hewart who, though an outstanding judge, was probably an even better advocate. On elevation to the Bench he almost certainly missed the evening companionship of fellow counsel in the hotel lounge when on circuit, as well as the cut and thrust across the floor of the court during working hours. For this reason he relished more than most the occasional moments of comic relief that crop up in even the dullest of cases, though his inscrutable countenance never betrayed the extent of his enjoyment.

On one occasion he found himself trying what is known in the legal profession as an open and shut case—where the evidence on one side is so overwhelming that the outcome is a foregone conclusion. In this case a verdict of not guilty was so certain

---

* Something between a social secretary and an office boy.

73

that the leading defence counsel decided to leave what little there was to do as a suitable debut for his most junior of juniors, before hurrying away to another court where his services were more urgently required.

The junior, let's call him Jones, was staggered by his good fortune and determined to make a favourable impression on the Lord Chief Justice. He launched enthusiastically into his opening speech and after twenty minutes showed no signs of having even reached the middle, let alone the end of his remarks. In such circumstances it is quite normal for the judge to drop a hint to counsel that the case has been adequately made and the proceedings can safely be allowed to move forward to the next stage. Hewart dropped no less than three such hints without making any impression on Jones at all. He bowed to the judge each time with a friendly grin and ploughed relentlessly on.

Standing at the back of the court, waiting to take part in the next case which should have already begun, was an extremely eminent King's Counsel; he knew Jones, liked him and realized that he was doing his career no good at all first time out by ignoring not only the senior judge of the realm but one of the most outstanding legal brains of the period. He scribbled a note and handed it to an usher. When it reached Jones he merely glanced at it, then stuffed it into his pocket, while his flood of words continued unabated. The King's Counsel could hardly believe his eyes for his message had been brief and to the point:

'Sit down, can't you see the old bugger's on your side.'

Hewart was intrigued. He had observed the whole incident and guessed its significance.

'Mr. Jones!' The unwonted sharpness of the tone stopped him in his tracks.

'M'lud?'

'I could not help noticing that an eminent member of this Bar caused a message to be passed to you a moment ago. Might I ask if it has a bearing on this case?'

'No, M'lud—a purely private matter.'

'So you say, Mr. Jones, but knowing eminent counsel as I do, I am aware of his complete grasp of the etiquette of this court; I therefore find it hard to believe that he would pass you a private message while you were actually on your feet defending

74

your client—unless of course it had a bearing on this case, however slight. May I see it?'

Mr. Jones, crimson in the face, had no alternative but to give the crumpled piece of paper to the Clerk of the Court, who handed it up to Hewart. He digested it; then, with a minute shake of his head, he regarded Mr. Jones.

'Well, can't you read?'

It was sad that the end of his long and distinguished career went completely un-noticed. Even though illness had kept him away from the Bench for a considerable time, it would have been reasonable to expect the news of his retirement to make the front page. It would have done so on almost any day other than September 16th 1940 when every British newspaper was excitedly telling its readers of the great daylight air-battle over London in which our fighters were reported to have shot down one hundred and eighty-three German aircraft for the loss of forty of our own.

On the face of it, to have a godfather who is the Lord Chief Justice might sound like a head start over the rest of the field. I thought of it as something of a handicap and kept it very quiet. Long before I made the decision to abandon the law as a possible career he was dead.

After the exams many of us who were cadets in the S.T.C. and had still not been called up, were persuaded by our officers, who were university dons on a similar voluntary basis, to stay in Cambridge and help out the tiny number of regular troops in the area. We wore battle-dress made from a fawn denim that stained very easily, khaki forage caps, gaiters and black boots. That was the theory. As unpaid guerrillas our company produced some interesting variations of this uniform, which at best defied any attempts to make it look smart and was not helped by the fact that we often had to sleep in it. 'Helping out' the regular troops mostly meant endless guard duties round the perimeter of Marshall's Aerodrome. Our withering fire-power consisted of a few Lee-Enfield rifles which, judging by the dehydrated grease with which they were encrusted when we got them, had lain undisturbed in some deserted armoury since 1919; we also had four eighteen-pounder field guns of the same vintage which we had regarded during the winter as lovable museum pieces on which to practice gun drill and other parade ground exercises.

Now, with a paratroop invasion of East Anglia expected daily, we realized it was about time our dummy shells were replaced with real ones.

It was something of a shock when we were told by the gunnery officer, who came to conduct our Cerificate B examination, that none of these four guns was capable of being fired more than once. Some essential part of the recoil mechanism had apparently been mislaid during the previous twenty-five years and, while one shot could be fired quite satisfactorily, it would damage the guns beyond repair. He gave us this highly classified information at the top of his voice as we stood on parade at the end of the day.

'You will appreciate, gentlemen,' he continued with a grim smile, 'that that one shot must tell. For obvious reasons it will not be possible to have a practice shot—so should you find yourselves the object of attack, you must make sure that the enemy is not only dead in the line of fire, but close enough to be virtually unmissable. I would say at a range of twenty-five to thirty yards. Then on the command Fire!—pull the lanyard and run like shit out of a goose.'

A week later they took our guns away—rumour had it they were urgently required in the Middle East.

The last part of my Cambridge summer was spent guarding the post office, which had strategic importance, for the building also housed a telephone exchange and a battery of teleprinters. We had guards posted all over it and at night it was often my job to sleep, locked in the teleprinter room beside the night operator, who was supposed to wake me if he heard anything suspicious. We were going through a parachutist-under-every-bed phase of security. The night teleprinter operator was quite a character. He transmitted his telegrams in rhumba rhythm with complete accuracy, usually whistling 'La Cucaracha' at the same time. By day, instead of sleeping, he preferred womanizing, and though he was not the sort of man to boast of his conquests or regale acquaintances with the details, it was obvious from the steady deterioration in his energy and high spirits that he was in heavy demand during his leisure hours. About two o'clock one morning I was on duty in the command post when a series of heavy crashes reverberated through the silent building. I and another cadet grabbed our revolvers and ran to the scene, certain that the Germans had arrived. The door leading to the teleprinter room had a glass panel. Our roving patrol man, making a routine check, had noticed that not only was our sentry asleep, which was permitted, but that the operator was slumped over his instrument, a victim, in the opinion of the highly imaginative patrol, of a poisoned dart. The crashing sound was his rifle butt, which he was using as a door knocker in an effort to rouse the sentry. It failed. When we got the door unlocked we discovered that the sentry was merely exhausted by non-stop guard duties, two hours on, four hours off, round the clock for weeks; as for the teleprinter operator, his condition is described very well by John Betjeman:

> 'Ah, love, for love I could not speak
> It left me winded, wilting, weak.'*

One night I had reason to be very grateful to him. Around eleven thirty a few of us were having cocoa in the Command Post when our officer, John Grace, arrived.

'They're on the way,' he said quietly, 'I've had the code word Cromwell.'

There was nothing to do but wait. I went up to the teleprinter room.

'You once said you could get straight through to London even when there's a delay.'

'That's right,' he said. 'And without paying for it—who do you want?' I gave him my home number. When my mother answered I tried to sound my normal self, apologized for ringing so late and explained that I'd had the call in for hours. Before ringing off I said,

'I just want to say that whatever happens I've enjoyed my life and I'm very grateful to you both.'

I meant it for the best, but it must have made them very anxious even though Cromwell never showed up.

By mid-July three of us shared responsibility for organizing our force of irregulars, having attained the exalted rank of cadet sergeant. My fellow N.C.Os were a short-sighted classical scholar called Finn and a volatile Welshman, Colwyn Williams. The principal advantage of our three stripes was that, by day at

* The Licorice Fields at Pontefract.

least, we could be above ground—the command post was a small room on the second floor. For the rest we slept and lived in the basement, which had a dusty concrete floor. There were no bunks, only the small square mattresses known as biscuits which were placed on metal stretchers. When we were tucked in our brown windsor blankets in the gloom we looked like patients in a singularly ill-equipped field hospital. Entwined round its walls and support pillars was a mass of pipes and conduits. These comprised a water main, a gas main, an electric main and a sewer. Despite the proximity of these services we had no heat, no water and precious little light.

One afternoon everything seemed to be under control and Colwyn and I were about to desert the command post for a quick half pint before the pubs shut, when we heard a sharp, muffled explosion. It clearly came from below.

'That was a shot,' I said.

'Nonsense, boyo, it was a door slamming, look you.'

'Somebody must have given it a hell of a bloody slam then.' At that moment our 'phone from the basement rang. Colwyn picked it up, listened for a moment, banged it down without answering, rose to his feet, ran to the door; before disappearing he shouted over his shoulder:

'Some silly bastard's shot the fuckin' water main.' He was gone.

The telephone exchange was on the floor above. I dialled O.

'Can I help you?'

'Well, it's rather a question of us all helping one another. I'm on the floor below you, and our basement is rapidly filling with water.'

'You're joking.'

The borough engineer also thought I was joking, and it took about twenty minutes to get it turned off. When I went down to have a look, the basement resembled the sequence in the film, *Ice Station Zebra* when they couldn't get the torpedo tube shut at four hundred feet below the surface; the biscuits were all floating above the stretchers and confusion was rife.

The culprit was poor Sergeant Finn. He had just changed the guard and faced a boring afternoon in the bowels of the earth. To enliven the proceedings he decided to give the cadets who had just come off duty a refresher course on the rules of aiming. As a boredom reliever it was dazzlingly successful.

'Supposing you were going to shoot that pipe over there,' he began, taking the loaded rifle from one of the guards. 'You line up the foresight with the U of the backsight and take the first pressure . . . ' Despite his defective vision, his aim was perfect. If he'd selected the electric main and got the gas on the ricochet, the results would have been even more spectacular and this book might never have appeared.

It took us till midnight, working with stirrup pumps and buckets, to get it pumped out—the fire brigade couldn't get their big sucker round a corner—so it was up to all us little suckers to perform one of those labours of Hercules that figure in mathematical problems.

Certificate B lived up to its promise. Instead of being called up as a gunner to a regiment I went in October straight to 123 Officer Cadet Training Unit, Bourlon Lines, Catterick. It was one of the new Sandhurst Blocks recently built to house the peace-time National Service intake. The course was five months and we emerged, it was hoped, as fully fledged troop leaders, or gun position officers capable of positioning, firing and looking after four twenty-five-pounder field guns and their crews under the supervision of a battery captain.

We were square-bashed by Sergeants and Warrant Officers who called us sir one minute and questioned our parentage the next in traditional army fashion. We progressed to ceremonial gun-drill, attended lectures on the internal combustion engine, the recoil system of a field gun, the angle of sight, map reading, organization, personal hygiene and V.D. and then gave back lecturettes to our class on the same subjects in an effort to prove we'd taken it all in. We rode large motor-bikes up and down precipitous, rocky slopes of the Yorkshire Dales, played 'catch' with the Green Howards, using bayoneted rifles and grenades instead of a ball, lived in constant apprehension of being returned to our unit as non-officer material and, in my case, only came alive when volunteers were called for to take part in a Christmas pantomime. The choice was *Cinderella*. A Cambridge friend from the A.D.C., Alec Gunn, was an ugly sister, Anthony Nicholls, the actor, was Prince Charming and I was Dandini. I sang 'A Nightingale Sang in Bourlon Square', and was supposed to follow it with my old stand-by, 'The Rose of Tralee'. Unfortunately the pianist misunderstood me when I nominated

A flat as the key. He preferred E flat. It was far too high and, to use a favourite phrase of professional singers, I couldn't have managed it wearing a fur-lined jock-strap standing on a chair. I broke down in the middle and got the bird.

Alec and I passed out pretty near the bottom of the class, which made us all the more surprised to be posted to the very smart 98th Field Regiment, Royal Artillery, formerly the Sussex and Surrey Yeomanry, then stationed at Fort Southwick, just inland from Portsmouth, which was under heavy air attack.

As the train meandered through Hampshire I couldn't help feeling a little smug.

'It just shows what rubbish it all is that you do best if you come out top. It's a matter of horses for courses, old boy.'

That's just what it is. When we were shown in to the Colonel's office he looked at us and chuckled.

'Ha, ha, so you're my ugly sisters.'

We froze.

'Yes—you see this regiment's pretty well equipped for most things, so I asked for a couple of young officers who could make us laugh a bit—organize the odd concert—that sort of thing. All right, dismiss.'

In enterprise of martial kind

(The Gondoliers)

My period of service with the 98th Field Regiment was brief.
It was also something of an ordeal. They had begun the war
volunteers to a man, territorials who had trained every week in
drill halls and then gone to summer camp while most people
were on holiday. These were the sort of men who hadn't just
worried about the rise of Hitler in the years before 1939. They'd
done something about it. Small wonder that the officers' mess,
made up of peace-time friends from the same part of the country
viewed outsiders like me and Alec with indifference. After a few
vain efforts to converse with our neighbours at meals we relapsed
into silence. Our equals would pass the salt or give mono-
syllabic replies to questions; but if we were rash enough to
address our seniors—there was literally no response whatever.

From the attitude of the battery sergeant-major—a builder's
foreman in civilian life—made it clear that it was only King's
Regulations that kept his contempt for my ludicrously inadequate five months training unexpressed, until one day when,
by the purest fluke, I gained his respect.

We were at Okehampton, the famous artillery range on
Dartmoor. On the first evening as I was about to dismiss my
troop and head for that unsociable mess, he approached me at
the run, the hint of a wolfish grin on his lips.

'Number 3 gun not running back properly, sir. What shall I
do about it?'

This meant that when the gun was fired and the barrel
recoiled, instead of returning smoothly to the firing position, it

was doing so in a series of jerks. If it had to be taken out of service the crew would miss vital training. The sergeant-major must have been sure that I hadn't the slightest idea what to do about it, and was already looking forward to telling his cronies so over his evening pint.

Now I've always had something of a flair for remembering scraps of useless information. I studied history at school at sixth form level yet my clearest memory is that the Gas Light & Coke Company was founded in 1810. During my officer cadet course at Catterick I found the lectures on the components of the 25-pounder field gun among the most wearisome I'd listened to since those on reversions in real property at Cambridge. I was frequently fighting sleep as the warrant officer droned on about calibration or the hydraulic system that absorbed the recoil. Fortunately I had been awake when he had talked about eradicating faults.

'When something goes wrong with the goon, gentlemen, the safest thing is to send for the artificer. Boot if she's not roonin' back smooth there's woon possibility . . .'

'Right sergeant-major,' I said, trying to look nonchalant. 'Fetch the drag-ropes and the tool-kit.'

The drag-ropes had rings at one end which could be attached to projections on the barrel so that the crew could pull it back manually to simulate a recoil.

'Thank you, sergeant-major; right, lads, pull her back.'

When they let go, the barrel jerked forward like a learner driver at his first traffic light. I selected a small spanner from the tool-kit, walked over to the gun, and turned a nut on the side of the breech a quarter turn clockwise.

'Pull her back again,' I said, assuming the air of a man who did this sort of thing every day. The barrel ran forward without a tremor.

''ckin 'ell!' muttered the sergeant-major, who was no more surprised than I was.

The next day was my first in sole charge of a troop of four guns. I had to lead them along the sandy tracks to a map reference supplied by my troop commander then get them into position. When I was given the map reference of a target I had to work out the range and angle of sight and then fire at it with live ammunition. When we arrived at the gun position it was immediately clear that because the ground rose steeply behind us, the lightly armoured trucks (known as quads) that pulled the guns would have to be parked fifty yards in front of them— not an unusual situation and perfectly safe provided we weren't shooting at very short range. When all was ready I reported by phone to the troop commander half a mile away in his observation post. He responded by barking out the map reference of the target and I galloped over to my map and protractor, set up on a tripod. It didn't take me too long to work out that the guns would have to be manhandled 10 degrees to the right.

'More one o degrees,' I yelled. 'Angle of sight zero, one thousand yards.' When the crew of number one gun, that's the one that fires the ranging rounds, reported ready I gave the order to fire to their sergeant. Nothing happened.

I repeated the order, but the crew of number one stood or knelt round the gun like statues waiting for their sergeant to shout. The chain of command is a vital part of service discipline, and I would have gone to the crew over the sergeant's head at my peril.

'Sergeant Wardrop,' I screamed, 'Are you deaf?'

'It's my brother, sir. I don't want to kill 'im.'

It turned out that Private Wardrop, driver of number one gun, was lying asleep in the cab of his quad directly in the line of fire.

'He's quite safe, sergeant,' I said. 'The shot'll clear the quad by a mile.'

'You come and look, sir.' I had to admit that looking down the barrel, the quad and its passenger appeared to be at some risk. However I felt that once again I was being put subtly to the test.

'Tell your wretched brother to get out and lie on the grass and then fire the bloody thing.'

'Yessir.'

I shut my eyes and waited for disaster, not to Private Wardrop, but to His Majesty's property and my reputation. Luckily the shot disappeared harmlessly over the quad and a moment later came my next order from the observation post.

'Less two o degrees.'

The crews cursed as they sweated to lift the heavy guns and shift them a whole twenty degrees to the left. I realized that something must have been wrong with my first calculation. A correction of twenty degrees was unheard of. This time the order to fire was obeyed without demur and from the observation post came a message I could hardly credit:

'Target destroyed. Cease Fire.'

In the mess that evening my troop commander spoke to me socially for the first time.

'Good show, Wallace, your map reading's pretty decent. Only one thing. Be a good chap and don't put your protractor on the map wrong side up when we're firing in anger. Never saw your first shot at all, so I thought to myself, bet the silly bugger's got it upside down and means left when he says right. What'll you have?'

* * *

I must be the only troop leader in the history of the Royal Artillery to have a one hundred per cent record of direct hits. I never had a further opportunity to spoil it. The day after we returned to Fort Southwick I was confined to bed with what at first seemed like 'flu, but which left me weak and easily tired. I was also losing weight. Eventually the M.O. sent me on three weeks' sick leave, which meant that I would have to report back to the R.A. Depot at Woolwich for a new posting and be immediately replaced in the 98th. My departure was greeted, except by Alec, with the same indifference as my arrival, though not for the same reason. Many years later after the regiment had fought with distinction through North Africa, Italy, and then from Normandy to the end, I ran into one of the officers in the Savoy Grill.

'Hello,' he said. 'Are you better now?'

'Yes, thank you.'

'Good. We heard you had a rough time; but of course when you left we thought you were swinging the lead. Didn't know you were so ill.'

'Neither did I,' I said, and we exchanged an embarrassed handshake.

My replacement in the 98th was Maurice Stride, one of my instructors at Catterick. They'd obviously gone off the ugly sister idea and settled for someone who knew what he was doing. Maurice is now a near neighbour, but one day in battle, standing where I might have been, he lost a leg. I also lost something; but not as a result of enemy action.

During my sick leave I became aware that all was not well with fifty per cent of my manhood—the right one. When the discomfort forced me to report it to the M.O. at Woolwich, he asked me some searching questions about my sex life, which at that time had hardly got off the ground.

'A pity really, because then it might only be V.D. As it is I think you'd better go into hospital for some tests. By the way, are you fond of milk?'

'Not particularly, why?'

'Well, milk that hasn't been pasteurised and comes from a tubercular cow can be dangerous.'

'I can't think of any time that I ever drank unpasteurised milk.'

'Good—any way, it's only an outside chance.'

On my way home I remembered, with a prickle of anxiety, that during the previous summer at Cambridge, while guarding Marshall's Airfield, a nearby farm had provided us with milk 'straight from the cow'.

I was sent to a civilian hospital in west London that had set aside a number of beds for military personnel. One morning a small, plump, white-haired man in a grey suit came to my bed which, was near a large window. He had an air raid warden's badge in his lapel. I thought he'd come to inspect the blackout.

'How are you feeling?' he asked.

'Fine, thank you.'

It's extraordinary how one always replies to such an enquiry in this way unless actually in agony or being sick.

'Good. We're going to shine an electric light into your bladder on Wednesday.'

Fear must have shown in my eyes as my imagination tried to grapple with the horror of an Osram 60 watt bulb, like the one hanging over my bed, in such a confined space—and how in God's name would it get there?

'Don't worry, you'll know nothing about it.'

It began to dawn on me that this was no warden, but the surgeon in charge of my case.

My incurable optimism had a final fling.

'Is there any possibility that what I have isn't serious?'

'Afraid not. You see we found T.B. in your water. See you on Wednesday.'

Before I could speak he'd gone, and I was left wondering whether I had six months to live or three. It was a moment when I needed a word or two of reassurance. I got them—not from the medical staff, but from a failed medical student in the opposite bed.

'You're probably not going to die,' he said and refused to elaborate. In 1941 there were no drugs, as there are now, to combat, tubercle bacillus. Treatment was rest, fresh air and, where possible, radical surgery. To most people the initials meant a short life dogged with ill health. To older generations it was regarded as a prostitutes' disease, and therefore unmentionable. Even my eminently sensible parents at first refused to believe the diagnosis, and then kept the truth from all but their closest friends.

The surgeon decided to operate, assuring me that I would soon be as good as new. I believed him—until one morning about ten days later I noticed that my remaining fifty per cent was displaying the same symptoms.

'What's the matter, Mr Wallace?' enquired the ward sister, who had poked her nose round the door of my side ward and noticed that I was crying.

'I think the other side's affected, sister.'

'Rubbish. It's sympathetic pain after the operation.'

'Sister. What if it isn't? What if it's the same thing all over again?'

'In that case, Mr. Wallace, I'm afraid we wouldn't bother to operate.'

Whether she, too, thought I was shamming or was merely trying to put some fight into me by deliberate provocation I don't know. But I did know that I was in a very serious condition and on the edge of despair.

Next day the registrar came to see me.

'I think you've lost confidence in us here.'

'I'd feel a lot happier if your genito-urinary man wasn't away with the R.A.F. in the Middle East.'

'Yes . . . well . . . I won't deny that you need an expert now. Look here, do you think you could fool a medical board of elderly R.A.M.C. brigadiers with Boer War medals into believing you're better?'

'I don't understand.'

'If you can bluff your way through that I can get you discharged from here on indefinite sick leave; but I'll only do it on condition that you promise to see a top G.U. specialist within twenty-four hours.'

I had the enormous good fortune to be given an introduction to Terence Millin, an Irishman of formidable ability and the sort of good looks that would have got him the name part in 'Dr. Kildare' against all comers.

'I tell you what,' he said, after a long look at what remained of my reproductive system.

'We'll shine a mercury vapour lamp on it at intervals for a month. It won't do a blind bit of good, but that's what it says in the text-books.'

'Shall I let you know how it's getting on?'

'No, I'll get the fellow who's going to do the treatment to keep me posted. But if by any chance it comes away in your hand give me a ring.'

For the first time in many weeks I had a feeling that I might be going to get better.

When the month was up Terence Millin's prophesy about the lamp was fulfilled. Things were worse, not better.

'If we're going to save that testicle I'm afraid it's going to mean more surgery. If you want another opinion I wouldn't blame you, but I think you ought to get it tomorrow.'

'I don't want a second opinion.'

'Right. We'll go ahead. Now cheer up. Always remember two's a luxury, one's a necessity, but I'm bound to admit that none's a disaster.'

It was, by all accounts, a long and very difficult operation, which left the theatre staff of a Hampstead nursing home speechless with admiration, and me still with a twinkle in my eye. Soon Millin became a household word in his field by inventing a simplified operation for the prostate gland that has removed one worry from the declining years of a sizeable percentage of the world's male population.

Some years after our encounter it was announced on the

87

six o'clock news that the Irish surgeon, Mr. Terence Millin, was flying to Ankara to treat the Sultan of Turkey.

'Good grief,' I said to my wife. 'It must have come away in his hand.'

* * *

I was soon fit enough to look for a light job and, on the strength of my career in amateur theatricals, applied for a posting to the Army Entertainment Branch. There was a vacancy at South Eastern Command Headquarters for an assistant to the Command Entertainment Officer. To my surprise he told me at the interview that I could start the following Monday, though I had no experience of the work I was to do. I discovered later that I was the only applicant. He had to find a 2nd lieutenant of low medical category or go without.

Command Headquarters was at Reigate and I was billeted at a small unlicensed guest house, long since defunct, near the level crossing at the foot of the hill. Whoever decided to call it the Castle Hotel was over-playing his hand. It was run by a cheerful young woman, Mabel Ena Rogers and her elderly mother with no visible assistance beyond an invalid boy with a severe speech impediment, who was willing to try his hand at anything with a winning smile, and varying degrees of success. The guests were mostly old ladies, permanent fixtures, who spent their days in the small lounge knitting comforts for the forces, their current preference revealed by the colour of the wool—khaki or blue. Most of them had been forced to leave comfortable homes when their staff or the relative who looked after them had joined up. Though they put a brave face on it, the chances of a return to their old life seemed slender in the spring of 1942 and they relied heavily on the other male guest at the Castle Hotel to liven things up: Major Jack Hobbs, my new boss.

Without detracting a whit from the reputation of the celebrated cricketer who was one of the heroes of my youth, there's no doubt that Jack Hobbs, actor and musical comedy star of the twenties and thirties, was a more entertaining personality with whom to share an office and lodging than the man who so often saw Surrey and England off to a good start. The old ladies were enthralled. All Naval and R.A.F. knitting was

88

suspended on his arrival and enough khaki mittens, balaclavas and scarves were produced and presented to have seen him through the Hundred Years' War. Jack had been something of a matinee idol and the passing years had only matured his good looks. The old dears couldn't have been happier if they'd had Rudolph Valentino at the breakfast table.

Our office was in an old mansion two minutes walk up the road that had probably belonged to a successful business man in the days when two thousand a year could sustain a cook, a parlourmaid, a car, public schools for the children, holidays abroad and still leave something over for retirement after tax. We had two desks in one of the spare bedrooms, where Major Hobbs treated me with a mixture of informality and blood-curdling threats that would have been quite out of place in the 98th Field Regiment.

'Well,' he said on the first Friday afternoon I was there, 'I'm off. You can hold the fort till Monday. Nothing'll happen; everything's been taken care of.' He paused at the door: 'If that nosey swine of an A.A.G. rings up, tell him I've gone to the War Office to see Basil Dean. If Basil Dean rings, say I've gone to Aldershot.'

'Yes, sir—er, where are you going, sir.'

'Mind your own bloody business.'

We had a similar conversation each week, which only varied in the vituperative epithets aimed at the Assistant Adjutant General, who might decide to check on his whereabouts. Basil Dean, the famous theatrical producer, who was head of E.N.S.A. did call once, seemed not in the least surprised that Major Hobbs wasn't at his desk, and rang off before I could get the cover story started.

Jack was an efficient officer, who had seen service in World War I. His present job could be done to a turn between Monday morning and Friday lunchtime, and he saw no reason to let the weekends go to waste. Once I dared to call him back as he started to make his Friday exit.

'Sir?'

'What is it?'

'Just in case that "snooping bastard of an A.A.G." doesn't believe me, or Monty wants to see you, wouldn't it be safer to leave a phone number?' (Monty was our G.O.C., shortly to go to the Middle East and possessing an unnerving reputation for turning up unannounced at any unit and asking awkward questions.)

He pursed his lips and frowned:

'Um—yes, perhaps it would.' He scribbled on a piece of paper. 'Now remember, that's only to be used if the balloon's on its way up. By the way, if any woman rings and you give her that number I'll have you court martialled and shot.'

Our sparsely furnished ex-bedroom of an office was a clearing house and distribution centre for all kinds of live entertainment from Shakespearean drama to concert party. Films were the concern of Army Kinema at the other end of the passage. The command was divided into three districts, each with a captain whose job was to get the available shows to the greatest possible number of troops, not forgetting very small units on anti-aircraft gun-sites miles from anywhere.

All three captains were theatricals of one kind or another. The Aldershot incumbent was an elderly character actor, D. A. Clarke Smith, who once sent me a requisition for a horse in protest against his meagre petrol allowance. His occasional visits to our office were apt to develop into an anecdote contest between him and Jack with 'Clarkie' a clear winner every time. Jamming his monocle into place he would settle his bottom on the corner of the desk and launch forth.

'Jack, did I ever tell you about the time I went with Sybil Thorndike and John Gielgud to read *The Merchant of Venice* to the prisoners at Wormwood Scrubs? The Governor, an awfully nice chap, escorted us personally to the hall and on the way he absolutely forbade us to exchange a single word with the prisoners. I was quite surprised when I saw them. Thought they'd look evil and twisted, but they were people like you and me and half of them were wearing gold-rimmed spectacles. When we'd finished I was just putting on my hat and coat when a little fellow, who'd been sitting in the second row darted up to me and hissed out of the side of his mouth: "I'm an old pro, Mr Smith, and I enjoyed that very much." Well—you couldn't just ignore him could you? So out of the side of my mouth I said "In that case you'll be glad to know we're coming back to do *The Taming of the Shrew*." "Ooh, lovely!" he whispered. "When?" "In about three months." "Bugger it," he muttered, "I shan't be here" '

I didn't see much of Bevan Williams, a theatrical manager, who quietly got on with it down in Kent, but Sussex was in the hands of a peace-time cinema organist and composer, Phil Park, who had rounded up a group of amateur talent in the Horsham area, and was keen to form them into a concert party to entertain the troops. Jack had all the professional's reserve about this volunteer effort, found Phil's advocacy of the project tiresome, and referred him to me. Within ten minutes his charm and enthusiasm had convinced me that it was not only a good idea, it was also my big chance—he was short of a male straight singer.

When I asked Jack's permission his reply was predictable:

'I suppose if you're stupid enough to drive 40 or 50 miles in an uncomfortable truck after a day's work here to make a fool of yourself in front of a lot of soldiers, there's not much I can do to stop you.'

And so 'The Fiddlesticks' began its brief career. We were quite a small concert party. Phil played the piano, and our star attraction was 'The Three Loonies', a description which concealed the identity of three privates from Bomb Disposal. They had professional experience on the halls and in provincial pantomime as eccentric and acrobatic dancers, and their act was interspersed with running gags and well worn comedy routines. They were a sure fire success, but very seldom did all three turn up. This had nothing to do with de-fusing bombs. Their nomadic existence in show business had left its mark, and they found it hard to resist the temptation to move on at the end of the week—without their unit. As a result they were frequently confined to barracks, fortunately for us, never all three at once. Occasionally we were down to one, and then I had to be pressed into service as the straight man for the question-and-answer gags, which involved me, among other things, in running on to the stage carrying two large potatoes and saying to the sweating 'loony' who had just finished a spectacular dance routine dressed in a morning coat, dicky, and army boots:

'Who's are these?'

'King Edward's, mate!'

If there were dog collars or A.T.S. in the audience I used to hide the potatoes, pretend I couldn't find them, and instead do the one about the gentleman farmer milking the cows with his gloves on; and if that sounds like prudish cowardice, it has to be remembered that in those days men didn't feel comfortable laughing at that sort of gag in front of the opposite sex, and Jack had more than once received complaints about it the following morning!

The supporting cast included a raven-haired tap dancer called Rene, a glamorous soubrette, Avis Scutt, and a plump little girl, with dark hair parted in the centre and gathered in a bun, who played the accordion and sang soprano. Her father had a large black moustache, never removed his tweed cap and always sat in the front row 'Just to make sure that nothing ever happens to Rosa.' So far as I know, nothing ever did. I used to sing a duet with her called 'Love's Garden of Roses'. Though it always went down well, I found it embarrassing. I'd never sung a love duet before and hadn't yet acquired enough experience to put my arm round a girl on the stage, gaze into her eyes and sing: 'Come, dearest heart, mid the flowers of June, come out in my garden so gay'—as if I really meant it.

Besides, I didn't find Rosa in the least attractive and was painfully aware of her ever-present father, stolidly puffing his pipe a few feet away. I could only get through it by facing away from her and singing diagonally across the auditorium. My embarrassment reached epic proportions one night to see Jack, an unexpected member of the audience, watching this travesty of a romantic scene and shaking with laughter.

I also had a solo spot—'On the Road To Mandalay' and 'Ma Curly Head Babbie', a touching ballad I've not sung since and can never recall without a touch of unease. Jack was very frank on the way home:

'You were bloody terrible in that duet. For Christ's sake take her hand and look at her. Poor kid! she never had a chance with you behaving as if you wished she wasn't there. Funny thing is, though, you ought to think about going on the stage. You're a natural if you know what that means.'

I didn't, but I kept breathlessly quiet.

'If you want a bit of advice, never be tempted to be a star. You'll do far better as "top of the withs".'

I didn't know what that meant and said so.

'Well, for example, "Jack Hulbert and Cicely Courtneidge *in* such and such *with* so and so, so and so, etc." *That's* the place to be on the bill. You don't earn a star salary, but then you don't have to live at that rate and keep giving expensive parties. What's more, as an established feature player you can work fifty weeks in the year if you want without being over exposed, and if you're in a flop, you'll find it's the stars or the author who get the blame, not the supporting cast.'

It was no doubt excellent advice that Jack gave me in that truck, picking its way through the Sussex lanes with headlights glowing behind the little crosses cut in the black discs pasted to the glass, though no one in their senses would have taken it. In show business success is achieved by doing your own thing as well as you can and hoping that the public will be interested enough to come and watch you do it. If you're an actor with star quality, you may well be a lousy supporting player. Many an actor has refused a leading role because the script was bad, the part was unsuitable, because he felt unready for such a part very early in his career and so on. I doubt if anyone ever turned down Hamlet and asked for Polonius instead.

If stardom had ever been mine for the taking I would never have heeded Jack's advice, but I've never been nearer than hailing distance to it. Oh, I know that most folk regard anyone they've seen on the telly or on the stage as a star and might accuse me of false modesty, but it's perfectly true. Though I've known the exhilaration of seeing my name in lights outside the Theatre Royal, Drury Lane, appeared in a Royal Command Variety Performance at the London Palladium and sung at the Rome Opera, none of these things make one a star in the eyes of one's fellow professionals or, more important, in one's own estimation. A star, by professional standards, is a person whose name alone will bring paying customers in large numbers to the theatre or cinema where they are appearing, not just in one success, which may turn out to be a flash in the pan, but in different productions consistently over a period of years. This involves the difficult task of pleasing both public and critics, though some stars have survived a good deal of critical abuse.

The part in all this that luck plays is enormously important, though not, perhaps, in the way that successful performers say it did when giving modest answers to television interviewers. The regularly out of work actor may be nearer the mark when he

93

curses his luck over a half of bitter in the pub after drawing his social security. Hundreds of thousands of people can act a bit, and a goodly percentage are tempted to take it up professionally. Inevitably the profession is overcrowded and quite certainly at any one time some fine artists are out of work while inferior players are in front of the public. That's not the sort of luck that operates in the making of a star. The particular kind of good fortune I'm thinking about concerns the combination of talents at birth, and it has to comprise acting ability, which, as I've suggested, many possess, a capacity for hard work, again very common, an unerring sense of timing, unteachable but not all that rare, plus a little whiff of undefinable magic without which the very top is an unreachable Everest. It's also important to stick to whatever it is you do best be it acting, dancing, singing, comedy or Shakespeare, giving you a chance to develop and become known as a serious contender for high honours. I, on the other hand, have moved erratically from one branch of the profession to another, changing direction as frequently as an inebriated football fan seeking the Glasgow train on a Euston platform.

But I'm getting ahead of myself. There's another reason why my career so far has followed a certain pattern and it manifested itself while I was at Reigate. At first I thought that I was suffering from a sort of mild lumbago; a doctor I consulted on a weekend leave dismissed it as post-operative rheumatism or a consequence of my being over weight. But as my weight began to go down the pain got worse. In the end it was Monty who probably saved my life. One of his final acts before departing for the Middle East was to test out the physical efficiency of the officers at Command H.Q. by decreeing that all those under forty and above category C would go on a cross-country run of seven miles. I had never been a runner, possessing a figure designed for comfort rather than speed, and I had certainly never run more than a mile at school, finishing an ignominious last, not only breathless but with an alarming red mist in front of my eyes. However, such was the reputation of our commander that I set off without attempting to obtain a medical exemption and somehow completed the course in a slow motion staggering lope that would have made a Goodies sequence look like a bunch of amateurs. I wasn't even last! The following morning I

94

was startled into wakefulness by a searing pain in the lower part of my back of which any self respecting torture chamber would have been proud. I lay motionless, praying it would go away. Gradually it dissolved into a bearable dull ache; I noticed I was drenched in sweat. I turned over only to be instantly back on that mediaeval rack. The pain was frightening.

'Has nobody suggested that you have that back X-rayed?' said the Command M.O. I'd managed to get to his sick parade with the aid of a stick, three Veganin tablets and the determination of the really scared.

'No.'

'How very odd in view of your recent medical history.'

'Surely you don't think I've got T.B. in my back?'

He looked at me sympathetically:

'It's a possibility that the X-ray may well exclude.'

I was no stranger to the Redhill County Hospital where I went for the X-ray. I had spent a few days there some weeks previously after an argument between my 150 c.c. B.S.A. motor bike and a large lorry belonging to Sainsburys on the Dorking–Leatherhead by-pass. A lacerated knee and a bump on the head was all the damage I sustained, and the only lasting effect is a little bald patch at the back, with which audiences may be familiar, and which marks the spot where my head hit the kerb as I fell off. It was what we call in our family a lucky light let off, but it gave me my second taste of a hospital ward. Those were the days of fantastically early mornings and rigorously observed visiting hours, though the nurses and staff were nothing short of angelic. The only major idiocy that took place during my stay occurred on the afternoon I was brought in. After a minor operation on my knee under a local anaesthetic and a sedative for shock, I was put in the male surgical ward of this civilian hospital. In the next bed was an old man with a shock of white unruly hair and a strikingly snub nose, who had hardly allowed me to settle between the sheets before he began regaling me with the lurid details of his ailment. Millin's simplified prostate operation was not yet in common use and this poor old boy had just had the first stage of the old fashioned method, which short circuited the normal way of evacuating the bladder by inserting a tube through the abdomen with a tap on it known as a spigot. Having described this to me in the compelling style of the Ancient Mariner he looked wildly round the ward calling out.

'Nurse, for Gawd's sake pull me bung aht, I'm up to the bleedin' top!'

Instead of a nurse the ward sister appeared accompanied by a bony looking clergyman.

'Sister, can I have a bottle? It's urgent!'

'Not till after the service, Jones. You should have asked earlier. You know perfectly well what happens on Thursday afternoons.'

The insensitive cleric smirked and started his cheery patter, oblivious of the quiet moanings and writhings of my agonized neighbour. At length the proceedings drew to a close and the padre, whose Adam's apple kept playing peep-bo with his dog collar, declared:

'Now we have a little custom that the newest patient chooses our hymn out of that little book I gave you all, and I believe we have a young member of the forces in our midst. Well, young man, what is it to be?'

'Make it a short one, mate, for Christ's sake,' gasped my neighbour.

'He who would valiant be,' I suggested.

We took it at a smart gallop.

* * *

After the X-ray I was to wait for the plates to dry and the result assessed so that I could take the report back to the M.O. I sat in the grounds or walked painfully round the quiet roads near the hospital in an agony of suspense. I just hoped I could get the sealed envelope in time for Captain Faber to put me out of misery that evening. It was nearly five o'clock before I was sent for. A tired-looking white-coated doctor with bushy eyebrows in a tiny bare office gave me a speculative look. In his hand was a small piece of paper.

'Have you found anything?' I managed to say. Without a word he handed me the paper. The writing was a typical medical scrawl, difficult to read and brief: 'Mucheal tuberculosis of 2nd & 3rd lumbar vertebrae.'

'No use prolonging the agony,' he said. 'You'd have to know soon so why not now?'

I had a friend among the nurses at the hospital, a friend to this day, called Elizabeth Solkhon. She found me outside the doctor's office in a daze and did all the tea getting and reassurance possible; but I was numb and miserable. My war seemed to be against a persistent, insidious enemy who could strike in a different place after months of apparent quiescence. It was a still day in late October and I felt that it was my autumn too.

My word, you do look queer!

(Music Hall song)

'Can you touch your toes?'

As I slowly stretched towards the floor, the red-hot vice that lay in wait to punish incautious back movements gave me a pretty good idea what those grisly relics in the Chamber of Horrors could achieve in the hands of an expert. Somehow I managed to make brief manual contact with my bedroom slipper. The return journey to an upright position had the laborious dignity of a circus elephant regaining its feet after shamming sleep at a Boxing Day matinee.

'Remarkable!—don't ever do that again until I tell you.'

'When is that likely to be?'

'I wouldn't like to say.'

That painful demonstration and terse exchange took place in the small clinic room in an isolated building a few hundred yards inside the gates of one of the largest mental hospitals in England. Nearby was a padded cell.

My interlocutor was a senior orthopaedic surgeon. Tall, straight backed and spare of figure, his face was pale, almost ascetic. He looked tired—not that I ever saw a doctor during the war who looked anything else. Holding an X-ray plate up to the light he ran his finger down what looked like an elegantly curved bamboo pole chopped into regular segments with daylight in between them. There were two near the bottom of the picture that had apparently encountered some misfortune. A sizeable chunk of each just wasn't there, and the daylight in between them was a mere chink.

'The treatment,' he went on, 'Is to immobilize those two vertebrae until they fuse together and you grow a lump of calcium round them to protect the area.'

'How long will that take?'

'Difficult to say—could be three to six months, perhaps even longer.'

'How do you immobilize them?'

'We'll make you a plaster bed to lie on.'

'Will I be able to sit up at all?'

'No.'

There was a rustle of sympathy from the audience—a large nursing sister wearing an enormous white linen cap shaped like the billowing sail of a Spanish galleon, and two young house surgeons whose stethoscopes dangled in front of their white coats like mayoral chains of office.

'You'd probably like to have lunch in the dining room before you go to bed, and we won't lock you in plaster for a few days— get used to lying flat first.'

There was one question that had to be asked sooner or later. I decided against a postponement.

'What are the chances of my making a recovery?'

'Fifty-fifty.'

In peace time that honest, unembroidered reply would have been a stunning blow. In October 1942 after two years of war that had already claimed several of my closest friends, the odds seemed perfectly reasonable. Fighter pilots and submariners accepted them every day, whilst sailors on Russian convoys would have regarded even money for survival as an improvement on the current betting. Certainly there was no doubting the accuracy of this assessment of my prospects. Hubert Wood of King's College Hospital was an unassuming, kindly man with a very high success rate in the shattered limb business. But when it came to calling the score he did so in a quiet matter of fact way that ruled out any suspicion of pretence. I ate the first of a long series of cottage pies—with sago pudding and stewed apples for afters—torn by conflicting emotions of euphoria and apprehension. Until that chat with Mr. Wood I'd thought I had no hope of recovery at all.

In case by now the reader is wondering whether the institution in which the above scene took place meant that a diseased spine was only part of my medical problems, let me hasten to reassure him or her that Horton Hospital, near Epsom, Surrey had been requisitioned as an emergency hospital for the duration of the war, and that the mental patients had been evacuated and dispersed among the other psychiatric units in the area, which included Long Grove, The Manor, St. Ebba's and West Park. The overcrowding which resulted was appalling and was only justified by the bleak necessities of a country facing the possibility of invasion at any time.

Horton E.M.S. Hospital was staffed from various sources. Many of the nurses were from hospitals run by the then London County Council, others were from King's College Hospital, which also provided much of the medical staff. The patients were both service personnel and civilians, many of the latter being victims of the London blitz. There was a number of celebrated names among the consultant staff, and the hospital had a reputation for getting cases that had defeated other establishments.

By no means all the doctors were from King's. The chest unit could call on the combined talents of Russell Brock from Guy's, Clement Price Thomas from the Westminster, Norman Barrett from St. Thomas and Tudor Edwards from the Brompton, who was the pioneer. In the comparative obscurity of this Victorian institution, built of dirty yellow bricks, and looking like an enormous rambling public convenience, these four men achieved break-through after break-through in the field of lung surgery. Backed up by the work of two brilliant consultant physicians John Clifford Hoyle and James Livingstone they progressed from the hopeless case who survived the removal of a lung for an hour to patients, who were able to go home looking well a month after the same operation. Over thirty years ago that was a triumph to rank with today's transplants, and brought extended life and hope to tens of thousands of people including the late King George VI.

The grounds of Horton were extensive with pleasant views of Banstead Downs, and B Hospital, where I took up horizontal residence, had an attractive garden shaded by a couple of large oak trees. I say had because when I went back to look at it recently most of the garden had become a car park. The two 25-bed wards were reserved for officers, who also had the use of a recreation room with a half-size billiard table, a dining room, a glassed-in verandah and, of course, the padded cell, which was occasionally used to restrain an obstreperous inmate. The decision to confine anyone there was not a medical one. It was generally made on the spur of the moment by his fellow patients late on Saturday nights.

In charge of this establishment was Sister Turner, her sail-like cap bobbing as she walked, the rustle of her lightly starched apron giving useful warning of her approach. Ethel Turner in those days was stout and occasionally stern. As a civilian in charge of officers she had an unexpectedly successful method of maintaining discipline. She called us all 'Mister' including a Lieutenant-General, who obviously found this form of address unnerving—but made no protest. Her effect on student nurses was more dramatic. They were apt to take to their heels at the mere slight of this blue and white galleon ploughing towards them at a stately pace. That was until they got to know her. She ran our little community with a mixture of threats, cajolery and belly laughs that would have made her father proud. He was a sergeant-major. So was she, with one important difference; she never raised her voice—she never needed to. Born within the sound of Bow Bells, she punctuated her pithy comments on life and people with a repertoire of sniffs and significant glances that made conversation with her a joy. I had a good deal for I stayed in her care for twenty months.

For the first few days it seemed as though the odds against me were lengthening. Even though I was lying flat, the pain in my back could be triggered off by anyone merely walking towards my bed or shutting a window. My ordeal by plaster was put off for a week or two; then one evening I realized that the staff of my lumbar torture chamber had taken a whole day's holiday. With any luck the painful part was over, and it was—nearly.

Making a plaster bed is fun for everyone concerned including the patient. The surgeon and his staff are relaxed and it's usually the last job of the day; there are no anaesthetics or incisions to worry about—just an indescribably sloshy mess of wet plaster of Paris, which finds its way into every unprotected crevice of your body or clothing. Anyone confronted by the scene could easily imagine that they had stumbled on a play-group for adults. The patient is laid face down on a table and covered from shoulders to knees with a length of thick felt. This is then tailored with shears round the neck and thighs, leaving a gap at the bottom for essential traffic, which is necessary though draughty.

Once the felt is pronounced a good fit, pounds and pounds of plaster are heaped on top. This has to be moulded and shaped before it hardens, which it does—rapidly. The urgent calls for more plaster, the splashing and slapping sounds, the white liquid flying everywhere and the general merriment made it an exhilarating experience. I lay there completely naked, convulsed by my first fit of the giggles for a very long time.

Right! We've finished; now roll over on your back and we'll make you a breast-plate for when you have to be turned over to wash your back.'

As I attempted the manoeuvre hundreds of needles jabbed me from neck to knee. The liquid plaster had run round from my back to my front and then set, glueing me to the table by every hair on my chest and elsewhere. I made no further attempt to move.

'Has anyone got a pair of scissors?'

As a comedy line this plaintive request went over very big. While they all roared with laughter I tried to cut myself free where it mattered most. Unfortunately, a busy surgical team weren't prepared to hang about until I had made sure that several hundred hairs had weighed anchor. They tip-toed up to the table, hoisted me firmly in the air, tossed me like a pancake and lowered me gently down again. Any horror-film director would have paid good money for my blood-curdling yell as I abruptly parted company with several square inches of short and curlies. This is always good for a laugh in medical circles, and I had to join in when I was finally lifted off the table and saw the plaster impression of my front—hairs and all.

*　　*　　*

For weeks I lay in the plaster in an ordinary hospital bed. I learnt to eat, drink, and read without any more movement than a pillow to bring my head a little forward. The muscles in my arms strengthened until I could hold up a book for a couple of hours without discomfort. My only dread was what would happen if something went down the wrong way. It never did.

There was no other treatment—except a stern warning that I must drink six pints of fluid a day to make up for lying still. That's quite an input of tea, coffee, cocoa, orange squash or plain water to keep up week in week out, particularly in cold weather; but when you're only on even money to survive you don't argue the toss about a few glasses of orange squash—and admittedly, a certain amount of beer found its way into B Hospital. Nevertheless, what goes in must eventually come out, and I was, throughout my stay, the undisputed champion bottle-filler. Mind you, to have on the ward a patient who constantly behaves like an ornamental fountain can be very irritating to overworked nurses trying, for instance, to resuscitate a pilot-officer who has tripped over a large dog at the top of the stairs of his officers' mess and fractured both arms and his skull on the way down. At such tense moments in a hospital ward a cheery call of 'Nurse, could I have a bottle, please.' is likely to evoke a rather tetchy response like 'Oh, tie a knot in it, Wallace, we're busy!'

*   *   *

It was not Mr. Wood's intention to leave me lying completely flat all the time in the ward. Even though my fellow patients were congenial company, most of them were in for a matter of weeks at the most, while I was one of only three long-term cases. The other two were both suffering from the after-effects of polio and were much worse off than me. I would either recover or die. The best they could hope for was a little extra movement in paralysed and wasted limbs. Bill Brewster had a wheel-chair, Eddie Goodger, his useless arms on an aeroplane splint, could walk, so it was a question of finding something to make me mobile. The old fashioned spinal carriage wasn't big enough to take me and the plaster bed as well, and in 1942 the vast range of equipment that now exists for the disabled had yet to be invented and developed.

He used one of the hospital trollies for transporting stretcher cases. They had two large wheels, sturdier, than those for a push-bike, though much the same size and positioned like the cart-wheels on a fire-brigade ladder. The stretcher was laid on a metal frame above the wheels like the plank on a see-saw. To prevent it behaving like a see-saw there were two retractable

104

metal poles back and front with small wheels rather like the nose-wheels of an aircraft.

Mr. Wood designed a wooden frame to be bolted to the top of the stretcher in which my plaster bed would lie at a slight angle to give me a greater field of vision and bring me up to a level where I could look the world in the face. When the front wheel was retracted I was at an angle of about 15 degrees to the ground—a tolerable situation.

At first I was only lifted on to the trolley for 'carriage exercise', but as this took the combined efforts of two hospital porters assisted by any four other people who happened to be in the vicinity and could be press-ganged into service, it was soon decided that I should live on the trolley all the time. This meant that my days in the ward were over. The trolley took up too much space, and in any case TB patients are always supposed to benefit from exposure to fresh air. I was parked in the glassed-in verandah, which looked out on the garden. Though it was peaceful I never lacked for company—with a welcome difference. In the ward, surrounded by people, conversation tended to be general. On the verandah folk drifted out in ones and twos, often for the purpose of unburdening intimate disclosures which were far more interesting. I became the receptacle of all sorts of secrets and confessions. One minute it would be old Moses, the retired jockey who swept out the wards, telling all about his brother's funeral where the pall-bearers were members of the local darts club, and he had fallen heir to the new suit delivered the day before the death ('It's an ill wind, Mr. Wallace.') the next it might be a decidedly nubile physio-therapist talking endlessly about the object of her affection, who was usually one of my fellow patients.

Before long I realized that I might be of some use as the moving spirit of a sort of 'lonely hearts' club.

'It's too sad. Peter never seems to even notice me. He just sat in the Spread Eagle all yesterday evening with Charles while Deirdre and I were only feet away, making a beastly gin and orange last a lifetime, and eating our hearts out.'

'The funny thing is, old boy, that Charlie and I get a bit tongue-tied when it comes to breaking the ice with those massage girls. Sat for an hour in the bloody boozer last night trying to think of an opening gambit.'

By setting both those sets of traffic lights at green I could save the four of them from wasting any more time on preliminaries. The likes of Peter and Charles would soon be discharged from hospital and could find themselves in the Western Desert within weeks, so time was precious.

Not all the problems were so easily solved, and I heard a good many sad stories on that verandah about which I could do nothing but listen. Maybe that in its way was some use. In a large crowded hospital no one had time to stop and listen : I had time unlimited, yet it seldom seemed to drag. Indeed the occupational therapists were quite worried that I had little interest in time consuming pursuits like tapestry, knitting dish-cloths from string, or fashioning amusing little puppets out of fir-cones or pipe-cleaners. If I wasn't conversing, listening to the radio or reading, I was quite content doing absolutely nothing beyond watching Sister Turner's pet ducks on the lawn, the squirrels scampering in the oak trees, even the rain running down the window could hold my attention for a surprisingly long time. It was like a sort of hibernation—my world had contracted, yet because I clung tenaciously to the idea that I was going to get better, it seemed only sensible to enjoy what this somewhat restricted life had to offer. I'd never be twenty-two again.

It had quite a lot to offer—excellent and varied company, cheap cigarettes, free beer and trips round the grounds whenever there was an able-bodied convalescent prepared to push my trolley and that was most days. Once every three months I visited the X-ray department full of hope that the latest picture would show sufficient improvement to get me upright again. There was a less attractive alternative to be faced on these quarterly occasions. Mr. Wood had indicated that should my natural resources show signs of failing to do a good repair job on their own, he would then graft a piece of bone from my thigh into the spine to act as a splint. I didn't like the sound of that at all, though one or two of his registrars and house surgeons, who longed to see this fearsome operation as a part of their education, always looked disappointed when he pronounced my latest X-ray an improvement on the last. I didn't blame them in the least, I was the best chance they had of seeing this graft and it must have been infuriating of me to improve without it. I'd probably have felt the same in their shoes—though at the time I could have risen from my trolley and thumped them for looking so down in the mouth. By the spring of 1943 I was presenting problems to the hospitals' X-ray machine. The starchy food had steadily added to my weight until there was just too much fatty tissue for it to penetrate. Fortunately a much more powerful machine arrived from America as part of the Lease-Lend programme, so I was spared a trip to London by ambulance. It was thought inadvisable to reduce my food, so that by the time I left Horton I weighed well over 17 stones.

Now if anyone is beginning to feel sorry for this large, stricken lad on his trolley, helping others to romantic adventures and then turning sadly to watch the squirrels as the lovers pedal away to their assignations, please don't. There are always girls about, who are switched on by incapacitated warriors, and, happily for me, one of them came to work on B Hospital. She was petite, extremely attractive and always seemed to have a special smile for me, often bringing presents of books and sweets, which I found embarrassing as I thought she did it because she was sorry for me. Then one day she appeared on the verandah on her afternoon off looking a million dollars in her ordinary clothes—and not every nurse can manage to do that.

'I've come to take you for a walk. I asked Sister and she says yes.'

I couldn't believe it. I knew for a fact that there was a queue of at least six trying to date her. I also knew that none of them was getting anywhere. My response must have seemed un-enthusiastic:

'Do you really think you can manage the trolley on your own?'

She was, as I've already said, petite, five feet four at the very most.

'I'm pretty strong.'

She didn't look it. The first part of the trip was plain sailing. The paths were level and the trolley was quite well balanced. It was a warm June day and I was, as always, enjoying the change of scene, though I wondered why Polly (that's not her real name) was so quiet. Suddenly she turned down a path I'd never been taken before—it was rough with pot-holes and slightly uphill.

'Where are we going?'

'You'll find out in a minute,' replied Polly through what sounded like clenched teeth. The exertion was telling on her a bit. Round the next corner my heart missed a beat—only two hundred yards more and we'd be in a wood! But that two hundred yards was up a steepish gradient with a few tree roots and stones as added hazards on the rough track.

'You'll never make it.' I said in a voice that was a thought unsteady.

'Want to bet?' gasped Polly. It was like expecting a Mini to push a goods train up Shap—but she did it.

What transpired in the wood is going to remain a matter for conjecture, though I'll admit that when on the way back Polly couldn't hold my heavy conveyance, and it lurched and bumped over the stones and tree roots, developing a speed-wobble halfway down, I didn't find that nearly so exciting. She never had to attempt that feat of strength on her own again. It hadn't gone unobserved (nothing does in a place like Horton) and on future occasions a discreet helper would casually appear from nowhere to give her a hand up the hill. When I think about it at this distance Sister Turner's part in the enterprise was one of unusual inactivity, bless her.

Student nurses did only three months on a ward. When Polly's time was up she got herself posted, not to another ward but to another hospital. I never saw or heard from her again. She covered her tracks completely. She had done wonders for my morale and therefore for my ultimate recovery, and I missed her dreadfully. I believe she went because I always refused to discuss the future so far as it might involve anyone else. Fifty fifty plus the possibility of my having to take care for the rest of my life didn't seem quite a good enough prospect to think of taking care of someone else, and I certainly didn't want to involve someone else in taking care of me. Perhaps my feelings weren't strong enough, I just don't know. It was a strange, unreal situation and I reacted to it in unusual ways sometimes. Any way to this day when I get a message sent round to a stage door or an artists' room, as still happens occasionally, saying that someone who nursed me at Horton during the war would like to see me, I always hope it'll be Polly, but it never is.

*   *   *

It was a warm, dry summer and I spent much of it in the garden wearing nothing but a towel and becoming more and more like a horizontal bronze buddha. Only twice in those pleasant surroundings was my prescribed treatment of peace and quiet put in jeopardy—on the first occasion by a harmless kitten. I must explain that the wooden frame on which my plaster lay (rather like a ship in dry dock) was high enough above the stretcher on which it rested to enable the bed-pan to be inserted. In between times this draughty corner was stuffed with a couple of old cushions to stop icicles forming on the largish portion of my stern protruding through the plaster. On the afternoon in question Sister Turner had given instructions that the cushions were to be pulled out to allow fresh air to circulate round as much of me as possible. I thought that this was overdoing it a bit—but it wasn't something worth arguing about. That part of my anatomy was quite out of my reach (I couldn't even see over the sides of the trolley let alone stretch over) so I shrugged and agreed.

Though I was soon engrossed in a whodunnit, I was also half aware of suppressed laughter from a group of patients sitting near me in deck-chairs; it was the sort of merriment one associates with the approach of the victim of a carefully prepared practical joke. I vaguely wondered what it might be. Strings stretched across ward doors to nip off those galleon caps, or a performance of ' The Dead March in Saul' as cases for the operating theatre were wheeled out past a guard of honour bowed over reversed billiard cues were every day occurrences— sometimes I would wake from a nap to find a little posy of flowers, plus water, in my rather deep navel, which had to be dried out with a sponge or blotting paper as I couldn't empty it by rolling over. But now, enjoying one of the 'Saint's' many adventures, I was unprepared for what was about to happen.

The kitten had been borrowed from another part of the hospital and persuaded to play near my trolley. Eventually, as everyone hoped, it decided to investigate this fascinating object. It climbed up the spokes of the wheel and hopped onto the stretcher. The deck chair brigade watched it walking along under the plaster—its erect tail brushing the smooth white surface until it reached the bed-pan area. I can still recall the sudden unbearable, unaccountable tickle as its tail swished my vulnerable cheeks. Was it a rat? A squirrel? or some sinister nervous disease? Almost as soon as the terrible sensation began it ceased, as the kitten continued its walk past the exposed area, but then encountering a solid piece of wood, it did the only thing possible and retraced its steps. The deck chair party were holding their sides and sobbing with mirth. They could see the whole performance and knew exactly when I would sound off and at the same time make a vain attempt at levitation. In the end the wretched creature apparently lay down and went to sleep while I implored somebody to tell me what sort of animal I was harbouring in such a sensitive area. For all I knew I might have just been goosed by one of Sister Turner's ducks.

* * *

Not long after this disagreeable invasion of privacy I volunteered to try a night or two sleeping in the garden. With my cushions firmly in place and a heap of blankets on top, it was rather romantic to look up at the stars before drifting off, breathing the balmy night air. For a night or two I enjoyed it, waking from dreamless slumber with an appetite for breakfast. On the third night I had a vivid, all too familiar dream. I was back home in London on a typical 1940 blitz night with the anti-aircraft guns firing, the drone of enemy aircraft above and the sickening swoosh and roar of the bombs. I woke to a sky pierced by search-lights and realized that the salvoes from the nearby guns were not in the least dream-like. Nor were the shell fragments, whistling down and thudding into the lawn as the guns tried vainly to get the range of the sneak raiders—the first we'd had over the hospital since I'd arrived. We were not the object of the attack, but it was all happening uncomfortably close—close enough to make it well nigh impossible for me to be heard shouting for help. The night staff had completely forgotten about me—but someone else hadn't. A majestic figure appeared out of the darkness, only visible in the light of a descending flare. She was clad in dressing gown and steel helmet.

'Can't have all our good work ruined by a bit of bloody shrapnel', observed Sister Turner as she restored me to the doubtful safety of the glass-roofed verandah.

* * *

As Horton was approximately twenty miles from home I couldn't, in the middle of a war, expect, and indeed didn't get, many visitors. The only regular was my mother, who made the journey by public transport at least twice a week. This involved catching a bus from the end of our road to Archway Tube Station, followed by a monotonous ride to Morden on the Northern Line—twenty-three stops in all—and then a longish journey on a 93 bus to the hospital gates. It must have taken at least two hours each way and had to be accomplished between cooking breakfast for my elderly father before he went to his office, and welcoming him back with an evening meal. On one occasion she was so exhausted she fell asleep in the train and was discovered by cleaners in a Morden siding. My father was rarely able to come. Though in his seventies he was working like a trojan for the war effort, and neither my mother nor I encouraged him to make the trip. He was a transparent man who could never disguise his distress at seeing his only son lying on a trolley. I did my best to get a laugh out of him but it was uphill work.

After my October X-ray Mr. Wood told me that I would certainly spend another winter at Horton, though the long-term prospects were still favourable. Faced with another six months of inactivity there were many who would have put the time to good use—who would have called for their law books or built a model of Windsor Castle out of match-sticks. I couldn't summon up that sort of resolution. I'd found studying law difficult enough with the help of university tutors—on my own it was out of the question.

Still, my increasing chances of recovery meant that from time to time I thought about the future. Superstitions about counting chickens made me shy away from making firm plans in the event of my being able to walk out of Horton, though I did reach a couple of conclusions. Firstly, that it wasn't in me to reach a position in the legal firmament where I could claim, like the judge in *Trial By Jury* that 'Many a burglar I've restored to his friends and his relations.' Secondly, that whatever else might befall me, I must first see if I could make a career doing what seemed to come most naturally—entertaining people.

I was not now required to lie quiet all the time. I was wheeled to dances and concerts and before long I was appointed M.C.

at one and sang a song or two at another. It was probably this resumption of activity that inspired me to try and write a show for the hospital amateur dramatic group. The script has long since disappeared and only the programme survives. I don't remember much about the story but it was called 'High Temperature' and the cast list contained such predictable names as Sergeant Gertie Gastric, A.T.S., General Anaesthetic, B.S.R., B.P. and Herr Sigmoid O'Scope, a spy! Having written the damned thing I was allowed to produce it, shouting up at the performers on the stage of the hospital hall from my trolley. I had a chorus line of massage girls whose costumes were made from old sheets and displayed considerable ingenuity. A civilian patient, Leonard Collins, an irrepressible Cornishman, who conducted the Wimbledon Philharmonic Orchestra, promised that they would be in the pit on the night, and they were. I had the invaluable help of two outstanding amateurs from Epsom, Doris Elphick and Aubrey Wyatt, who played comedy parts with panache and from October till the first night, the 20th January 1944, I had all the occupational therapy I needed. Composing is not my line but some old songs suffered the indignity of topical lyrics.

All amateur productions depend on a first class stage manager. Mine has remained a sort of right hand man ever since. John Partridge, a young surgeon, not only ran the whole thing on the first night with clock-work efficiency, but had to cope with a blown fuse and total darkness minutes before the off. None of us knew till afterwards that he was battling with some obscure virus and a temperature of 102. Doctors are a foolhardy lot on the whole. John has been for many years a highly respected doctor in Dorking, was best man at my wedding and if today I'm wearing a hole in the carpet over some important decision, he's the chap I'm most likely to ring.

A few days before the first night the Ministry of Information somehow got wind of this modest entertainment and decided to issue a press release. The human interest part of the story was too good for the papers to ignore and the national dailies jammed the hospital switch-board. The Superintendent of the hospital, Dr. Nichol, came over to B Hospital, looking decidely put out. A distinguished man, his speciality was treating a disease called general paralysis of the insane—a form of tertiary syphilis—

by allowing patients to be bitten by malaria carrying mosquitoes. The resultant fever and rigors apparently worked wonders. It was a revolutionary idea that was a success, and he was carrying on with it as best he could despite his hospital's change of role. The press in full cry was outside his experience.

'I've a good mind to keep them out,' he growled looking at me as if I'd invited them all personally. I knew something of the way press-men react from my father's political career.

'I wouldn't do that, sir, if I were you. Don't forget that letter in *The Times* by Sir Shane Leslie complaining about food here; I dare say you'll be hearing more about that—let's face it, it isn't very good.' (In fact a question was asked about it the following week in the House of Lords.) 'At least this can be a bit of good news to come out of the hospital, but if you ban them, they'll climb over the wall and start poking their noses into the kitchens.'

The catering wasn't poor Nichol's department, but he would bear the brunt of any public outcry and he knew it.

'All right. I'll tell 'em to come at eleven o'clock tomorrow morning.'

In the end the *Daily Mirror* did it as an exclusive with a large photograph splashed across the centre pages under the heading 'BEDRIDDEN, HE PRODUCES A SHOW!' There I was in the foreground with my banjolele lying across my knees, a script in one hand and pointing an admonitory finger at a row of dancing girls on the stage.

The article revealed the nature of my illness, which greatly upset my parents, who as I've mentioned were unwilling to admit, like others of their generation, that any close relation could possibly be suffering from this particular malady. I was a little shocked myself to realize that millions of people were reading exactly what was the matter with me.

Two days later Sister Turner handed me a bulky package of letters. 'Looks like fan mail' she observed with a characteristic sniff. It was. The letters were all from fellow-sufferers and could be divided into two categories. Most of them were from patients who said that reading about the show had brought them new hope of recovery. Several were from children. The smaller batch were from people who had recovered and wanted to give me hope. One in particular I remember. It was written on a scrap of lined paper and it ended:

'I had what you had and was given up for dead, but I got over it and have stood twenty years at a capstan lathe. Good luck and chin up!

Mrs. Carter.

High Temperature did two nights in the hospital, and collections from the audience raised seventy pounds for the Red Cross. The company called themselves The Horton Barnstormers, and they decided to do a performance a month later in Epsom itself—also for the Red Cross. Mr. Wood reluctantly but firmly refused to let me go, but I had a pretty good deputy. The local paper reported that in the interval 'Sir John Wallace thanked the audience for their support and appealed to their generosity for a retiring collection.'

It must have been a good appeal. Over £120 was collected. If you multiply that by the necessary amount to relate it to today's values, it comes to a tidy sum. I asked for it all to go to helping prisoners of war. After all I was a sort of prisoner myself.

It must have been about the end of March when Mr. Wood began to make plans for my release. I was measured for a spinal jacket to be made of leather reinforced at the back with steel strips.

'Your latest X-ray is fine, but you're now so heavy that no self-respecting spinal column should be asked to support you. We'll give the calcifying process a little longer and take one more picture at the the end of May. If it's all right we'll get you up.'

The great day came. My mother had prepared for it too, by putting an enormous gusset in the back of a pair of grey flannels —clothes were rationed and I had hopelessly outgrown my wardrobe. Two days before the final X-ray the tube in the American machine went phut.

It's the most extraordinary thing. I had lain there for twenty months perfectly serene, not showing any noticeable signs of depression or impatience. Yet now, having been promised an X-ray on one day and to sit up the next if all was well, I behaved like a spoilt prima donna when they told me I might have to wait a week or two longer.

My behaviour must have been really outrageous because they sent for my father! Instead of coming to see me, he went to

114

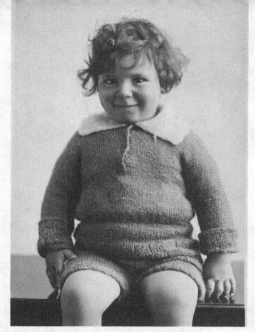

Above: Ian Wallace circa 2 years.
Below: The Hydro Hotel, Kilmacolm, Scotland. A Fancy Dress Ball in the early 1930s with myself as a Belisha Beacon with my father and mother.

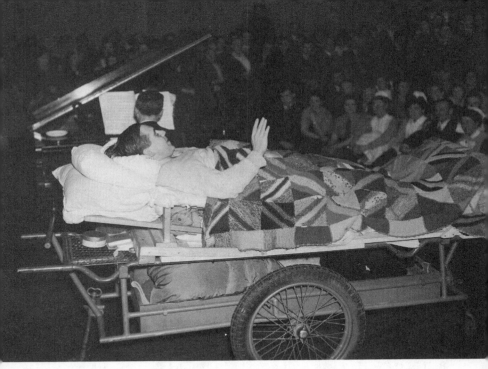

Above: On my trolley singing at a concert, Holton Hospital, near Epsom, 1943. *Below:* 26th June 1948, Cupar, Scotland. Ian and Patricia with Dr John Partridge as best man.

Dr. Nichol. (People like my father always go to the man at the top.) I was told afterwards that all he said was 'My name's Sir John Wallace—I don't know why, but that's what it is. Is there anything I can do to get my son X-rayed a bit sooner?'

Dr. Nichol found this direct and engagingly modest approach irresistible and between the two of them they must have had some fairly profitable telephone conversations that afternoon. Within forty-eight hours a Liberator had flown in a new tube and I was carted down to X-ray.

'Hold your breath and count up to five,' the usual instructions, but there was no accustomed buzz and click from the apparatus. The radiologist looked puzzled.

'Try again,' she said.

Again silence from the machine.

'Terribly sorry, Ian, I'm afraid the new tube is u.s.' I felt like bursting into tears but instead I clutched at a straw.

'There's a switch up there on the ceiling—do you think it might have been put off while they changed the tube?'

'I wouldn't have thought so.'

'Isn't it worth a try?'

She sighed, but pushed a chair into the middle of the room and used it to climb up onto the slab where I lay. As she stretched up to the switch I had an invigorating view of viyella undergarments.

'I can't believe it'll make any difference, but here goes.' She jumped down and lined me up again like a ham on a slicer.

'Right, breathe in, hold and count to five.'

The machine buzzed and clicked merrily.

Next day I gingerly sat up, supported on one side by Sister Turner and on the other by Bebe Costello, an Irish staff nurse. There was no pain and sentimental observers swear that a tear coursed down my cheek, but I don't think it did.

A day or two later I was on my feet wearing the extended grey flannels. My legs felt like sacks of potatoes, and with great caution I managed about half a dozen steps, at which moment my trousers fell down. I've always been a one for the comic touch.

The fact that I could even put one foot in front of the other at snail's pace with the help of two sticks was due to a course of gentle leg exercises during the weeks before the X-ray, carefully supervised by the massage girls. They promised that once I was up they would really get to work on me in the gymnasium and have me running round in a matter of weeks. Running seemed optimistic. Over seventeen stone plus my leather saddle put me among the Clydesdales rather than the colts.

They never got a chance to try. The very next day the hospital was evacuated in preparation for the massive casualties expected—and thank God, not experienced—from the invasion of the French coast, which was due to start any day. So, round about the first of June 1944, with barely time to gather my possessions and say my goodbyes, I was popped into an ambulance and taken home. After nearly two years of gentle progress on a trolley the journey seemed to be made at break-neck speed.

* * *

Free from his fetters grim

(The Yeomen of the Guard)

As I lay in bed in the drawing-room—stairs were still beyond me—I reflected on my last conversation with Mr. Wood. His instructions were clear: I was to take it easy, to come for a check-up fairly soon, and not to think of work of any kind for a year.

'By the way, what sort of career are you planning? It's legal isn't it?'

'You'll probably think I'm mad, but I want to go on the stage.'

'I thought you wanted to be a barrister.'

'No, that's what my father would like me to do.'

He thought for a moment.

'I've got a feeling,' he said slowly, 'that you may come to less harm doing what you want even if it's pretty strenuous. Remember, you can't lie around in the sun for the rest of your life.'—Then he had an afterthought. 'Funnily enough, it's the ones who take too good care of themselves who seem to relapse; but don't take that too literally! Good luck.' And he was gone before I had time to thank him.

Well, now I had to teach myself to walk with the help of dear old Miss Groser, the local masseuse, who had kept going because the young ones were all away in hospitals or abroad. She really hadn't the strength to do more than squeeze my calves—but she brought in the local news.

There was one bit of news that I saw for myself. I was woken up very early one morning soon after my return by what sounded like an armada of aircraft. I got to the window in record time to see the incredible sight of large planes towing trains of gliders. It was breathtaking and awesome. I could well imagine what those men in the gliders must have felt like, some silent, some cracking jokes, all with a sick feeling in the pit of the stomach. During that day, as we listened to the triumphant progress of the invasion on the radio, I kept thinking that not all those men who'd passed over the house in the early morning would be still alive.

*   *   *

Within a week the flying bombs had begun to fall on London. The first night we were all very optimistic. We kept hearing what sounded like a new enemy plane with an engine that had the dull growl of a powerful motor-bike. As the guns banged away the engine would suddenly stop.

'Hooray!' We cried several times. 'At last the guns are giving them what for.'

'Must be some new radar development,' said my father with a knowing look as he went up to bed. However bad the raids, he always spurned any idea of taking shelter.

'I sleep so badly unless I'm in my own bed,' was his answer to any suggestion that it was dangerous upstairs.

As the night wore on and no 'All Clear' was sounded my mother and I began to notice that all these shot-down planes were crashing with a mighty explosion. It wasn't till morning that we learnt the truth. We also heard in the next few days that there were definite 'lanes' along which the bombs were directed. As we could hear them we were presumably in the line of fire.

One morning about a fortnight later I heard one approaching and yelled to my mother and Mrs. Page, our daily, who were washing up the breakfast dishes in the scullery, to come into the study, which was our shelter. It was strengthened with wooden struts and the window was sand-bagged. They were gossiping so intently that I had to yell some barrack square language to attract their attention. They arrived at the double and we all lay down. The motor-bike seemed to be right overhead when the engine cut out. After a few seconds of agonizing silence the house gave a lurch and there was a noise like every Chinese lantern in Peking reacting to a force eight gale.

My mother knew what it was. As she rose from the floor she picked up the phone and dialled the local builder, on the old fashioned principle that thrice armed is she who gets her call in first. Every single window at the back of the house was shattered, the lead lights twisted into grotesque shapes. In the scullery, where my mother and Mrs. Page had been, daggers of glass from the window were embedded in the plaster of the opposite wall. The bomb had landed about 250 yards away on one of the playing fields belonging to Highgate School. The back of our house got more than its fair share of the blast.

Soon after, our doctor, in consultation with Mr. Wood, decided that I must get out of London. I felt very badly about once more leaving my parents to brave it out—but there was no doubt that disturbed nights and the perpetual anxiety of having an ear cocked for one of those infernal machines was not the best of convalescences after a protracted illness, that had a reputation for coming back if it wasn't treated with respect. There was another reason. My mother was worn out, and though my father was delighted to have me home, he was anxious that the extra work I undoubtedly made would be too much for her. It wasn't a selfish reaction on his part. He had an important job to do, but without her help he couldn't make a piece of toast.

I went first to dear friends in Cambridge, the Nourses, who only made one stipulation about my visit. I was forbidden to get on their bathroom scales. Curiosity got the better of me the second day, and I stepped on carefully. The needle flicked up near the maximum, which on those scales was 18 stones. I got off as quickly as I could. To my horror the needle only went back as far as 4 stone 2 pounds. When I confessed to Harry Nourse, he was justifiably angry.

'Just one thing,' he concluded after expressing himself quietly but forcibly on the subject. '*Don't* try to repair it.'

I usually do what I'm told, but on this occasion some devil got into me and as soon as he'd gone out on his rounds, (Harry's a doctor) and his wife had gone shopping, I nipped upstairs and managed to get it working properly. I decided to say nothing and just let them discover that it had made a spontaneous recovery. When I got married five years later the Nourse's present was a set of bathroom scales.

From Cambridge I went, via a brief holiday with my mother

in Norfolk (while my father sampled the delights of his club), to Kilmacolm, which, you may recall, was where my parents met. The Hydro was now a naval hospital and my grandfather and auntie Peggy had moved to a hotel in Glasgow's west end. Auntie was a postal censor, and could just about manage to support the two of them. I put up at a guest house, which I shared with a number of old ladies of both sexes.

For the first time since my illness began I was really bored. I couldn't walk very far, there was no company of my own age, and apart from reading and letter-writing my only diversion was an occasional trip to Glasgow to see grandad and auntie or to go to the pictures. As autumn gave way to winter I even thought nostalgically of B Hospital now and again. Then one day I read something in the show business column of a Glasgow evening paper that decided me to ignore at least some of Mr. Wood's instructions.

It was an article about Howard M. Lockhart, the chief variety producer of the B.B.C. in Scotland. It mentioned, almost in passing, that Mr. Lockhart was always prepared to see ex-service artists and give them a chance if they had something to offer. I wrote and asked if I could drop in and see him one day. He was as good as his word—but this tall, thin, black-haired man wearing horn-rimmed glasses raised his eye-brows as I entered his office in Queen Margaret Drive carrying a banjolele in one hand and a music case in the other.

'Hello,' he said. 'Glad to meet you, but I didn't know this was to be an audition.'

'Neither did I—but you never know,' was my cheerful response.

Within a quarter of an hour I was sitting on a corner of his desk regaling him with songs accompanied by the few basic chords on the banjolele with which I was familiar. I ploughed through 'Chinese Laundry Blues', 'Lazin'' and a cloyingly senti-mental offering of my own composition entitled 'It Won't Be The Same'.

He listened with patience and good humour. When I'd finished—or he'd politely hinted that he'd heard enough; I used to go on a bit in those days—he said with the air of a man choosing his words with care. 'You know, I'm afraid we really couldn't offer you a radio date—not for at least three months, but of course if anything comes along I'll let you know at once.'

I was ridiculously disappointed. Swaying down Great Western Road in a number 10 tram, known as 'a blue caur', I realized that my self-esteem had taken a nasty jolt. For several years now I had lived with the reality of a disease that might prove fatal, but maybe I had been shielded from some of the other realities of life. Perhaps the audience reaction to my singing and the show at Horton had been no more than an emotional response to a brave gesture; maybe I was deluding myself by thinking that I had anything to offer in a professional capacity.

As the train for Kilmacolm pulled out of St. Enoch's station I remembered that he'd not entirely closed the door. He'd said something about three months. I don't know what I'd expected. Looked at rationally the idea of walking into the office of a senior B.B.C. producer with a few old songs, no training, one hopeless piece of original material and expecting him to lie on the carpet and wave his legs in the air before leading me to the nearest microphone was absurd. By the time I was back in the guest house I had made the painful mental adjustment from amateur pipe dreaming to professional pessimism. The remark about three months, I told myself, was merely to soften the blow—I'd never hear any more. Even if I did, what could I do in the meantime to improve my chances? I knew so little about the business and there was no means of learning any more in Kilmacolm. I had no act, no real repertoire, nothing. By the next morning I had resigned myself to a resumption of boredom. It was raining, as it occasionally does in the west of Scotland, a fine, persistent, wetting drizzle that sentenced me to the sitting room with the *Glasgow Herald*, the *Bulletin*, and three sets of clicking knitting needles—and tongues—for company. By lunch time I was morosely considering spending the afternoon in bed when the phone rang. It was Howard Lockhart.

'I've been thinking. This is nothing to do with the B.B.C., but I'm producing a play at the Park Theatre in Woodside Crescent. It's only semi-professional and a tiny theatre—104 seats, but if you're interested there's a part in it I think you could do—as a matter of act it's the male lead.'

I nearly dropped the phone. 'I'd love to!'—I hadn't yet

acquired that off-hand telephone manner of the true professional, which conveys—or tries to convey—that the offer will have to take its place in the queue of even more fascinating possibilities that have arisen in the past hour.

'The play's *The Man With A Load Of Mischief* by Ashley Dukes and the part's the nobleman. Of course I'll have to audition you before I make a final decision.'

'Of course,' I agreed—all my optimism had returned in a flash. The audition would be all right. I was convinced of it—without even seeing the play.

'There's just one thing,' I said, 'I'll have to ask the surgeon in charge of my case if he'll let me do it. Can I let you know tonight?'

Getting on to Mr. Wood at Horton wasn't easy, but the personal call operator was a persistent angel, and at tea time I got him. I tried to make it sound as if the whole thing would be a quiet doddle that would keep me out of mischief. He wasn't deceived.

'Before you embark on anything like that you'd better come down here and have another X-ray.'

'Can I come the day after tomorrow?'

He laughed.

'You sound pretty keen—all right.'

By the time I rang Howard Lockhart, another call to the hospital had put the reservation of sleepers in motion through the Red Cross. I was paying, but getting a berth was impossible without some service department behind you, and this seemed the time to pull a string or two. When I told Howard that I couldn't give a decision until my return from Epsom he sounded worried.

'But, Ian, I have to warn you that if you're not right for the part at the audition I will have to give it to someone else. I can't audition you before you go—I leave Glasgow for a week first thing in the morning and I just hate to think of you going all that way and spending all that money perhaps in vain.'

I assured him that I was determined to go ahead and would quite understand if he had to turn me down—I even quoted him that line from *Julius Caesar* about a tide in the affairs of men, which taken at the flood leads on to fortune. He rang off and I suspect that he probably thought he'd involved himself with an enthusiastic nut-case.

Mr. Wood agreed to let me do it, but he laid down a series of conditions. I must live within easy walking distance of the theatre, I must wear my spinal jacket all the time, except in bed —and while on the subject of bed he insisted that I retired there as soon as the show was over. No parties, except after the last night and three good meals a day. When the six weeks were over (three of rehearsal and three of performances) I was to have a good rest. Any pain or feeling of malaise and I would have to stop at once. All this assumed that I'd pass the audition.

When I got back I had two days to prepare for the ordeal and the only place where I could look at a copy of the play was the Mitchell Library in Glasgow—and I wasn't allowed to take it away. I spoke the lines in a stage whisper in a corner of the reading room amid glares and shushing sounds from old age pensioners trying to enjoy their free read of the daily papers.

The Park Theatre had been used as a viewing theatre by film distributors in the west of Scotland. It was comfortable but tiny. The stage was minute. When I stepped on to it to do my reading I thought that however well I did, he'd have to look for someone who took up a little less room. As I began I was suddenly aware that I was shaking like a leaf, and for the first time experienced a sensation, that has since become very familiar, of a detached part of me, a little above the right hand side of my head, looking down and watching me do it. After a few lines Howard Lockhart stopped me:

'All right, Ian, I can put you out of your misery; you'll do.'

I think he was even more relieved than I was. He's a sensitive man of complete integrity. If I'd not been right for the part he'd have said so, but knowing my background, it would have upset him for days afterwards. Then he introduced me to the owner of the theatre, and my boss, John Stewart, a Glasgow business man, who suggested in his appearance and precise speech both a bank manager and a presbyterian minister, with a dash of Tweedledum thrown in for good measure. He was passionately fond of the theatre and determined to bring plays to people in Scotland who had never had a theatre within striking distance of their homes. This Glasgow venture was a pilot scheme which led to his founding the Theatre In The Hills at Pitlochry. His premature death prevented him enjoying the high and lasting reputation of this arts centre in Perthshire, which is enjoyed by tourists and residents alike, some of whom come long distances to see the plays and other events including celebrity concerts. It is fortunate that his business associate, Kenneth Ireland was not only prepared to pursue Stewart's ideal but has had the necessary flair to sustain it over a long period.

However, on that day in early November 1944, if I thought I was going to buy my Christmas presents out of the proceeds of *The Man With A Load Of Mischief* I was in for a swift disillusionment. John Stewart handed me my contract, which informed me that my total salary for the engagement was three guineas. As my face fell he added that it was more than he'd ever paid before. Still, I had been warned that this was a *semi*-professional company. It certainly was! I make no secret of the fact that at this time in my life I relied on my father for money. I was in receipt of a small disability pension, but, apart from that and the income from a few shares that he had made over to me just before the war started, I had nothing of my own. I was now within a year or so of becoming financially independent, but that moment had not arrived when I looked at my Park Theatre contract!

I moved into Green's Hotel in Woodlands Terrace, only a few hundred yards away, which was where grandad and auntie Peggy had been staying for some time.

Almost the first thing that grandad said when I arrived was 'What are ye gettin' for this?'

As an old theatrical journalist who had memories of Henry Irving it was right up his street.

'Three guineas.'

'A performance?'

'No.'

'A week?'

'No.'

'For the whole bloody thing?'

'Yes.'

He shook his head. 'That's what I can only describe as an alarmingly low salary!'

Alarming or not, I enjoyed every minute of rehearsals. *The Man With A Load Of Mischief* is a marvellously written play, which takes place in an eighteenth-century inn. The nobleman is a lecherous, conceited, arrogant fellow, who makes passes at the two other guests at the inn, a mysterious lady and her maid. In the end he gets his come-uppance, partly due to some adroit manoeuvres on the part of his manservant. It was first presented at the Haymarket Theatre in 1925 with Frank Cellier and Fay Compton as the nobleman and the lady. Leon Quartermaine was the manservant. The two other main parts in our production were played by distinguished Scots, who are both still very much in front of the public, Madeleine Christie and Bryden Murdoch.

When my costume arrived from the hirers in London it had the illustrious name of Robert Morley on the label inside the collar. Unfortunately the breeches were much too tight. When I tried to sit down my legs shot straight out in front of me.

'Ian, what's the matter? Your performance has lost all its edge.' From the gentle Howard this was severe criticism.

'I think I'll be all right when I get my breeches off,' was my ambiguous reply. Once again in my life it was a question of gussets. Today Robert would be incredulous if I told him that one of his costumes was too small for me. It certainly was then, and I couldn't blame the spinal jacket for filling out the breeches!

They had a pleasant custom at the Park Theatre of asking the person playing the principal part to choose a piece of music to be played on the panatrope as an overture before the play. I suggested the overture to *The Marriage of Figaro*. You could call it a prophetic choice.

The morning after the first night auntie burst into my bedroom with the papers.

'You've got rave notices from everyone!' she cried. I had too. There were flattering comments about my ability to throw away a line, one went much too far and described it as a Laughtonish performance. The consequences were rapid and exciting. I was almost immediately offered the lead in an hour long radio play called *The Frontier*. My money went up as well. For one performance of *The Frontier*, live on the national network, I got four guineas.

I remember nothing about the play except that it had a supernatural theme and was produced by Moultrie Kelsall, who startled me at the first read-through by producing an amazingly authentic imitation of an old creaking door when this sound effect was indicated in the script. Thrown in at the deep end like this I had to learn the rudiments of broadcasting very quickly, so it was lucky that the rest of the cast were experienced and kindly radio actors, who helped me all they could during the two days of rehearsal. The most important thing I learnt was that on radio dialogue must not be projected as it is on a theatre stage. The more natural and relaxed it is the better. As the listener's imagination has only sounds to inspire it the producer is always trying, among other things, to achieve perspectives of sound, something much easier to do since the invention of stereo. For instance, if someone enters a room in a play and then walks to the centre of it—the radio actor does just as he would on television or in the theatre. Reading from his script, he starts some distance from the microphone and moves towards it, being careful not to collide with his colleagues and making sure that while speaking he's 'on mike'—that is within the area of its sensitivity. It's also important to modulate the voice carefully when speaking close to a microphone. If you're giving a talk there's no problem. The sound engineer will ask you to speak a few lines so that he can decide how far away from you the microphone should be, and he knows that your voice level will probably be much the same throughout, because you'll be sitting at a table in a set position. In a play, one minute you may be shouting, while a few lines later you could be down to a whisper. However carried away you may be with the dramatic interpretation of your part, you must always be close in if you're speaking quietly and well away if you're going to bawl your head off. Microphones are delicate and expensive pieces of electronic equipment; if in a live performance (and they were all live in those days) you make a loud noise too close which the engineers are not expecting, it can blow a fuse and put the transmitter off the air. An experienced broadcaster leans back as he raises his voice and forward when he's being confidential. Another lesson that has to be learnt by all broadcasters is script management. The B.B.C. always type their scripts on a paper that hardly rustles at all, but unless great care is taken those incredibly sensitive instruments will pick up the tell-tale sound of a turned page. A news-reader can get away with it—in fact it may enhance the impression that the pages are hot from the type-writer; but in the middle of a tense drama obvious script noises will quickly wreck the illusion for the listener.

So, you have to insert your thumb or finger between the page you're on and the next, and then lower the script towards the floor letting the page you've just completed drop down, then with the other hand you quietly fold it behind. This is quite easy because scripts are held together by one large paper clip at the top left-hand corner. It does present problems, though, if the speech you're reading continues on the next page. B.B.C. secretaries skilfully avoid this whenever possible. There is the old chestnut about the radio actor whose script had been rather inexpertly typed. His last words on one page were: 'What's that lying in the road—pause for turning the page—ahead?'

The curse of all radio and television directors is the necessity to tailor every programme to the demands of the clock. No playwright or author can possibly think in precise terms of 30, 45, 60 or 90 minutes, even when they are writing for radio or television, and so the director is usually faced with having to make cuts—sometimes on a ruthless scale. Moultrie Kelsall had a reputation for leaving some of these cuts until fairly late in the proceedings. He gave me one or two hair-raising ones in *The Frontier* about five minutes before the transmission.

'Ian, halfway down page 23 from "and", halfway through the sentence on line 36 to "you see what I mean", which is three words into line 13 on page 24. I had hardly time to cross it all out, let alone try out how it would now read.

A producer making cuts in a live show depends greatly on the performers maintaining the same pace during the performance as they did at the final rehearsal. Shortly after *The Frontier* Moultrie was directing a play in which the noted Scots character actor, James Woodburn was appearing. Jimmy had a very long speech, which ended the play and took up the whole of the last page of the script. When he reached this moment in the transmission he discovered to his horror that, as can easily happen in several days of rehearsal, the final page had frayed round the paper clip and dropped off. He looked despairingly round the rest of the cast, mutely appealing for one of them to hand him their script—alas, no one else had that page. There's a tendency to lighten a long script by slipping out the pages that don't concern you—and only Jimmy had anything to say on that last one. At that moment the director's secretary tip-toed into the studio and handed Jimmy a piece of paper—nodding gratefully, he prepared to deliver the end of the play—but all that was on the paper was a scribbled message, which read:

'Speed it up—we're thirty seconds over—Moultrie.'

Disaster was averted by the discovery of the missing sheet in a corner on the floor, but poor Jimmy's pulse-rate must have been at least 120 as he read the dignified ending a shade faster than he'd intended.

For the next three months I appeared regularly in dramatized episodes broadcast for schools. The parts could hardly have been more varied. I could be anything from a Roman centurion to John Knox, and it was a marvellous way to learn something about radio. I worked for people like James Crampsie, Lennox Milne, Harry Hoggan and Robert Kemp, occasionally making the trip to the Queen Street studios in Edinburgh. The amount of work, too, was ideal for someone in my situation, though it seemed odd that I'd stormed Howard Lockhart's office as a singer and entertainer and emerged as an actor.

My winter in Glasgow ended with something of a flourish. The Glasgow Citizen's Theatre had its home at that time in the old Athenaeum, St. George's Place. The company was a strong one that could call on such talents as the late Duncan Macrae, Molly Urquhart, Denis Carey, Yvonne Coulette, James Gibson, and Archie Duncan and that's an incomplete list. The director was Eric Capon, and he invited me to join the company as a guest artist for a production of Gogol's play *The Government Inspector*. I was to play the Charity Commissioner. Frith Banbury was coming up from London to play the leading role.

I can't say I altogether enjoyed it. Some of the company regarded me, quite reasonably, as a complete amateur, who had no right to be sharing their dressing-room. There was also, perhaps, another cause for their resentment. Some of them, for one good reason or another, had not been required to join up and had instead done an excellent and necessary job providing entertainment in war time in a large city for very moderate remuneration. I was the first sign in that dressing-room that the war was nearly over and that the competition for jobs would inevitably stiffen. I presented no menace myself, except as a sort of storm signal.

Some of them, including Duncan Macrae, Molly Urquhart, Jimmy Gibson ('Gibbie'), and the ingenue, Lucille Steven were kindness itself, while the gruff, generous-hearted Archie Duncan and I shared a common feeling that neither of us was very good in our respective parts, which drew us together.

I was quite dazzled by finding myself on the same stage as Frith Banbury, a West End star, within a couple of months of my debut—so much so that I was quite bereft of speech when we were together, though this probably worked quite well in the play itself as I was supposed to be scared stiff of him!

By the time I went back to London I had a hundred pounds in the bank and had earned none of it singing. Indeed I only sang once in public the whole six months I was in Glasgow. I was reminded of it coming across a letter in an old press-cuttings book. It was from a lady called Kathleen Stewart, who described herself as Hon. Organizer of Service Entertainment for Glasgow Corporation. Writing from the City Chambers she said:

'I confirm my telephone conversation with you today that you will open the Show at "Garrison Theatre", St. Andrews Halls, Glasgow on Sunday first 15th April. I shall want a 10 minute spot, and shall be glad if you will introduce as much comedy as you can without spoiling your act. Please also bring your ukelele. I have billed you as Ian Wallace "With a Smile and a Song". I have telephoned Miss Sutherland of Galts and told her about you, and she is going to try and come along. Who knows what may come of it—I hope something good for your sake.' This engagement was unpaid.

I made my first appearance in the famous concert hall, which was so tragically destroyed by fire some years later, singing 'Sweet Rosie O'Grady' with one chorus whistled. Then, if the *Glasgow Evening Citizen* is to be believed, I did impressions of Robb Wilton, George Formby, crooners in general, and ended up with the sentimental ballad 'Without a Song'. The *Citizen* notice was headed 'V For Versatility'. I wonder if there are many other artists who, like me, would love to be able to see one of their early performances thirty years later. Now, videotape and film make it possible, but I'm talking of the really early efforts like that one. I'm sure it would seem hilariously funny, especially those impressions.

Miss Sutherland of Galts' Theatrical Agency who did come was good enough to offer me a summer season at Rothesay—and who knows what might have come of that if I'd taken it. But it was time to go home, for I knew by now that the tubercle bacillus hadn't entirely given up hope of getting me in the end, even at this late date.

*　*　*

'I think we'd better go in and have a look.'

Mr Wood was now contemplating, not my back, but a swelling between two ribs on my chest, which had gradually increased during my last few weeks in Scotland. I was back in B Hospital, back on the verandah—in a bed this time—though I was no longer the sole occupant of this pleasant area. There were so many casualties from western Europe that the verandah had become an overflow ward. At least this time I hadn't come for a long stay. Next day I made the trolley journey through the grounds to the operating theatre in the main building—it wasn't far short of a quarter of a mile away. Everyone we met was in tremendously high spirits—and no wonder, the Germans had finally surrendered the previous evening. I'd chosen VE Day to have a major operation!

Mr. Wood's assistant was John Partridge (I mentioned earlier what a right-hand man he's been in my life!) while Sister Turner was awaiting my return from the theatre with an oxygen cylinder at the ready. They were two familiar faces that I was delighted to see. So many of the others were new, though I'd only been away eleven months. It turned out to be some kind of residual abscess, and it continued to trouble me for another three years before it finally healed completely. Still, the operation had satisfied Mr. Wood that I could live a normal life—always with the proviso that I didn't get too tired. Before leaving hospital—after only twenty days this time—I once again asked him that sixty-four thousand question—would it get all right in the end?

'Oh yes,' he replied. 'Eventually.'

That was good enough for me.

It was about this time that my father and I had the conversation recorded on the first page of this book. He was by now resigned to the fact that I would pursue a theatrical career—

and there wasn't a great deal he could do to stop it other than cutting my allowance unless I agreed to go back to university for an LL.B., and he wasn't that kind of man. On the contrary, I think he was secretly proud that I was striking out on my own. I heard much later that the afternoon *The Frontier* was broadcast he had insisted on gathering fellow members of the Reform Club round a radio and daring anyone to speak until it was over.

He hated retirement, had outlived many of his friends and was desperately worried about falling share prices and the threats of a capital levy voiced by the new socialist chancellor, Sir Stafford Cripps.

My career, too, was in the doldrums. I had had to leave Scotland just when I was beginning to make something of a name for myself. It's always dangerous in show business to lift a boiling kettle off the stove.

Then out of the blue and quite unsolicited I got a post card from the Old Vic Theatre Company inviting me to give an audition the following morning at the New Theatre (since re-named the Albery). It had obviously been held up in the post. I was to attend at 10.25 and it went on to say 'Two contrasting pieces are advised, preferably one of a classical style and one of a contemporary style.' The directors were listed as John Burrell, Laurence Olivier, Ralph Richardson and Eric Capon, who had produced *The Government Inspector*. That was the link. He lived in Highgate and I rang him up at once, a mixture of breathless thanks and anxieties about the short notice. He told me that he was forming an Old Vic company for Liverpool and wanted me to be in it. It was the policy of the Old Vic that everyone had to be auditioned by all the directors, even though he knew my work and was satisfied.

'I know nothing by heart!' I wailed. Within half an hour I was in his flat where we sorted out the 'If it were done when 'tis done' speech from *Macbeth* and a comic slice of 'Doolittle' from *Pygmalion*.

Next morning I nervously joined a cluster of young actors in the wings. I watched the ones ahead of me with deepening misgivings. They seemed so assured and all were word-perfect. The one immediately before me stalked on to the stage, gave the directors halfway back the stalls a haughty greeting and then, with a series of balletic gestures, indicated where all the scenery was before launching into 'To be or not to be' with such bravura that I nearly went home on the spot.

When my name was called I shuffled on—still very large, still wearing my spinal jacket, still very ungainly.

'May I crave your indulgence to read, gentlemen, I only got your postcard last night.'

My copy of Shakespeare had tiny print that now seemed to dance in front of my eyes. I was shaking again and when I got to 'Blow the horrid deed in every eye' something seemed to collapse in the back of my throat and the word 'eye' came out as a sort of breathless groan. There was one chair on the otherwise bare stage and I decided to use it for the 'Doolittle'. I hoped it would look as if I was lolling vulgarly at ease, which seemed suitable for the dustman in 'Professor Higgins' study. My real reason was to take the weight off my trembling legs. When I'd finished I heard the unmistakable voice of Mr. Olivier courteously thanking me for coming. I was nearly into the wings when Ralph Richardson called after me:

'By the way, Mr Wallace, do you sing?'

I left him in no doubt on that score. While waiting to hear the outcome of this audition with no confidence whatsoever, I engineered another. It had been announced in the papers that Alastair Sim was going to appear in and direct a musical version of James Bridie's play *The Forrigan Reel* in London. During the winter I had seen the Citizen's Theatre's excellent production of the straight play and felt that, with songs added, the part of Mr. Grant of Forrigan would suit me down to the ground. From the admirable *Spotlight* casting directory I got hold of Mr. Sim's phone number, rang him up, told him I was a Scots actor who could also sing, and would like to be considered for his forthcoming production. If he was taken aback at the cool effrontery of this assured approach from a total stranger he gave no sign, inviting me to come to his flat the next morning.

He greeted me at the front door in dressing-gown and pyjamas.

'God bless my soul, boy, I'd forgotten all about you—come in, come in.'

While we chatted he kept glancing at me in what I found a disconcerting manner; soon he excused himself only to return in a few seconds carrying a shirt. It had the identical pattern of the one I was wearing.

'I was sure of it!' he said delightedly. 'That's a good omen—what about some coffee?'

He told me that when casting a play he always looked for one thing—'I have to be able to see the boy or girl still in the face—even in an old man or woman. If the boy or girl has gone—as a performer they're dead.'

He was engagingly frank about himself:

'Though most people enjoy my performances, there's a small percentage who can't stand me—it has to be so if you've a positive style. I know that on some people I have the same effect as drawing a nail across a rusy corrugated-iron roof. The sad thing is that one of them's my mother—now what are you going to read for me?'

I didn't think he'd want to hear 'Macbeth' so I socked him the 'Doolittle'.

'Not bad—not bad at all; but you must understand that I couldn't possibly give you an important part like Mr. Grant unless you had had far more experience. We're talking about a West End production, laddie, and even if you were a terrific actor I just couldn't take the risk—you do understand?'

'Of course.' (I didn't really, but it seemed the correct thing to say.)

'However, if you'd like to understudy the part . . . how would that appeal to you?'

I accepted with alacrity.

The next day John Burrell phoned and asked if I could come in and see him. My father and mother and I were catching the night sleeper to Scotland for the first holiday we'd had together since the war began.

'You can't possibly go into town today,' protested my mother. 'You haven't done your packing and there's a lot of things to arrange.' It takes quite a long time for people outside it to adjust themselves to the vagaries of the theatre. I was halfway down the path before she had said the half of what she intended.

John Burrell gravely thanked me for coming so quickly. He was probably quite used to such telephone summonses being responded to within the hour.

'I've been asked by Mr. Olivier and Mr. Richardson to offer you a contract with the London Company—we're doing *Henry IV*, parts 1 and 2, *Oedipus* and *The Critic*.'

'B-but I thought I was auditioning for Liverpool.'

'So you were—but we want you here.'

'I'm delighted of course, but I read, I wasn't by heart, and all those others knew their parts from memory.'

'Don't you believe it. The mistakes and misquotes drove us all mad. A lot of what we had to listen to was bluff and bull-shit. Can I take it you're interested?'

That motion was carried unanimously.

'It's a thirty-two week season followed by an American tour and of course as soon as the first play is on we'll be rehearsing the next during the day. The parts won't be large, but you'll be in all four and it could lead to all sorts of things. There might be a bit of singing too.'

'Dear Mr. Sim,

I have been offered a season by the Old Vic. Would it be possible for you to release me from our verbal agreement that I would understudy the part of Forrigan . . .?

The written offer from the Old Vic arrived a few days later. I was to start rehearsals in a few days, for which I would get a weekly salary of £3, rising to £8 when we opened. I couldn't really take it in. I had landed the sort of job that any young actor would be delighted with today—working with two of the greatest actors in the country—in the world, come to that. When I think back on it, I conveniently forget that in July 1945 there probably wasn't much serious competition around.

My parents were distressed and uneasy at my joyous excitement. They implored me to consult Mr. Wood before accepting. Reluctantly I rang him up. He refused point blank to let me do it. I'd never heard him express himself so vehemently. The season was too long, too strenuous; to imagine that I could rehearse all day and then be in the theatre all evening as well was nothing short of madness. When I mentioned the American tour at the end, he was positively angry. I told him that I'd never get a chance like it again (which was true!).

'If you don't give yourself more time to get over that operation and work up your strength and resistance gradually, you won't be fit to take another chance,' was his bleak reply.

I'm sure there are plenty of brave people about, who would have disregarded his advice. After over four years in which there

134

had been more than one setback, I felt I had no choice but to take it.

Sorrowfully, I wrote the inevitable letter and for several days can't have been too easy to live with. About the only bright spot in the gloom was the evening that one of my father's oldest friends and business colleagues, Michael Black, came over to dinner with his wife and three daughters. They lived at Cupar and we were staying in a hotel at Elie on the nearby Fife coast. After dinner there was dancing to the gramophone, and I temporarily forgot my disappointment, gliding clumsily round the floor with Ann, Patricia and Marion. Ann was a W.A.A.F., Marion still at school, while Patricia, the fair one, worked as a land-girl on their home-farm, which could boast a fine herd of pedigree Aberdeen-Angus cattle. The last time I'd seen her she was about eleven. Now at nineteen she seemed to me what was known at that time as 'a bit of all right'.

But next day it was back to sitting in a deck chair on the beach, gazing at Berwick Law wondering if anybody in the theatre would ever bother with me again. It's a profession where you're very much 'in for a penny in for a pound'. If your part demands that you fall downstairs, get soaked to the skin, stand for a quarter of an hour on a draughty stage in nothing but bathing trunks—or nothing at all, you must do it or refuse the engagement. You can't make your own conditions—at least not until you've achieved some sort of fame; even then it doesn't always work out. Newspapers frequently report clashes between stars and directors, which end in the star walking out; sometimes that walk is assisted from behind.

Though I hadn't the sort of physique that would inspire directors to cast me in swashbuckling roles full of sword-fights and tomato ketchup, I realized that I'd have to be careful not to try for anything else from which I'd have to withdraw for medical reasons. Such news travels fast in show business, and I could soon be a dead duck before I'd begun. When I returned to the hotel for lunch the porter said that there was a personal call from London coming through for me in about five minutes at one o'clock.

'Ian! Alastair here—listen, if you've not clicked with Vic, how would you like to play the part you were going to understudy? Peter Sinclair has dropped out.'

Signor Caruso told me I ought to do so.

(from Wilkie Bard's song *I Want to Sing in Opera*)

I arrived for the first rehearsal of *The Forrigan Reel* a month later to discover that the cast included Duncan Macrae and Molly Urquhart from the Citizen's Theatre, while among the English contingent, who visit the Highlands during the course of the play, were two stalwarts of The Players' Theatre, Geoffrey Dunn and Joan Sterndale Bennett. I was indeed fortunate in my colleagues. The music was by Cedric Thorpe Davie—now Professor of Music at St. Andrews University— who was energetically writing successful film music and rearranging Scots folk songs by the score. Bridie himself appeared from time to time and would join us for a drink before lunch. Standing in a saloon bar in his black overcoat and brown trilby, he looked a slightly incongruous figure holding a cigarette between finger and thumb, often wearing chamois leather gloves, and eyeing us benevolently over his gold rimmed glasses. I don't know what a typical playwright looks like, but he certainly resembled his alter ego, a consultant physician, who only retired from medical practice to become a full time dramatist when he was fifty.

Working with Sim was an education. He did not suffer fools gladly, and my lack of training and purely instinctive approach rightly earned the rough side of his tongue now and again. However his anger was always short lived and he was just as quick to join in the bouts of helpless giggles that inevitably occur from time to time during long hours of rehearsal. I was there, incidentally, with Mr. Wood's blessing. The extra

137

month's holiday and the fact that it was only one show had made it a different proposition. Though I had to have regular checks for several years, it was never again necessary for me to get his permission to undertake a job.

Only one thing marred this happy scene; we all sensed it from the start. We were in the wrong theatre. The whereabouts of Sadler's Wells in Rosebery Avenue has always been known to opera lovers—and in recent years balletomanes and the afficionados of Gilbert and Sullivan have also found their way there. The public for a Scots play with music is quite another thing. Even with such a popular figure as Alastair Sim in the lead it was asking too much of them to go so far from London's traditional theatreland, and we had no chance of picking up any passing trade. Apart from a few water board officials and post office sorters on their way to put in some unsociable hours, the pavements of Rosebery Avenue in the early evening are deserted.

There was something else. Although we were offering a musical, it wasn't on a big enough scale to fit comfortably into a large opera house. Despite the tuneful music, some prodigious acrobatic dancing from Macrae, a vintage performance from Sim as a reprobate old Highland fiddler, Bridie's resoundingly funny lines and, according to the critics, one or two promising supporting performances we folded in two weeks. Even my startlingly effective tartan trews, mentioned in several prestigous papers, couldn't save us. There's nothing like the theatre for making the graph of your emotions like a relief map of the Austrian Tyrol.

All was not lost. Alastair promised he'd use me again if the opportunity presented itself and Geoffrey Dunn, with whom I'd shared a dressing-room, diffidently asked me on the last night if I'd be remotely interested in doing a singing part in a Christmas show at the St. James's Theatre called *The Glass Slipper*, a delicate and original treatment of the Cinderella story by Eleanor Farjeon with music by Clifton Parker. Geoffrey had played in it on a previous occasion, making the part of The Herald his own. Now that we had closed and he was free, the management had pounced on him and Joan Sterndale Bennett. She was to play an ugly sister. He had·been asked to suggest a singing actor for the part of The Toastmaster and other bits and pieces throughout the evening.

Dear Eleanor Farjeon with her heavy brown boots, long, tweedy overcoat and enormously magnified spectacles was, unlike Bridie, in fairly constant attendance at rehearsals, easily wounded if her text was misused, but warmly encouraging, particularly to the younger members of the cast. There was something of a fairy-tale character about her. It would have been quite easy to believe that this rather ugly woman, who had some difficulty in walking, was really the good fairy in disguise.

The St. James's, alas demolished a few years later, was a lovely old theatre of great elegance and atmosphere with a horseshoe shaped auditorium. Back stage it was badly in need of modernisation. The dressing room I shared with several others was at the top of at least four flights of stone steps. After two performances, which involved many costume changes and therefore several hundred steps I was quite exhausted, though by now I had thankfully discarded the spinal jacket.

Cinderella was played enchantingly by Sara Gregory, who is married to Richard Stone, a school friend, who had taken part with me in Charterhouse theatricals, and was now embarking on a career as an agent after a war in which he had attained the rank of colonel and a Military Cross. I had no agent at that time and didn't yet feel the need of one, but we mutually decided that when the day arrived I'd go and see him. A year or two later he became my agent and remained so for nearly a quarter of a century. Sara had given birth to their first child a very short time before rehearsals began, and there was a moment of unusual charm when halfway through the dress rehearsal Robert Donat, the marvellous Scots actor whose life was cut short when he succumbed to asthma and heart trouble long before the allotted span, and who was presenting *The Glass Slipper* announced to the cast, 'There will now be an interval while Cinderella feeds her baby.'

When I arrived for that dress rehearsal there was a strange apparition standing in the passage outside the dressing-room. He was well over six feet tall with uncombed, wiry grey hair and wild bushy eyebrows. There were several days of stubble on his gaunt, sallow face and the high cheek bones were so prominent that he couldn't have seen a square meal for weeks. He wore an ancient and threadbare overcoat, parts of which were completely missing. It was tightly secured round his waist by coarse string.

The collar was fastened as high as it could possibly be with a safety pin. The bare legs, which protruded from the tattered relics of a pair of grey flannels were protected from the hard, wet London pavements by nothing more substantial than a pair of tennis shoes that could only have been salvaged from a dust-bin.

'Good afternoon, sir, I have the honour to be your dresser,' he said in the sort of voice that wouldn't have been out of place in the Athenaeum, and I'm not thinking of the club servants.

For the whole of the first week he appeared punctually—never removed the overcoat—we could only guess at what lay beneath—or didn't. On the Monday after the first pay day I walked straight past the distinguished looking man standing in the passage and did a genuine double take when the familiar voice bade me the time of day. His jacket and flannels weren't new, but they were well-cut and carefully pressed. The black brogues gleamed, while the shirt fitted so neatly that it could have been hand-stitched in Piccadilly. He made no reference to the dramatic change, nor did it seem possible to ask him about it. Old Harry Brindle, a veteran opera singer, whispered something to me about his having probably got his clothes out of pawn, which was undoubtedly what had happened.

For three or four weeks this enigmatic, courteous man did the job of dresser quietly and efficiently, maintaining a liaison with the wardrobe over laundry and repairs, helping with quick changes, handing us personal props in the wings and faithfully carrying out important errands like fetching the odd pint of beer from the pub next door.

Then one Monday afternoon the overcoat and the stubble were back. On Wednesday he didn't turn up. I've never seen him since. It was impossible to penetrate his reserve.

The conductor of *The Glass Slipper* was Ernest Irving—certainly the oldest person on our pay roll—enjoying a busman's holiday from his regular job of musical director at Ealing Film Studios. He was reputed to have had more heart attacks than it should have been possible to survive, and an iron determination to keep going. It was generally believed at Ealing that Ernest would only leave there for the last time feet first. For an old man with a weak heart, I would have put him about seventy, he

140

could produce surprisingly energetic bursts of temper when he would say things to his players that might have caused industrial action from anyone else—except perhaps Beecham. In his own field of film music he commanded that kind of respect.

Putting the music on a film sound-track is one of the most important jobs in the studio. We tend to take film music for granted; few films have none, so it's hard to judge the considerable contribution it makes to our enjoyment unless we've seen a long sequence of film before and after the music has been added. The difference is often startling. The director of the film and his music man will be working hand in glove at the planning stage, when it must be decided how much music will be needed, what kind, where it will come and, most vital of all, who shall write it. At that stage, enter the composer full of splendid original ideas, which may mean that all the plans have to be altered. After the film has been shot there comes the intricate and often frustrating job of fitting the music to coincide with exact moments on the screen. Most difficult of all is conducting a passage so that it lasts a precise length of time. It has to be done with one eye always on the stop-watch.

Then there is another time factor which can't be ignored—money. The musical director may have booked a famous orchestra for two three-hour recording sessions at considerable cost, certain that, barring accidents, there should be ample time to get all the music for that part of the film safely 'in the can'. It turns out to be one of those days when nothing goes quite right. The musical performance of one bit sounds marvellous when they play back the tape, not a blemish. The only trouble is that it lasts thirty-nine seconds instead of thirty-seven and a half! Next time through it's spot on for time but, alas, the poor wretched horn player has split a couple of notes, so they must do it again—and again with everyone getting more and more uptight until the session goes into overtime rates. It's a situation that every musician understands, it can happen so easily to the best. The person who doesn't understand is the man in the office who's putting up the money.

After years of working in this atmosphere where perfection has to be achieved by 5 o'clock it was no wonder that Ernest's temper could be fiery. He had inexhaustible mental energy, and enlivened the pauses between musical numbers in the show by playing chess with several members of the orchestra simultaneously on miniature sets. Up on stage we would be in the middle of a dramatic scene while Ernest would be lost in thought, staring at a pocket chess set. Then, having made a move, he'd pass it back to the second viola and accept another from the first clarinet. Still holding it in his left hand, he'd pick up the baton and begin the next musical number with hardly an upward glance. Along with Howard Lockhart, Alastair Sim and Eric Capon he was one of my great encouragers, and of them all, he was the one who wrote a letter that changed the whole course of my life.

One other member of the cast of *The Glass Slipper* must be mentioned here though I've never seen her since. She probably made more impact on the audience than anyone else, playing the mute part of a zany with unforgettable comedy and pathos. Her arresting appearance was achieved very simply by wearing a straight, short blonde wig to conceal her dark hair. The contrast with her huge brown eyes was, to say the least, effective. Her mother is Dame Marie Rambert and her father wrote *The Man With A Load Of Mischief*. When I was introduced to Lulu Dukes at the first rehearsal it seemed a remarkable coincidence.

I suppose I could be said to have made a reasonably good start. I'd had quite sizeable parts in two London musical shows and though I'd not been through a drama school or musical college, the critics had written pleasant enough things, and one night at Sadler's Wells a man with black hair brushed straight back and rather sharp features had poked his nose round the dressing room door to tell me he'd enjoyed my singing.

'By the way,' he added before disappearing, 'My name's Stanford Robinson of the B.B.C.'

It was like a vote of confidence. Yet if anyone had asked me then what were my ambitions, I'd have been stumped for a reply. What had already happened exceeded my wildest dreams in such a short time. I'd never expected to be in the West End of London for years. On the other hand, if I'd been asked what sort of work I hoped to get, I could have been more specific. I was still stones over weight and had been forbidden to diet, which meant that I could never aspire to anything except character parts, and that probably meant playing people much older than my twenty-six years. This was a bore, but I was extremely lucky to be alive, let alone able to pursue the career I'd always wanted. The best bet was musical plays, and I felt that I stood more chance of landing something if it involved making people laugh.

If anyone had suggested after *The Glass Slipper* that my future would lie in opera I'd have dismissed the idea with a shudder—not only would have, I did. An old school friend, Ted Jackson, who, unlike me, had decided to be a lawyer, wrote about this time strongly urging me to consider an operatic career. I hated the idea. I'd only seen three operas in my life; *La Boheme* at L'Opera Comique in Paris, which I didn't enjoy half as much as the Folies Bergere, *The Shepherds of the Delectable Mountains*—a school expedition, which was unbearably tedious, and *The Marriage of Figaro* at Sadler's Wells which, admittedly, I loved, not so much for the music as the comedy, a delightful surprise in the course of what I expected to be a boring evening.

The only two opera singers I'd encountered were old Harry Brindle at the St. James's who tended to reminisce all night about the singers in the Carl Rosa and the Moody-Manners Opera Companies in his young days at the turn of the century. He was a dear old boy, who could still sing well, but I had little or no interest in this sort of conversation from which there was no escape as we dressed side by side. When I was staying at Green's Hotel in Glasgow I had met Norman Allin, who was still singing with the Carl Rosa on tour at the age of sixty-one. His speaking voice was like a deep organ pipe with a Lancashire accent—a tall dignified man of great modesty and charm, he was undoubtedly the finest English bass singer of his generation.

One evening in the lounge, for the benefit of several elderly residents who were too frail to venture through the black-out to hear him at the Theatre Royal, he took off his jacket and sang them Colline's touching song to his overcoat in the last act of *La Boheme*. Listening to that magnificent voice I remember thinking that if I'd wanted to sing in opera, which I didn't, I'd have no chance up against that sort of competition. As far as I was concerned opera was a high-brow entertainment that didn't appeal to me and in which I had no desire to participate.

It was therefore something of a shock when about ten days after the last performance of *The Glass Slipper*, at the beginning of March 1946, I got a letter from Josephine O'Donnell, secretary to the Administrator of The Royal Opera House, Covent Garden telling me that they were in process of forming a new company and inviting me to present myself for an audition. My name, she added, had been put forward by Mr. Ernest Irving, who felt that I was worthy of consideration.

It's fascinating how quickly one can change one's mind. I wrote at once accepting, giving no thought to the appalling gaps in my muscial education and repertoire, which included nothing operatic at all beyond the Prologue to *Pagliacci* and an aria by Handel from his opera *Berenice* called 'Love That's True Will Live For Ever'. I decided to rely on the latter because, being more of a bass than a baritone, I couldn't sing The Prologue in the original key. Even I knew enough to realize that they wouldn't be impressed with one of the best known arias in the world transposed down a tone.

The great day came for me to attend what was described as the preliminary audition. The atmosphere was quite different from the Old Vic. Each person had been allotted a quarter of an hour and the only other singer I saw was Owen Brannigan, who was in the middle of what sounded to me like a most strenuous and difficult aria—it turned out to be the celebrated Catalogue Song from *Don Giovanni* by Mozart, and I heard him sing it before me at every other audition I attended there; whoever else had been eliminated, we always seemed to be among the survivors. The cheerful and sympathetic Eric Mitchell played for everyone, possessing a rare talent for putting nervous artists at their ease, though I think I was really much less nervous than I'd been at the New Theatre. Probably this was because I didn't think I stood an earthly—it was all a bit of a joke. Standing on that famous stage marvelling at how resonant my voice sounded would be something to dine out on—no more. I can't remember if I sang anything else. If I did it would only have been a folk song. Anyway, when I'd finished I was called down to the stalls. In place of Olivier and Richardson were David Webster, the Administrator, and Elena Gerhardt, a distinguished German mezzo-soprano who since retiring had been a respected singing teacher in London for many years. Webster had been persuaded to turn his back on a highly successful career managing department stores in order to build a new opera company from the very foundations. He told me many years later that he didn't need much persuasion. In fact when he was offered the job at 'The Garden' he had to persuade the chairman of The Metal Box Company to release him from a much better paid job he'd just accepted there. He was a classic example of a man going to work where his heart lay and making a success of it.

He introduced me to Madame Gerhardt of whom I'd never heard. Her enthusiasm about my singing took me by surprise, especially when she told me to go away and learn the Papageno arias from *The Magic Flute*. I'd be called back to sing them at a later date when the qualifying auditions would be held. I felt as if I'd got through the first round of a sort of musical tennis tournament.

My first appearance in the qualifying round can still bring a blush to my cheek. So unaware was I of the significaace of what was happening that I merely got hold of the score of the opera, found the songs and worked them out with one finger on the piano. Despite my early piano lessons I had only the haziest ideas about sight reading and I'd never seen the opera. I had no idea that, scattered about London, were people who, for a guinea or two, would have helped me—opera coaches or repetiteurs as they're called. Any one of them could have taught me those arias and how to interpret them within an hour. Unaware of the availability of such skilled assistance, I turned up at the appointed time not exactly equipped to knock them cold with my rendering.

The two who had heard my first effort were now joined by Karl Rankl, the newly appointed musical director. I was still taking the whole thing rather lightly. I certainly had no idea that I was about to make a complete idiot of myself.

At the end of the first verse of 'A Fowler bold in me you see, a man of mirth and minstrelsy', Herr Rankl held up his hand.

'Meester Vallace, pliz; don't you theenk eet go a liddle faster, hein?'

It turned out that I was singing it at less than half speed and accenting all the wrong notes. I was politely dismissed and told to restudy it. They would call me again in a few days. I was very lucky they didn't tell me to get out and stay out. In the meantime I bought a record of Dennis Noble singing the arias and broke into a cold sweat when I compared his interpretation—and tempo—with mine.

My luck held. When I returned and gave a somewhat better account of Mozart's joyous music, they told me that I had qualified for a place in the final audition. This might not take place for weeks. I was naturally delighted to have got this far, but the fact remained that there were longish gaps between these auditions and I began to feel it was time I earned some money. All my eggs seemed to be in this one exciting, but so far unproductive, basket. To mix the metaphors, I was also wondering what would happen when I tried to learn to swim at the deep end. I'd had a good square look at Papageno by now and it seemed a hell of a big part for an operatic debut at a place like Covent Garden for a man who hadn't even got a singing teacher! More than that I just simply couldn't believe that my voice was good enough for opera. Truth to tell, I didn't want to believe it. I did believe something else, though; if opera *was* going to play a part in my life, it wouldn't be a bad idea to try it out in rather less exalted surroundings than the Royal Opera House to get the feel of it.

Once more my guardian angel was on hand; this time to guide my footsteps into the path of Helen Lawrence, who had been in the chorus of *The Glass Slipper*. She told me that she had just landed a job in the chorus of a new opera company that was opening in a few weeks at London's Cambridge Theatre.

'Why don't you apply for an audition?' she suggested.

I wrote at once—only to get a reply saying that they were fully cast. But I ran into her again a week later, and when I told her what had happened she said.

'Take my advice and go and see them at the office. They're at 141, Park Lane, I'm sure they have vacancies—you might be lucky.'

I was. As I arrived and stood indecisive in the large hall of what had once been a gracious town house, a man, obviously leaving, came down the stairs. He was dressed all in black including an impressive Homburg with a curly brim. He looked like a bishop, who would do the football pools when no one was looking.

'Can I help you?' he said.

I explained my business.

146

'I see. Can you sing a top F?'

'Yes.' It was true—just.

'Come upstairs.'

He waved me into a comfortable chair in his spacious office overlooking Hyde Park.

'Do sit down. My name's Owen Mase and I'm the Managing Director of The New London Opera Company. Tell me, do you know the part of Schaunard in *La Bohème*?'

'I'm afraid not.' I hoped it sounded as if this was one of a small number of parts that I had unaccountably let slip through the net. I prayed he wouldn't ask me which parts I did know!

'Have you any music with you?'

'A little,' I said, guardedly.

'Good! It just so happens that our Schaunard had to withdraw today—he hadn't realized that there was an option in a contract he signed for a show last summer that compels him to appear on the south coast from June till September this year, bad luck, but there it is, perhaps good luck for you,' he chuckled. 'Now, do you feel like singing for our vocal director, Mr. Borgioli? With any luck he'll still be here.'

Dino Borgioli was a celebrated Italian tenor, who had sung many times at Covent Garden. He had appeared in *La Bohème* with Dame Nellie Melba and had sung 'Ernesto' in the pre-war *Don Pasquale* at Glyndebourne, he was now the most fashionable singing teacher in London. When I was ushered into the large rehearsal room which I was later to know so well, he came forward dressed in a dark blue suit which could be accurately described as magnificent, a jewel shone in his tie pin, but on his head was a terrible toupée of auburn curls that could have deceived nobody but the wearer. I couldn't keep my eyes off it as I ploughed through *Love That's True* and the Papageno arias. I was more nervous than I'd been at the Garden, I scented some kind of victory I suppose. He never asked me what I'd done before. Opera people don't seem so obsessed with one's antecedents as theatre people. If they like your voice they're not so concerned with what's gone—or not gone—before.

'You dont'a knowa da Schaunard?'

'No.'

'You learna da first act by Thursday and singa for me again, no?'

'Yes, please.'

'Buono. Arrivederci.'

On my way out they handed me a vocal score of the opera—that's the music arranged for piano accompaniment including all the singing parts. It's what singers use to learn an opera before rehearsing it with the orchestra. The vocal score is also used for production rehearsals, which are accompanied on the piano until a very late stage in the proceedings. The orchestra doesn't arrive until the dress rehearsal, except in opera companies where there is a lot of money to spare! Even then they will only play for the last two or three rehearsals.

If ever there was a time when I would have profited from the services of a repetiteur it would have been that week! Instead, still not knowing of their existence, I made do with Auntie Peggy, who was staying with us. She bashed out the notes by the hour, though even she wasn't too certain of the tempo here and there. When I returned to Park Lane on Thursday I didn't know it all that well, but I managed to stumble through. At the piano was George Coop, an Italian, who had done everything in opera houses from repetiteur to chorus master and from prompter to conductor. He sang all the cues in a voice like a corncrake, puffing out clouds of smoke from the cigarettes he smoked incessantly in a long holder. Every now and then he would have to play my melody loudly as I strayed from the correct notes.

'Brava!' said Dino and smiled.

I was in.

Next day I signed a run-of-the-operas contract. I was to play Schaunard in *La Bohème* and any other parts required by the management for twenty-five pounds a week.

I hadn't even started rehearsing when my summons to the final audition at Covent Garden arrived. I went along and once more trotted through my Papageno arias. This time Mr. Webster took me on one side.

'We're rapidly coming to the conclusion we can use you,' he said in his precise, rather over-pronounced style. (It had already taken them three months!) I told him what I'd been up to—making the point that it seemed to me only common sense to get some experience under my belt in a smaller company before aspiring to an enormous house like Covent Garden.

'Excellent,' he replied, 'That'll last about a couple of months and then you'll come to us.'

It lasted a couple of years, and by that time he'd changed his mind.

* * *

And the brass will crash and the trumpets bray

(The Mikado)

Jay Pomeroy, the Russian impresario of the New London Opera Company was a person to be reckoned with on the London musical scene during and immediately after the war. On a first meeting he struck me as a man it would be inadvisable to cross. Though below average height, he was broad and solid. His head was permanently a little bowed so that he peered up at you, blinking rapidly as he spoke, which didn't make for easy conversation. He spoke excellent English, but with such a thick accent that it was hard to catch every word. His heavily lidded eyes that could flash with anger or amusement, the gleaming black hair, brushed straight back without a parting and the flat Slav nose were a combination of features that left no room for speculation about his nationality. He always wore double-breasted blue serge suits and, even indoors, seemed loath to remove his dark blue overcoat with black velvet on the collar. I can't recall in three years seeing him casually dressed or wearing a hat.

Rumour had it that he had been Trotsky's secretary and had left Russia as male nurse to an ailing Soviet official who was seeking a cure in a Swiss clinic. Having safely delivered his patient, he headed for London. Whether true or not, it was a colourful story, which we were happy to believe.

As a business man he had considerable skill and during the war he made a great deal of money using an ingenious plan which, though legal when it was conceived, didn't quite fit the spirit of the times. The Government, determined to prevent the terrible profiteering which had caused such anger and bitterness during World War I, had introduced the Excess Profits Tax which, over certain levels of profit, was levied at the punishing rate of 100 per cent. An example of its effect was a reduction of business in the whisky trade. To avoid the range of the tax, which would have meant working for practically no return, distillers and bonded warehouse companies drastically reduced their output and were only supplying regular customers with rationed quantities.

Pomeroy and his associates was only one of several groups of business men who decided to buy a controlling interest in various distilleries and replace the directors with their own nominees. The nominees then sold large quantities of whisky to other members of the syndicate at knock-down prices, which avoided bringing the transactions within the scope of the tax. They in turn sold it at the full price to anyone who would buy, and, due to some anomaly that these keen-eyed chaps had spotted, those sales didn't attract Excess Profits Tax at all. They made fortunes and it was said that they even managed to export some of the precious liquid to America at the height of the submarine blockade.

In 1943 the Government became aware of this loophole and closed it—retrospectively, which meant that the Commissioners of Inland Revenue could move in and sue Mr. Pomeroy and others for unpaid tax on what had been tax-free profits according to the law when they were made. Pomeroy's personal liability was reckoned to be in the region of £400, 000—a hell of a sum in the 1940s, especially when one was a victim of retrospective legislation, something which has always been hated in Britain and avoided by politicians in normal times. But those were not normal times.

The case was hotly contested by both sides. It went to the Court of Appeal and then to the House of Lords where the Tax Collectors were finally declared the winners. Before the 1943 legislation Pomeroy had started using the money for theatrical enterprises, and after it, convinced that he would come out on top, continued to do so. He began with a Russian opera *Sorochintzi Fair* by Mussorgsky followed by the Strauss operetta *A Night in Venice* and finally The New London Opera Company. They were impressive achievements in those austere times, whatever the source of the money.

Above: Daria Bayan as *Mimi* in *La Boheme*, Cambridge Theatre, talking to Fiorello LaGuardia, Mayor of New York, 1946. Ian as *Schaunard* in the background. *Below:* As *Dr Bartolo*, Cambridge Theatre in *The Barber of Seville*, 1947. Make up pretty rudimentary.

Above: Carl Ebert directing Hilde Gueden and me in *Don Giovanni*, Edinburgh Festival, 1948. *Below:* Left to right: Alda Noni, Ian and Fernanda Cadoni in *La Cenerentola* at Glyndebourne 1952.

How much was left for the Inland Revenue when their hands were held aloft by the referee in the House of Lords is anybody's guess. It evidently wasn't enough; they declared him a bankrupt. There are various degrees of bankruptcy—but to go bust with the Inland Revenue as your chief creditor is the worst. You have to pay tax on all your repayments. Trying to run up an escalator that's going down is child's play by comparison.

Whatever were his reasons for becoming an impresario, making money can hardly have been one of them. If that had been his aim he would never have founded an opera company! The events which led up to this major enterprise were as follows. In 1942 *Sorochintzi Fair* was presented at the Savoy Theatre to mark Russia's entry into the war—a gesture on his part to promote friendship between the two countries. He called his production company The Music, Art and Drama Society (we affectionately referred to it as the mad society), and its principal activity was presenting symphony concerts in London —in 1943 there were no less than 132 of them.

A girl called Daria Bayan from Leningrad made her debut in *Sorochintzi Fair* in an otherwise experienced cast that included Oda Slobodskaya and Parry Jones. She had travelled extensively with her family and spent her early childhood in China; after touring Europe she went to school in Switzerland and then to art school in Vienna. Presumably her parents were well off, for when she expressed a strong desire to give up painting in favour of singing, they sent her to London for lessons with Borgioli.

She proved an apt pupil. When Pomeroy presented *A Night in Venice* at the Cambridge Theatre in 1944, Miss Bayan was in the lead and the production ran for over 500 performances. I never saw it, but this beautiful woman with the dark chestnut hair captivated audiences with her appealing performance, both as singer and actress.

Those of us who were lucky enough to be engaged to sing for The New London Opera Company owed our opportunity to her, for there can be little doubt that one of the reasons 'Pom', as we all called him, formed the company was to create a setting for her talents. There was another reason. I think he felt that if things did go badly in the law courts, it would count as a point in his favour that the money had been spent bringing worthwhile cultural experiences to the nation's capital. It was a naive belief, but I think he held it, and it cost him very dear in the end.

Of course when I turned up for my first rehearsal I was unaware of all this background. I had been engaged by one opera company while a bigger one waited in the wings. This was heady stuff and I confess to revelling in the situation.

First of all I had to learn the role (you can't rehearse an opera with the score in one hand like you do a play, it's too heavy and the double tax on the memory of words and music makes rehearsing moves and business a waste of time till everyone is word and music perfect). I was assigned for several hours a day to Professor Maliniak, a middle-aged Polish Jew, who with his family had suffered badly under the Nazis. Very short-sighted, he was a gentle, soft-spoken man with an ironic sense of humour, but at the piano he was a tyrant, who wouldn't let the slightest error pass uncorrected. To singers, such people are worth their weight in gold—though they reduce us to shaking fury about once every quarter of an hour in the early stages of learning a role. When I say 'us' I'm referring to singers like me, who are not so hot at sight reading. Good readers get the music right first time and have only to memorize it—but there's the rub— for some reason those to whom the music comes easily often have more difficulty committing it to memory than we do. Perhaps because we have to hear it played through so many more times!

When you half know a scene and can reel off a page or two without looking at the score, it's maddening to be stopped in full flood and told you sang a crotchet instead of a quaver. Maddening, but necessary, because if you're allowed to get away with that error two or three times, it's apt to creep into your performance and take up permanent residence. Such perverse creatures are we that if someone like the Professor takes pity on our frailty and lets a few little things pass for the sake of peace and quiet, and we are later criticized for them by the conductor, we will at once round on the poor old coach and tell him he doesn't know his job!

When Jerzy Maliniak told the conductor you knew a role— you knew it all right. The scenery could fall down, the orchestra could suddenly break into The 'Blue Danube', but you'd still go forging ahead with Puccini, undismayed. One day at the end of a session he closed the score, shut the piano and held out his hand.

'Congratulations, tomorrow you can rehearse with the others.' Not for the last time in my operatic career I experienced the sensation of being back at school and passing an exam. I had never worked with opera singers before and imagined they'd be a temperamental lot. Instead they were friendly and welcoming. Though I was an unknown quantity and they had been working together for some time, they accepted me at once. The Mimi was, of course, Daria Bayan; Rudolph, the poet, was wearing the uniform of a captain in the U.S. Army. Lester Ferguson, a handsome athletic young man with rugged good looks, and, as it turned out considerable attraction for the girls, was within a few days of demobilization. Marcel, the painter, was an older man; Stanley Pope, in his forties, was tall and moved rather stiffly and if at that time I'd been asked to nominate someone to personify the sort of Englishman who could be described as the backbone of the country, it would have been him. He'd been a successful concert singer before the war, who had always yearned for the operatic career that hadn't come his way. This was his chance, and though his acting was never exceptional, his beautiful baritone voice and complete commitment to the role he was playing was to win him a new and admiring public over the next three years. I think we became friends in the first hour.

Colline, the philosopher, was one of the three biggest men I've encountered in opera (the other two were Bruce Boyce and David Franklin). Martin Lawrence, son of a tailor in the East End of London had served an apprenticeship in the Carl Rosa Opera Company on tour and was now getting the chance to establish himself as principal bass in this one. He was well over six feet and weighed not far short of twenty stones. Around this time there was a news story to the effect that the combined weights of Martin, Stanley, Fergy, (we never called him Lester) and myself was sixty-five stones and 1 lb. As the paper commented, 'Not a light opera!'

The fickle Musetta was Dorothy Vernon, a young fair-haired soprano, who started life as a shorthand typist and studied singing in the face of family opposition. War-time concerts and a tour with a youth orchestra was all the experience she could muster when she applied for an audition with the company. I was thankful that there was one other member of the cast who was as new to opera as I was. In fact there was a second, but he was widely experienced in a similar field. Tony Sympson, the diminutive musical comedy actor, was making his operatic debut doubling the parts of Benoit, the landlord and Alcindoro, the foppish old roué in the second act. His was hardly a voice of operatic proportions, but in the cameo parts of our repertoire he was outstanding. When we met recently he sang one of Spoletta's phrases from *Tosca* in impeccable Italian. Tony nowadays sports a magnificent white beard and never stops working, but his last opera was twenty-seven years ago.

Borgioli was our producer as well as vocal director, and the scenery was designed by the famous Alexandre Benois, who had worked with Diaghilev at the Ballets Russes in Paris. Two of the greatest successes of those legendary seasons in the early 1900s were *Les Sylphides* and *Petrouchka*. Benois created the settings and costumes for them both. Though now an old man, he produced three marvellous sets, on which he worked in his Paris studio; like Rudolph's attic it overlooked the rooftops. When he borrowed a score of the opera to remind himself of one or two points, he found it had been autographed by Puccini himself.

If we had a great designer, we also had the most important ingredient of any operatic success—a fine conductor. Alberto Erede, a pupil of Felix Weingartner had been associate conductor with Fritz Busch at Glyndebourne before the war. He was not only an experienced musician, but spoke German, French and English as well as his native Italian. His appearance was strikingly unusual to someone like myself, who had never met an Italian before. His olive complexioned face was long and sad, terminating in a massive and prominent chin, which he often stroked—perhaps in anticipation of the beard which he has grown in later years. Despite his melancholy expression, he could call on a lugubrious sense of humour and over a meal he would convulse us with casually thrown away remarks about his colleagues, revealing insight and acute observation. He played the piano as if it were an orchestra and would often rehearse us round it for a couple of hours till he was satisfied with our performance, singing as an ensemble. For me, to whom such musical sublteties were at that time a closed book, it was a marvellous opportunity to learn from a man who was, to my great good fortune, a teacher as well as a musical director.

The date of the first night was several times postponed and we rehearsed, off and on, for nearly two months. At last it was fixed for 12th June—about three weeks ahead—and it was to be a charity gala in aid of The Returned British Prisoners of War Association in the presence of H.R.H. Princess Elizabeth. We were to start stage rehearsals in the sets at the Cambridge Theatre almost at once. The main reason for the delay in announcing the start of the season was Pom's determination to open with a big splash. The gala was just what he wanted.

Now I began to feel apprehensive. Not only was I nervous about how I would get on in performance with the orchestra (an accompanist at the piano can jump a few bars if you make a mistake, an orchestra of sixty-five can't), but I was also seized with a dread of catching cold just before the first night. I was afraid of taking part in it and equally afraid of being prevented from doing so! Fear of the latter possibility afflicts most singers throughout their careers, until they reach an age when colds are less frequent and their inevitable sense of insecurity comes to terms with the truth that a cancelled engagement does not necessarily mean that no one will ever book them again! Incidentally, it's not a nose cold that worries a singer—it can even improve the voice for a day or two—it's the possible complications. The onset of infection at the top of the chest as a result of a cold 'slipping down' can stop the voice even more effectively than laryngitis—while tracheitis (inflammation of the inside of the wind-pipe, which can be caused by singing with a severe chest infection) can put a singer out of action for weeks. Unless you're under contract to a large opera house, it's a case of no singing, no money. Bronchitis is another menace because though this may not affect the voice, the strenuous singing necessary in opera houses and concert halls is impossible if you can't breathe properly.

Having said all that, though I have had to cancel the occasional performance because of chest colds and other ailments, I've managed to struggle through thirty years of never being ill on a first night. There must be a lesson in that somewhere—if only the old cliché that the things you worry about most never happen.

Of course we don't just worry, we do what we can to minimize the risks and there is now a useful repertoire of antibiotics to come to our assistance, th' ugh it is unwise to make more use of these than is absolutely necessary. On many occasions on my way to an engagement I've reluctantly left a comfortable reserved corner seat in a crowded train in search of an odd place elsewhere because my immediate neighbour was all too obviously in the throes of a bad cold. Catching it could cost me money, let down audiences and cause managerial headaches. Naturally the chap with the cold isn't ill enough to stay at home and can do his job perfectly well with anything short of double pneumonia. I'm sorry for him: but I hate him. Whenever practical, most of us travel by car—and this is one of the reasons why. We are not, on the whole, hypochondriacs. I play golf in the rain and go out immediately after a hot bath. I will drive over 200 miles, get out of the car, have a cup of coffee, change and then sing and talk to an audience for a couple of hours. For over twenty-five years of my career I smoked cigarettes, I drink both wine and spirits, though not before singing, and I'm a late bedder. I don't exactly coddle myself, and most of my colleagues seem to have similar depressingly normal habits.

When the date of our opening was announced Fergy decided to play a joke on Pom. Disguising his voice, he rang him up.

'Mister Pomeroy?'

'Yis.'

'This is Colonel Hackelberger, United States Army here.'

'Yis?'

'I believe you have a Cap'n Ferguson under contract, is that right?'

'Yis.'

'Waal, Mr. Pomeroy, I sure have some goddam bad noos for you.'

'Yis?'

'Yeah. Cap'n Ferguson has misunderstood his demobilization order. He ain't doo for release till the Fall and I'm havin' to post him to Germany at the end of this week.'

The vocal disguise was not quite good enough to deceive Pom.

'Don't you worry, Colonel,' he replied, 'You sind 'im where you like. I found out yesterday 'e's a pouf so I don't want him any more.'

The first night was a great success, and though I was very nervous beforehand, the Professor's careful preparation and the sheer excitement of the occasion carried me along. The first thing I discovered about an operatic performance was that you have to pace yourself through it like a long distance runner. I came bouncing on in the first scene and made a mistake immediately. Schaunard is bursting with the good news that he's had an unexpected windfall, a wealthy eccentric has given him money in advance to teach a parrot to sing, which means that he and his three companions can go out for an evening's celebration. As Schaunard is a musician, Benois designed a top hat for me which, as I entered the attic, I was to take off and throw onto a chest by the window. I was so keyed up that when the moment came I took it off, threw it into the air and it went straight out through the sky-light and disappeared. This would have been all right as a comic happening if the sky-light had been open. As it was I merely revealed to the audience that the illusion of glass was only given by clever lighting. Then I launched into the scene with all the voice at my command, and Schaunard has quite a lot to sing as soon as he comes on. Long before the scene was over I was beginning to run out of steam. What had been easy in rehearsal was suddenly a great effort, I was soon panting for breath and wondering how I would manage to get to the end of the act without the audience noticing. I wished I hadn't hit it so hard at the beginning. I made it, but it taught me to spread my efforts more evenly over the whole performance. Like everything in life, one learns by experience, in this case a frightening one.

The critics were kind and were clearly wanting to give such a brave venture a good send off. Pomeroy did all he could to woo them. There were marvellous supper parties at the Hungaria Restaurant after all our first nights, to which critics and columnists were invited, and the seating plans put them next to singers rather than other guests. It was one of Pom's short list of illusions that the press wouldn't pan a show if they'd had a good dinner at the management's expense. It didn't work, and it would have been scandalous if it had. On the other hand, it was interesting to meet the critics every few months, and in conversation with them I got a far better understanding of their job and their point of view than I had had up to then. For one thing I realized that it is no part of the critic's task to be concerned with the personal problems or illness of an artist whom he is reviewing, nor can he be sensitive to all the weeks of slog that a cast has put in if he feels that the end product is poor. He has to remember that the public rely on his judgement and may decide whether or not to book for a show on his verdict. All artists find adverse criticism hard to accept, especially when we're aware that thousands of people are reading over their breakfast the words that are putting us off ours. It does slightly assuage the anger and resentment that criticism often inspires to know that the man who wrote it is knowledgeable, responsible, loves opera and is concerned with keeping up high standards. We may dismiss him as a failed singer or a composer who could never get his works performed. It may be true. The fact remains he may be better at his job than we are at ours.

We performed *La Bohème* three times a week, sharing the theatre with the Monte Carlo Ballet while the second opera in the season was prepared—*Don Pasquale* by Donizetti with Martin Lawrence in the title role, one of the great buffo roles in the Italian repertoire. Andrew Macpherson, an excellent Scots lyric tenor had won the part of Ernesto against numerous rival candidates at the audition and Tony Sympson was to be the comic notary. But to be honest, the news that was exciting London opera lovers about this production was the return to this country of one of their great pre-war favourites, the Italian baritone, Mariano Stabile to sing the part of Malatesta and the intriguing information that with him was coming an unknown, but promising soprano, Alda Noni.

We had sung *La Bohème* in English, which suited us fine, there wasn't an Italian in the cast. *Don Pasquale* was to be in Italian, and it was obvious that if international stars like Stabile were going to join us, all the operas would have to be sung in their original language. All the subsequent productions were in Italian, and we eventually converted *La Bohème* as well.

The conversion as an upheaval could well be compared with North Sea Gas. We sang it in English one night and Italian the next—hair-raising.

If *La Bohème* had been a success, *Don Pasquale* was a triumph. Martin Lawrence, who was acclaimed by the entire London press, had worked tremendously hard on the role with Borgioli before Stabile arrived. He was amazed to find that this elegant, flamboyant, beautifully dressed Sicilian, fifty-eight years of age, with husky speaking voice and mischievous hooded eyes was prepared to teach him how to play it. It would have been impossible to find anyone better qualified to do so.

It's no disrespect to the late Michael Benthall, who produced the opera, to say that Stabile took over the production in all the scenes where he was on the stage—and some where he wasn't! Michael, very sensibly, made no protest, sat calmly in the stalls and confined himself to setting the few scenes in which Stabile showed no interest, and making such a tour de force of the famous chorus scene that it never failed to stop the show.

Alda Noni gave a delicious performance, her enormous, expressive eyes making every male heart beat faster, even those located at the back of the upper circle, while Stabile himself used this light comedy role to captivate his audience and get himself match fit for the sterner tasks that lay immediately ahead. It's a mystery why Martin Lawrence never managed to scale the same heights again. His was a performance of tremendous vigour and character, which roused audiences to a high pitch of enthusiasm every night. The patter duet between Stabile and himself, encored as a matter of course, was that rare combination, funny and exciting. Perhaps some artists are unfortunate enough only to find one role that enables them to express their talent to the full; on the other hand there are a great many more whose search is completely in vain.

Mr. Wood had made one stipulation about 1946—I must have a month off in the summer. I went to see Pom in trepidation. After all I'd only been working for him for about three months. I needn't have worried. He was kind enough to tell me that I'd proved my worth to the company and he'd arrange for someone else to sing Schaunard in my absence. Then as an afterthought he added.

'You know something? You could have been a second George Robey; but you are too well brought up so you will never be.'

That rather depressed me in view of the fact that, so far as I

161

knew, George Robey had had much the same sort of upbringing as I'd had. I defiantly decided that I'd try to be the first Ian Wallace instead.

I only mention the holiday because we went back to Elie, where I contrived to see a bit more of Patricia Black. I'd scraped together enough petrol to drive up to Scotland, which made it easier to nip over to her parent's home.

My main source of transport from the time of *The Forrigan Reel* onwards was a 1930 Austin 12, which had been a commercial travellers' car in the Michael Nairn fleet, and which had lain unused in their Greenwich warehouse throughout the war, where it had suffered slight blast damage from a nearby bomb. It had a number of idiosyncrasies—the choke lever was missing, so I had to devise an alternative—a piece of string which came in through the window from under the bonnet. One day when I gave Stabile a lift and he watched me pull the string as part of the starting process, he grinned broadly, an expression which displayed a splendid array of golden dentistry, and said

'Charlie Chapo, eh?'

The front wings trembled and clattered when the engine was started and the way into the bonnet was by means of two hinged portions, which were fastened with four clips, two either side. At least two of these didn't work and when driving in wind the hinged covers would move up and down as if the car was shrugging it's shoulders.

I was lucky enough to get, with financial help from my father, one of the early post-war Austins, though when it arrived I kept on Old Faithful for the combined petrol ration, and I still used her to get to the theatre. A can of water to top up her leaky radiator and a walking stick to dip the petrol tank were necessities, while on cold mornings I used to put the plugs in the oven for a quarter of an hour and pour a kettle of boiling water into the radiator. There's nothing like the cooling system for heating up the cylinder block.

Opera number three was *Tosca*, in which I was to be the Sacristan. Scarpia, the cruel police chief, was, of course, Stabile and Tosca, the opera singer, was Margherita Grandi—a tall, dark dramatic soprano from Tasmania, married to Giovanni Grandi, who designed and painted the sets. She had sung Lady Macbeth with great success at Glyndebourne before the war and so, like Stabile, was no stranger to London. The tenor, Antonio Salvarezza, completed the Italian contingent.

Stabile was the official producer this time and devoted hours to teaching me and the other British singers in the cast the correct way to pronounce Italian. His patience in this respect was remarkable. Not only that—the Italian trio in the cast, for I always think of Margherita as Italian, sang and acted their roles with a style and panache that was infectious. Just as Martin had been inspired by Stabile and Noni in *Don Pasquale*, so now were Ian Wallace, Sidney Snape and Tony Sympson in *Tosca*. Our parts were small, but we were supporting three superb main principals and that helped to raise our game!

On the first night I came onto the stage five minutes before the curtain was due to rise. There was Signor Grandi still painting the backcloth. About a square foot of bare canvas remained in the midst of gilt railings and a shaft of sunlight from a stained glass window. He sat on a small canvas stool, his brush carefully filling in the detail. The orchestra could be heard tuning above the buzz of excited conversation from a full house. I watched, not daring to distract him. He finished as the applause broke out for the conductor's arrival in the orchestra pit. He folded his stool, picked up his paints and said, 'I theenka you say in England it issa best to hasten slowly.'

That performance was delayed for a few minutes, not by Signor Grandi, but a failure of communication. At the time the Maestro arrived in the pit Ronald Perry, the stage manager, rang Salvarezza's dressing-room to call him down to the stage.

'Pronto,' said the tenor, which, of course, means 'ready'.

'Grazie,' said Ronnie and put the phone down. He didn't know that in Italy 'pronto' is what you say instead of hallo—in other words 'ready to receive a message'—not 'ready to come down and sing the first act of *Tosca*.'

A few moments later Ronnie tried again.

'Pronto.'

'Grazie.' Still no sign of Salvarezza.

'Pronto.'

'Grazie.'

Finally the desperate stage manager ran upstairs and said to a surprised Salvarezza, who had little or no English, 'If you're pronto why don't you come?'

When he did come he scored a notable success, which was all
the more laudable as he found the English climate trying and
suffered from chest trouble all the time he was in London.
Margherita was also in sparkling form, but the evening belonged to Stabile. His Scarpia was the best I've ever seen. It had
power and control, a mixture of amiability and temper, of
sadism and passion and a personality that dominated the stage
with the sort of ease that only comes from long experience of the
big occasion. He knew every note of the opera, and could
correct anyone's musical mistake, even during a performance.
This was something of a feat in view of the fact that he could not
read music at all. He had learnt all his roles from ear, but it was
no handicap to him.

One or two critics thought my Sacristan very overdone,
while others called it refreshingly British. Neither opinion
brought me much comfort—but among those who gave me
warm praise for my interpretation of this Catholic church
official was *The Jewish Chronicle*.

We had a new Colline in *La Bohème* now that Martin Lawrence
was occupied with *Don Pasquale*—Martin Nowakowski, who had
come to Britain during the war with the Polish forces. He had a
voice of beautiful timbre and his appearance was impressive.
Opera was almost as new to him then as to me and, though he
had a successful operatic career, singing more than thirty roles,
many of them at the Royal Opera House, at this early stage he
was concentrating so hard on his moves and business that other
things could occasionally slip his memory, just as happened to
the rest of us.

One night in the last act of *La Bohème* Mimi was, as usual,
dying while Schaunard and Colline were striking attitudes of
grief leaning against a chest of drawers upstage. The moment
was approaching when Colline decides to take out his overcoat
and sell it to provide money for a doctor's fee and medicine for
the dying heroine.

'Psst.' I heard from his direction. I looked up and he leaned
forward confidentially towards me.

'I have forgotten the Coat Song,' he whispered.

'Vecchia Zimarra, senti,' I hissed.

'No, no, not the words—the tune!' This was incredible—
the words often leave you but not the tune.

'Mm, mm, mm-mm, hm, hm,' I hummed under my breath all on the same note, which is how it starts.

'No,' he whispered desperately. 'I know that bit. What happens next?'

By then it was too late. He stepped down stage and sang as always with beauty and taste—but the melody was unfamiliar; it would have surprised Puccini, if for no other reason than that it fitted his orchestration like a glove.

Most opera singers can reel off a list of hilarious happenings on stage and many regular opera-goers have seen comic disasters of one kind or another. I can't say that many have happened to me, though most of the funny things that I recall happened in *La Bohème* because in the two years it was in the repertoire I sang it many times, switching roles to Colline about half way through.

A unique and unforgettable incident befell poor Fergy in the first act one warm summer evening. Things seemed to be going along nicely when, during the scene with Benoit, he whispered, 'Have you got a pin?' As it happened I had one stuck in the lapel of my costume coat—I pulled it out and offered it to him. A look of horror flitted across his face and he shook his head.

'I mean a safety pin.' It was my turn to shake my head. I saw him go to the others in turn with no success. He came back to me,

'I guess I'll have your pin.' I gave it to him. All this whispered conversation had to be fitted in between singing and acting and concealed from the audience.

He took the pin upstage and, partly hiding himself behind an old wardrobe, seemed to be very concerned with the fly button area of his breeches—which was odd in view of the fact that those breeches had no fly at all.

'What's he doing?' said Stanley Pope to me while Tony Sympson was singing away about his conquests in drunken euphoria.

'I don't know,' I replied out the side of my mouth, 'But it looks bloody suggestive.'

Soon all of us except Fergy went off the stage leaving him for the scene with Mimi where he sings 'Your Tiny Hand is Frozen'. During this Stanley and I would sit in a little room just off the back of the stage where they kept the props. When Fergy reached the top C in the aria he cracked disastrously. Stanley grabbed me by the arm. There's nothing more likely to make a singer feel squeamish than to hear a friend in bad trouble in front of the public.

'God, I hope he doesn't try for the other C at the end of the act,' said Stanley, referring to the optional one at the end of the duet with Mimi. But he did, and with the same strangled, embarrassing result. As the curtain came down Fergy ran off the stage and pounded up the stairs to his dressing room. We followed and found him, acutely distressed, sitting at his table, head in hands.

'What happened?' asked Stanley.

'O, Jesus, you know how we all go down on one knee when we sing 'Sta Luigi Filippo ai nostri pie'?'

'Yes?'

'Well I split my pants down the front and because it's so hot I've nothing on undereath. That's why I tried to borrow a pin.'

'What happened on the C?' said Stanley.

'I'd tried to cover myself with my cloak, but when I sing the C I always hold my arms up, and as soon as I did that the cloak fell off and I knew they could see everything. Like a goddam fool I did the same thing at the end of the act!'

At that moment a furious Pom, who had been in the audience arrived.

'Why did you leave Dashinska (his pet-name for Daria) to take a call on her own at the end?' he demanded.

'I couldn't go out there!' shouted Fergy, 'My balls were showing.'

'If they'd seen them once it would do them no harm to see them again!' An extreme example of the determination that the show must go on. As it happened I never heard of anyone who had noticed anything amiss. It was announced to the audience that Mr. Ferguson had been afflicted with a sudden and passing laryngitis, and that he would resume the performance in a quarter of an hour. Meanwhile the wardrobe mistress carried out lightning repairs. Fergy was a splendid Rudolph with a voice of great appeal and he is still before the public.

The high point of the long Cambridge season came for me on the 8th January 1947, when the fourth opera, *The Barber of Seville* was presented. Some two months earlier Maestro Erede had asked me if I would be interested in singing the part of Dr. Bartolo in *The Barber*.

'It's a part I've always wanted to sing,' I said without hesitation. I didn't tell him that I'd never seen *The Barber* and had no idea who Dr. Bartolo was.

'Buono—you will starta to study it witha Dino at once.'

My fellow principals in *The Barber* turned out to be three-fifths Scottish—the Dickie brothers and Bruna Maclean. The other two were both Italians and new to our company.

Preparing for the most important role I'd yet sung was a strenuous business as I had my *Bohèmes* and *Toscas* to sing four evenings a week after rehearsing all day. Incredibly I still had no singing teacher. Billy Drew lived in Cambridge, but was a sick man, and the various others I had tried didn't seem to suit me. Even dear Norman Allin, who gave me useful advice on many aspects of an opera singer's life, wasn't able to help me vocally. So characteristic was his own sound that I emerged from a lesson with him only able to give a pale imitation of his voice which added nothing to my own. Dino Borgioli was the vocal director of the company and in theory he was supposed to give us all lessons. He was too busy to do this. He was producing the operas as well as keeping his own private pupils going. If he'd given lessons to every member of the company as well he'd have been putting in a twenty-four hour day. He did give me a few sessions to check and correct my Italian, threw in some ideas about interpeting the role and that was that. When I asked for vocal advice he would say, 'You 'avea da natural production—aparta that there are others who needa me more.'

The Dickie brothers arrived from Scotland in a flurry of publicity. William, the baritone had worked for the Burmah Oil Company and Murray, the tenor, ten years younger, had been, among other things, a sound effects boy at the B.B.C. in Glasgow. Both were pupils of Professor Polman—a dignified man who looked like a retiring elder brother of Groucho Marx. He'd certainly delivered the goods as far as these two were concerned.

Bill had sung a little in Italy at the end of the war while serving in the army. He'd ended up as a Lieutenant-Colonel, so we pulled his leg by saying that he'd ordered the defeated enemy to let him use their opera houses. He'd met and sung with one or two famous personalities like Gino Becchi, and he made a very authentic Italianate high baritone sound. It was ideal for Figaro.

At first sight it was hard to see how Murray could get away with a romantic role like Count Almaviva unless he could find a short soprano to match him for size. After ten minutes in the company of this small man it was hard to think of anything that he couldn't get away with. He exudes self-confidence that never becomes offensive because it is leavened by an equally strong sense of the ridiculous. Unlike most singers he is an excellent business man, and Bill once said wryly of his younger brother, 'If Murray fell in the Thames he wouldn't get wet.'

During the rehearsals for *The Barber* they succeeded in getting an interview with Gigli, who happened to be in London, and sang for him at his suite in the Savoy Hotel. The great Italian tenor declared that they were the best British singers he'd heard. The rest of us were tasteless enough to point out that this would have been a more impressive statement if they had not also been the only ones.

Murray's tenor voice and personality have given him a lasting career of great distinction, much of it as a member of the Vienna State Opera. He has been there for over fifteen years and is a Kammersanger—an honour for a singer which is roughly the Austrian equivalent of a C.B.E. plus a pension. For many years he was the automatic David in *Die Meistersinger* all over the world.

The three of us became firm friends concealing affection and respect behind an exchange of pungent insults, and we carry on in much the same way when we meet nearly thirty years later.

The fourth Scot in the cast was a cheerful, plump mezzo called Bruna Maclean, who had the small part of Berta. She had a Rabelaisian sense of humour, less usual in a girl then than now. She made a useful contribution to the opera, but our paths have not crossed since.

The two Italians in the cast had quite a task on their hands— to inspire the four of us to perform the opera with Italian bravura. Liana Grani was an experienced coloratura soprano who would never put a foot wrong vocally—but if *Tosca* was Stabile's evening—our mainstay was Andrea Mongelli—a great hippopotamus of a man, who played Basilio, the rascally music teacher. He insisted on his soutane being filthy, his umbrella on the point of disintegration and his wig wildly dishevelled. On his first entrance one could only think of a very knowing tramp who had spent the morning scavenging through all the dust-bins of Seville. He ended his Slander Song with a top G that had such reverberations on it that one feared for the safety of the folk in the dress circle. Basilio is quite a short part and it takes a really accomplished artist to use it to steal the opera. With no disrespect to the rest of us he did so night after night.

I can claim to have given him a little help. In the Slander Song where Basilio tells Dr. Bartolo that the best way to get rid of an unwanted suitor for his ward Rosina is to start unpleasant rumours about him, depends for its success to some extent on the old doctor's reactions. Every night after we had made our exit together at the end of the aria, this forty-five year old, stout, completely normal Italian would enfold me in a tight embrace and kiss me with garlic-ridden fervour.

The reason was that in Italy Bartolos are sometimes jealous of Basilios and won't lift a finger to help their performance (or didn't in those days). This is understandable, because though Bartolo's aria, which follows later, is much more strenuous, it never gets as good an applause as the Slander Song; it shows Bartolo in an unsympathetic light, and any way it's not such a good piece of music. On the other hand, if Bartolo sits through Basilio's aria and does nothing, he's digging his own grave by passing up a wonderful opportunity to establish his character for later in the opera.

I've rather got ahead of myself because I've not yet men-tioned the first night and the critics' verdict. They liked it and they praised us all. What they said doesn't matter. All that was important to me was that I could apparently sustain a big character role and earn the respect of a hard-bitten Italian professional singer like Mongelli. That meant that opera must play a big part in my future. I was therefore speechless with indignation when Owen Mase told me that my next role would be the Count Ceprano in Verdi's *Rigoletto*. My anger was delayed because, as in the case of Dr. Bartolo, I didn't know what I was being offered until my more knowledgeable colleagues told me. It was, they said, a tiny part usually sung by what the Italians call a comprimario—the operatic equivalent of a bit-player on the films. Often such a singer would return to the chorus on nights when his small part service wasn't required. A fine reward I thought, for my success in *The Barber*. I took a deep breath, rang Mr. Mase and said I wouldn't do it.

'Under the terms of your contract you can't refuse.'

'I won't do it,' I repeated and put the phone down. It wasn't like me at all—but I felt that I was being forced into something not only unfair but a dangerous step back as well. Besides, as I now had three operas in the repertoire and we were doing Saturday matinees, which occasionally involved me in two different operas in one day, I was quite ready to sit the next one out.

Before long the phone rang again. It was Maestro Erede with whom I had become very friendly, and who had done everything he could to plug some of the more obvious gaps in my musical education.

'Ian—il Conte Ceprano iss veree eemportant—'e, 'ow you saya dominatea the first scena.'

'Now, Alberto, for goodness sake, it's about the smallest part in the opera.' There was what the Italians call a lunga pausa; then, 'Ian, trusta me, I can't say why, but eef you do thees it will be veree good for you. It issa my idea you do it not Mr. Mase's.'

With considerable reluctance I allowed myself to be persuaded. Thank God I did. The company had approached Carl Ebert with an invitation to direct *Rigoletto*. Ebert had, of course directed every opera at Glyndebourne from the beginning in 1934 till the war. Now that they were about to resume activities they were determined not to lose him. The negotiations were delicate, secret, and in the end satisfactory for everyone.

No wonder this man Ebert was once described in *The Observer* as 'The Master Opera Producer of the Western World'. He had been an actor in Germany, and a very good one—roles in which he had excelled included *King Lear* and *Cyrano de Bergerac*. When he abandoned that career to produce operas he must have been convinced that it was possible to make the producer a much more important figure in the opera house than he had been in the past.

It's no part of this story to delve into the history of opera production. Sufficient to say that until Ebert's generation arrived on the scene, the function of the producer—or director as he is called now—in an opera house was little more than re-hashing old productions, telling singers where to stand, positioning the chorus and trying to co-ordinate the traditional business of the various visiting principals, who probably brought their own wigs and costumes, which might or might not match the scenery for colour or historical period! Rehearsal periods were sometimes a matter of hours rather than days and the producer was a hard-working nonentity attempting the impossible and wielding little or no power or influence.

Ebert approached an opera with the same attention to detail as if it were a play. To him the set designer was vitally important, the singers must not only sound right, they must look right as well. He demanded not days, but weeks of rehearsal. He expected acting performances from the singers, who were discouraged from singing out to the front all the time like a concert in costume. They had to sing to one another as naturally as possible—not the easiest thing to do when it's also necessary to keep an eye on the conductor and project the sound to the back of the theatre. All of this could have been disastrously unsuccessful if Ebert hadn't been passionately fond of music and understood that there are times when singers need all their breath just to sing something strenuous without leaping about the stage as well. On the other hand where it was musically practical, he gave them moves and business which was often complicated and elaborate. He made demands that no previous opera director had thought possible, and after the singers had recovered from their initial shocked surprise, he charmed and cajoled performances from them of which they would never have believed themselves capable.

Professor Ebert is now living in retirement in California. I suspect his appearance won't have changed all that much. There is something of the lion about him—the large head with the long silver grey hair, the shrewd, slightly pouched eyes, the smooth brow and cheeks which instantly crumpled into lines and furrows as all the different emotions he wanted us to express marched obediently across his countenance.

At the first rehearsal of *Rigoletto* I had an impression of someone with great reserves of power. He would stand on the stage at the early rehearsals, his shoulders hunched, his eyes restlessly following the action till he would stop us and demonstrate, giving an arresting performance of one of our roles, even singing quietly in his rather unsteady but effective croon. Today a director who had the hardihood to get up and demonstrate would lay himself open to charges of invading the actor's territory and attempting to dilute his performance with someone else's conception of it. While that may well be the case with an experienced actor, I must confess that we all found it most helpful. Not too many singers can say that their acting is up to their vocal standard, and in an opera performance it takes the lion's share of anyone's concentration just to interpet the music and make a good sound. Any help on the acting side is gratefully accepted and to be shown, as we were, how a superb actor like Ebert would have played our part was an inspiration.

The surprising thing was that he didn't inhibit anyone. After he'd finished even the most inexperienced actor among the singers wouldn't be too conscious of his own inadequacy to have a go—and then Ebert would encourage even the slightest improvement with enthusiastic praise. Thus did performances build from day to day.

He was also capable of bouts of rage which could occur suddenly out of a clear sky. The cause was nearly always the same—a feeling in his mind that someone wasn't working hard enough, or paying attention—someone in fact, who had for the time being failed to have the same intensity of feeling about the production as he had. You had to tread carefully, never whisper or giggle, and give one hundred per cent effort—then he was one of the easiest people to work for that I ever encountered.

The morning after the first night, which was a great personal success for the Yugoslav baritone, Marko Rothmuller, Erede rang me up.

'I told you il Conte Ceprano issa eemportant—you are mentioned by the creetics. But I must be honest—thata 'as never 'appened before.'

I had been lucky. Ebert had decided to make a big thing of the Count's jealousy when the Duke of Mantua seduces the Countess, and he'd given me my head both then and in the other scenes. I was only doing what any competent actor could have done it if had been a play, but with Ebert's skilled direction it was evidently effective.

If I had to pick two years out of my life that I'd be happy to relive, I think it would be those two at the Cambridge Theatre. We lunched at restaurants like Gennaro's in Soho, we had parties on the slightest excuse, the Italians were easy to get on with and seemed to laugh at the same things as we did. We were living very much in a family atmosphere and as such had our rows. There was quite a dust-up during a rehearsal one day and two singers squared up to one another. Pom rushed onto the stage.

'Stop at once!' he shouted. There was complete silence. He glared at us all.

'The trouble with this company,' he growled, 'Is that there are too many bloody foreigners!'

When we all laughed he looked surprised—then he saw the funny side and joined in. It was touching that he didn't till then think of himself as a foreigner in London. At that moment I noticed that Dino Borgioli's toupée had been knocked off in the melée. He was clutching his bald head in embarrassment. As someone handed him his terrible hair-piece we all saw for the first time his distinguished domed forehead with the grey curls at the temples. One of the women, I don't remember which, had the courage to say,

'Don't put it on, Dino, you look so handsome without it.' We all applauded. He never wore it again.

During those two years I worked with a great many singers from Italy, Germany and elsewhere and gained priceless experience. The sets of all the operas were excellent, the costumes well made of the best available materials, (in *Rigoletto* the tights were all of real silk). I learnt and sang five useful roles, six if you count Ceprano, and that was due to the help, not only of Erede and Professor Maliniak, but the three young men whom Alberto had recruited to his music staff, Bryan Balkwill, Emmanuel Yourovsky and Edward Renton—all of whom coached the singers and conducted performances—it was a great opportunity, which they all seized, and in each case it led to greater things.

Apart from the singers I've mentioned we had performances from Erna Berger, Theo Hermann, Mirto Picchi, Ljuba Welitsch, Rachele Ravina, Emma Tegani, Bruce Boyce, George Hancock, Italo Tajo—and the list is by no means complete. Daria Bayan sang Gilda in *Rigoletto*, Nanetta in

Falstaff, Zerlina in *Don Giovanni*. Perhaps she didn't quite possess the vocal fire power for an opera career on the grand scale, but she gave convincing, appealing performances to which audiences responded.

Nobody was paid a great deal of money in that company and Pom kept a close eye on the accounts. I got a rise of £5 a week after *The Barber* and that was that. One person who was very dissatisfied with his remuneration was Mongelli, our Basilio. He decided to employ an elaborate tactic in order to get a rise.

He wrote to a friend in Buenos Aires asking him to send a cable as if it came from the management of the Colon Opera House there offering him a large number of performances at an astronomical fee. The Colon has the reputation of paying the highest fees in the world. When the cable arrived Andrea took it to Pom's office, convinced that one look at Mongelli's market value in South America would persuade him to double his Cambridge Theatre money on the spot. A few of us waited outside the office to see what would happen. We weren't disappointed.

'Buon giorno, Signor Pomeroy, io ho ricevuto questa telegramma.' Pause while Pom read it.

'Mongelli, you must go! What a wonderful offer—biliv me I will not stand in your way. Be kind enough, pliz, to sing tonight and I will replace you on Saturday.'

'No, no, no, no, Signor Pomeroy—I a man of 'onor, not breaka da contract—I justa showa you 'ow much others wisha to pay me.'

'Thank you, Mongelli, for letting me see it—and how good of you to stay—let me know if you change your mind.'

Mongelli emerged holding the telegram with the look of surprised bafflement on his face that the fans of the late Oliver Hardy knew so well.

By the time Pom's legal affairs reached the point where he had to call a halt to the two year season we had added the two more operas mentioned above—the notable *Falstaff* with Stabile taking London by storm in the title role which he had originally learnt from Toscanini, and *Don Giovanni* with the American baritone Bruce Boyce. I had the minor principal role of the peasant bridegroom Masetto. Ebert produced the first and had an anonymous hand in the second. We got a fortnight's notice at the beginning of May 1948.

For a reason that had nothing to do with the opera, the last year in particular was a happy one for me. I had been courting Patricia at long range and we had become engaged. Though this wasn't a time when one wanted to lose a good job, it did at least mean that we could fix a date for the wedding.

During the final week at the Cambridge two letters arrived for me at the theatre. One was from the Royal Opera House inviting me to re-audition, the other was from Glyndebourne offering the part of Masetto in *Don Giovanni* at the Edinburgh Festival—it would be produced by Carl Ebert. Now I could see why Erede had been so keen for me to do the Count Ceprano.

The Royal Opera House episode was short and to the point. I sang 'The Catalogue' aria from *Don Giovanni*—the one I'd heard Owen Brannigan sing two years earlier, and the 'Coat Song' from *La Bohème*, these were both operas that Covent Garden were about to do, and though 'The Catalogue' aria comes, not from Masetto's part but the much larger role of Leporello, I thought I'd have a shot at it. In addition to Rankl and Webster my audience included the famous Scots tenor Joseph Hislop, who had become vocal adviser to the opera house.

'Come and have a drink,' he said afterwards, the other two had vanished. In the pub he smiled at me and said,

'You have a good voice, and you act well, but it's that,' he held his hands six inches apart, 'instead of that.' He increased the distance to a foot. 'But I'm sure that can be put right.' He was, of course, referring to the fact that in a house the size of Covent Garden a voice had to be fairly large to carry, and that mine was still comparatively small. I told him that I would re-apply when I thought it was worth while. I had just found a new teacher—or rather Erede had at last introduced us— Rodolfo Mele. He was an old friend of Alberto's and both of them had felt unable to suggest a course of lessons so long as I was under contract to the New London Opera Company with Borgioli as vocal director. Apparently Mele had often sat in the stalls at the Cambridge muttering to his Scots wife Meg, 'Eef only I could get my hands on 'eem!' Well now he had, but it was not in time for us to work before that audition. In fact all my subsequent efforts to get into Covent Garden were unsuccessful.

I would be politely told that there was no vacancy for a voice like mine at present, but though I expressed a willingness to re-audition, the opportuntiy to do so never arose. I'm sure this had nothing to do with Joseph Hislop, now a sprightly nona-genarian living in Fife, and able to display the hall-mark of a fine teacher—pupils of renown. One of them is Birgit Nilsson. I may have been a victim of the curious antagonism which existed in those days between Glyndebourne and the Royal Opera House and which was usually given an annual fillip by John Christie's foreword to the Glyndebourne programme.

Then, some years later when I was rehearsing at Glynde-bourne, I noticed one morning that my British colleagues were distinctly cool. At lunch time I discovered the reason—a letter in the *Daily Telegraph* criticizing the Royal Opera House for spending public money on bringing so many foreign singers to London while ignoring British singers who had proved them-selves worthy of a chance to appear at Covent Garden. It listed a number of such singers with my name at the top. The letter was signed by Martin Cooper, the paper's senior music critic. It seemed that everyone thought that I had inspired it or at least given approval for it to be published. Even as late as the 1950s such brash behaviour was considered in poor taste. In fact Martin Cooper would never have lent his name to a singer's conspiracy of this nature, and was simply bringing a contro-versial issue to public notice. But in the opera world, with its volatile emotions and struggles for survival, such cool assess-ments are not always made. Fortunately, the look on my face as I read the letter convinced my colleagues that it was a complete surprise to me; and while I was flattered to be rated so high by Martin Cooper, I was only too certain that it would not improve my chances with the Royal Opera House. I rang Cooper and suggested that it might have been better if he'd consulted me and the others on the list first.

'I suppose I should,' he said, 'would you have objected?'

'I don't know,' I replied, 'but I'm sure of one thing. You've said that in the first post-war decade they haven't used me. I think you've probably ensured that I shan't sing there for the next ten years.'

'Yes, perhaps I have,' he agreed, rather quietly, 'Do you mind?'

I indicated that the prospect hardly made me jump for joy and rang off. In fairness, two offers did come in the early 1960s; one was for a part I didn't feel was quite suitable vocally, and the other caught me unavailable. That's the way the cookie crumbles, but I would be less than honest if I didn't confess to a few regrets. To sing a performance on that stage is an unfulfilled ambition, which I haven't quite abandoned. Only a few years ago the late Sir David Webster kindly agreed to take part in a television series I was doing in Scotland on opera called 'Singing For Your Supper'. He was about to retire from his post as General Administrator of the Royal Opera House and I asked him out to lunch to discuss the programme. He told me about his early life when his talent for running retail shops threatened him with a life of wealth and dullness. I recalled my early days and all the auditions he'd heard me sing.

'There's no chip on my shoulder, David,' I said, 'and I've had an absurdly varied and interesting career, but that was a disappointment.'

He looked at me gravely and said, 'At that time it was my job to say yes to this one and no to that one. I sometimes think that if I had said no to this one and yes to that one, the final result would have been just as good.

* * *

Pat and I were married in Scotland on 26th June 1948, and after a honeymoon in Paris and Dinard during which the papers were full of the Berlin airlift and we were literally pursued by cyclists taking part in the Tour de France, we went down to Lewes and put up at the Tatler Guest House for the rehearsals of *Don Giovanni* at Glyndebourne.

The Stately Homes of England.

(Noël Coward)

I was probably more aware of what lay in store for me than
most singers arriving to work at this great Elizabethan house
for the first time. Erede had graphically described the hours of
meticulous ensemble rehearsal, the insistence on the highest
standards, the necessity to arrive word and music perfect and,
of course, he'd told me about the legendary beginning in 1934
when only seven people from London joined the local audience
for the first night of the first ever Glyndebourne season. The
opera was *Le Nozze di Figaro* in Italian; the following night it
was *Così Fan Tutte* and the same small London contingent came
down. Two of them were the music critics of *The Times* and the
Daily Telegraph and what they had to say about these two productions ensured capacity houses at every subsequent Glyndebourne performance until the war put a stop to the summer
festivals for the duration. I had also seen a production in 1947 of
Gluck's *Orfeo* with Kathleen Ferrier and been bowled over by
the whole evening. For a start there was the unusual sight of an
opera house standing only a few hundred yards from grazing
sheep; then there was the orchestra playing croquet in the interval on a lawn discreetly hidden from the public by ancient
yew hedges; most startling of all was the audience, many of
whom must have walked down a platform at London's Victoria
Station in full evening dress shortly after lunch to be at the
opera house for a 5.30 start. Those who had arrived similarly
attired by car had, in some cases, brought picnic baskets as an
alternative to the restaurant that served dinner in seventy-five

179

minutes flat between the two halves of the opera. Though I knew what to expect and was suitably dressed, I still found it unbelievable. There was one small, unique touch. The name of the head gardener appeared in the programme. Why not? Two of the delights of a visit to Glyndebourne are the herbaceous borders and the beautifully kept lawns.

Above everything I was knocked out by the all-round excellence of the production and Kathleen Ferrier's moving performance. Now that my moment had come I knew it wouldn't be easy to live up to that sort of standard. At least I had performed the role, with the added advantage of knowing what it was like to work with Ebert. Of one thing I was sure. None of the stars I was about to meet would be given star treatment. They would be expected to work as a team and leave their star status hanging up in the cloakroom.

When the taxi arrived, a thin man in a short sleeved shirt and linen trousers flung open the door.

'Mr. Wallace and Miss Ayars?'

'Yes.'

'Welcome to Glyndebourne! I'm Harold Chapin, the stage manager. Now, let's all go and have coffee.'

He pointed towards the canteen with both hands like a boy scout practising semaphore, and Ann Ayars, the American soprano who was singing Zerlina and I followed him in. At the counter was a middle-aged man wearing one pair of glasses while another pair dangled on a ribbon round his neck. He was dressed in Austrian lederhosen shorts and a white linen bolero jacket with green frogging and brass buttons down the front. White stockings and heavy brown brogues completed the outfit. He leant on what resembled a short shepherd's crook. Chapin introduced us.

'Mr. Wallace, Miss Ayars—Mr. Jani Strasser, the chief coach.'

He looked all set to give us a yodelling lesson or show us a quick way up the Matterhorn. I had heard of Jani Strasser and knew he was responsible for delivering the singers to the conductor prepared to the last detail, not only for solo work but ensembles as well. Speaking in his carefully articulated, rather nasal style with the slight Hungarian accent that all British singers love imitating he said,

'Hello, I hope you'll both be very happy here. Now, Mr. Wallace, when you've had your coffee, perhaps you'd like to go through your part with me.'

'Of course,' I said, and then incautiously added, 'I know it pretty well, I've been singing it at the Cambridge Theatre.'

A look of pain crossed his face. 'I know,' he said with a touch of sadness and a slight shake of the head, 'I've heard you.'

It was a year or two before I found out, comparing notes with other victims, that this was a Strasser tactic, employed in one form or another on all singers arriving at Glyndebourne for the first time. It certainly dented my confidence for a day or two, but it also made me determined to show him that I didn't deserve that critical thumbs down. It was exactly the reaction he wanted—the start of a process which in the end made one realize that Glyndebourne had brought the preparation of opera to a fine art. The stage rehearsals and music sessions were designed to be complementary. Inevitably, working on acting and movement takes the edge off one's attention to musical detail, so we were constantly hauled back round the piano to repair the defects and recall the subtleties introduced in an earlier run-through. Jani or one of his acolytes would be ever-present, noting down imperfections for our later edification, and this also happened at public performances. Ebert, too, in those days attended virtually every performance and would come to our dressing-rooms afterwards if we had deviated from his production—he would mournfully enumerate those bits one had missed, though he was happy to accept something happening spontaneously in a performance, which was in the style of the character, and he would allow it to be 'kept in'. The average rehearsal time for a new production was five weeks and during the final rehearsals we worked with the orchestra for more than twenty hours. We usually put in about six hours rehearsal a day, some of which might well be individual coaching to brush up a few difficult passages or to work on Italian, German or French pronunciation. There was always a coach there who was a native of whatever country the opera came from.

I say all this in the past tense because I'm speaking of my own experience. I've little doubt that the preparation is much the same today, with one difference—the cost! Oh, and one other, Jani has retired, and he didn't wear those lederhosen every day.

In fact I never saw him in them again, which was a pity.

There is a danger that rehearsing to this sort of schedule can spoil one for anything else. During a career we often work under far less ideal conditions; we have to give performances after a fraction of the necessary rehearsal time with musicians and conductors, who are not quite so experienced or proficient as they might be. For a long time after my Glyndebourne indoctrination I used to feel apprehensive about any performance that hadn't been prepared up to that pitch, but then I was fortunate to be made aware of such a high standard so early on. To be 'brought up', as it were, first by Erede, Maliniak, and Stabile—then to graduate to Ebert, Strasser and Glyndebourne, all in two years, was the large dollop of good luck I felt I deserved after the long years of illness and uncertainty.

Glyndebourne has developed enormously since those days, but then the number of people involved was small enough for it to have the atmosphere of a large house party. We ate at big circular refectory tables, sitting where we liked. Jock Gough, the stage carpenter, who spoke his mind at all times, might be next to Ebert, with a member of the chorus on the other side. I might find myself sandwiched between John Christie and Paolo Silveri, the Italian baritone, who was singing the role of Don Giovanni. Next to him might well be one of the girls from the wardrobe—and so on.

The Christies made us feel honoured guests rather than artists in their employ, and the new young administrator, Moran Caplat, who had succeeded Rudolf Bing when he departed, to run the Edinburgh Festival *en route* for the Metropolitan, New York, was a cheerful and friendly ex-actor, who had spent the whole war in the Royal Navy and concealed his undoubted abilities behind a modest charm. He's no different today except that he's added a highly impressive beard to his managerial set-up.

The country house atmosphere pervaded the places where we rehearsed. No austere functional buildings in the grounds for us in those days. Individual calls were in small reception rooms with mullioned windows, while the ensembles took place in the large organ room or the green room, both oak-panelled with enormous oil-paintings on the walls. Their windows looked out on the gardens and the Downs beyond. The theatre itself, though small from the point of view of the numbers it can seat, has a very big acting area, a cyclorama, sophisticated lighting, and an orchestra pit worthy of the name.

Spike Hughes has written an admirable book on Glynde-bourne and therefore I don't propose to go over ground that has been so carefully and entertainingly documented, and which is familiar to so many opera lovers; but meeting John Christie and his adorable wife Audrey was to realize how it had been possible for them to persuade the world to beat a path to this compara-tively remote corner of the Sussex countryside.

He was about sixty-five in 1948, a mixture of Mr. Pickwick and John Bull, with twinkling blue eyes, and he spoke as if he'd just got his breath back after walking briskly uphill. It was easy enough to believe that he came of a long line of aristocratic landowners, harder to imagine him as a science master at Eton, and well nigh impossible to credit that he had married an opera singer in his middle age after a romantic courtship, and then insisted on building her an opera house in his garden at a time of grave economic depression—until, that was, you met Audrey.

What disastrous consequences there might have been if she had lacked the necessary character and judgement to make the most of this marvellously eccentric gesture. Audrey Christie was a beautiful woman with an inner radiance and repose that is seldom encountered. She was a sensitive artist and a good singer. She wasn't a great singer and she knew it. What's more, she sang roles which ideally suited her talent and never allowed herself to be tempted away from them. When she felt the time had come to retire, she did so gracefully and without fuss. Easy to retire, some might say, when you don't have to earn your living. That would be a misunderstanding of what motivates an artist. It is not uncommon for singers who are no longer young, and who haven't quite the voice they could call on in the past, to agree to appear for reduced fees, not because they need the money, but because they would miss the stimulus of an audience. If you don't believe me, just reflect on what takes Bobby Charl-ton, one of the greatest footballers of all time, out of his mana-ger's office to play for Preston North End, a third division side at the time of writing.

I'm not suggesting that John Christie didn't have visions of the sort of opera seasons that have delighted audiences ever since when he gave orders to dig the foundations, but I have a shrewd suspicion that it was Audrey's determination to create an opera festival that could rival any in the world, and the unselfish use of her own position and influence that eventually brought the dream to reality.

By the time I arrived on the scene she had retired and was our hostess and confidante. She possessed a natural dignity that prevented even the most brash extrovert among the singers from becoming over familiar, yet she could pass easily from being Mrs. John Christie to Audrey Mildmay, former soprano, who could share our apprehensions and technical problems—as well as our jokes. She could also create exactly the right atmosphere to get the best out of us. If she felt that rehearsals were flagging she would organize, at three hours notice, a block booking at the cinema in Lewes or a party in the organ room with dancing to the gramophone. One evening when I was staying in the house she asked me if I was coming to the party she'd arranged.

'Oh yes,' I replied, and added by way of a joke, 'but I thought I'd have a bath first and then slip into something loose.'

She thought for a moment.

'When you've had your bath go to your room, but don't get dressed. I've got an idea.'

I never disobey instructions like that. Soon there was a knock at the door. When I called 'come in' she appeared carrying a Susanna costume (once used by an enormous soprano) and a black lace mantilla. She got me into all this like an experienced theatrical dresser and made me up. Then she sent for Ronald Perry, the assistant stage manager who, like me, had come from the Cambridge Theatre.

'Ronnie,' she said, 'go down and tell the party that an old friend of the family and a tremendous opera fan has unexpectedly arrived. Then announce the Duchess of Surrey.' Ronnie did it perfectly. We heard the party groan at the thought of being polite to some effusive old girl, then Ronnie's stage whisper that she was in earshot and the sudden silence. As I glided in, Ebert came forward, a polite, mechanical smile on his face. I think I fooled them for about fifteen seconds—but people who were there still remember it, and other evenings as the Christie's guests, with affection.

There was no season at Glyndebourne itself in 1948 or '49—

we were there because the management had undertaken the artistic direction of the first Edinburgh Festival in 1947 and agreed to provide the operas thereafter, which they did for many years. The plain truth was that there was no money to mount operas in Sussex during those two years. From the beginning John Christie underwrote the whole enterprise from his own pocket—there was, and is, no public subsidy—and the days when industry and private individuals were to share the burden with him still lay in the future. For the time being he felt that to dig any deeper into his own money was to endanger his family's future and the continuity of his estates. Nobody could possibly blame him for temporarily pulling out.

While we rehearsed *Don Giovanni* another cast were preparing *Così Fan Tutte*. Ebert was producing both, but there were two conductors, Rafael Kubelik for the Don and Vittorio Gui for Cosi. Of the celebrated Fritz Busch, musical director before the war, there was no sign.

So we rehearsed in a theatre in which we were not going to perform. It was to be four years before I was to sing there in front of an audience of paying customers.

We moved to Edinburgh for the final rehearsals. Pat and I drove up ahead of the rest of the company and went down to greet them at Waverley. I donned the kilt for this occasion which made quite a splash in the papers. The Scottish capital was in the grip of what was called at that time festivalitis The city was a mass of flags and bunting; there were flowers in neat municipal rows on the centres of roundabouts; an infectious feeling of anticipation and excitement was in the air. We were entertained here, there and everywhere, we posed for photographers and cartoonists and, what's more, saw the results in next day's paper. We were bidden to coffee mornings, cocktail parties, and press conferences.

We also sang nine performances of *Don Giovanni* to packed and wildly enthusiastic audiences at the King's Theatre in Lothian Road. Among the soloists was one link with the past. David Franklin sang the part of the Commendatore. The last time he had done so was at Glyndebourne in July 1939. One day during rehearsals there he invited me to go for a stroll with him round the lake. He towered over me—he was 6 feet 3 inches —and in the sepulchral voice so familiar to radio listeners in recent years he asked me how a colleague who was a mutual friend was getting on with his attempt to alter his voice from baritone to tenor.

'I don't think,' I replied, 'that the metamorphosis is working out too well.'

He stopped dead and a huge hand clasped my shoulder bringing me to a halt.

'This is a significant moment,' he declared, 'till now I thought I was the only literate singer in England—metamorphosis!— there are two of us.'

David Franklin was christened William and was known to his family and friends as Bill. He changed his christian name to avoid confusion with William Franklyn, the actor. The above conversation is a fair example of his pomposity, which undoubtedly antagonised some people, while adding flavour to his radio personality for the rest. Beneath it lay a soft heart and a fear of betraying the fact. In 1948 he had no idea that his singing career was nearly over and that, following an operation, he would have to build a second as a broadcaster and lecturer. Courage and skill made *that* metamorphosis a brilliant success.

Paolo Silveri was a spendid Don, even if he failed to prevent Ljuba Welitsch, with her flashing eyes and red hair, from running away with the evening as Donna Anna. One critic was unkind enough to suggest that she could have eaten him for breakfast! Someone else made a quietly auspicious Glyndebourne debut in that cast. Don Ottavio was sung by Richard Lewis.

When the festival was over Pat and I went to stay with her mother near Cupar and I was able to draw breath for the first time since my operatic career started.

My Masetto had been well received by the critics. I had been singing in top class international company for over two years— yet I was now out of a job. Since my schools programmes in Glasgow my only radio work had been relays of the performances from the Cambridge Theatre, from where we had also televised a complete performance of *La Bohème* to the tiny audience in the London area that made up the viewing public of those days.

I was now on the books of De Wolfe & Stone, theatrical agents, which was possibly an ill-advised move on my part. In his own field Richard Stone was and is among the finest agents in London. Opera and concerts do not happen to belong to that field, yet here was I, an emerging opera singer with enough success to be exploitable, represented by a firm without any opera contacts. I take full responsibility for the decision to sign with Richard. Remember, I had studied law, not music. The refuge of all straight singers not engaged in singing opera is the concert platform, and I was ill equipped to mount it. The thought of endless Messiahs in Wales and northern England filled me with melancholy, recitals of Schubert lieder demanded a type of voice and an intellectual approach I didn't possess, even in opera it was clear that my future lay in the buffo or comic character roles, which weren't to be found in a distressingly large number of operas. I had an in-between voice, slightly soft-grained which, as Joseph Hislop had pointed out, wasn't all that big. Added to which I had started as an actor and still felt that my future might well be in plays or musicals. I didn't believe, even after that flying start, that opera would necessarily be my whole career. That assessment has proved correct, but things might have been different if, in the autumn of 1948, a good opera offer had come as a result of Edinburgh.

Instead, Alastair Sim honoured his promise to me after *The Forrigan Reel*, offering me the smallest part in a revival of Bridie's play *The Anatomist* at the Westminster Theatre. It was a bit of a come-down, but there was literally nothing else doing. The play deals with the activities of the two notorious Irish body-snatchers Burke and Hare, who undertook to provide the medical school in Edinburgh in the 1820s with subjects for dissection when the law, religious objections and public opinion were against this practice. At first they raided churchyards, but eventually resorted to murder in order to deliver the cadavers for which they were so well paid. Burke was played in rivetingly sinister fashion by Liam Redmond, who enlivened the dressing room with Irish stories that made such compelling listening that the rest of us were in danger of missing an entrance in the play in order to hear the denouement.

'Did I ever tell you,' he began one evening, 'about the character actor at the Abbey Theatre, Dublin, who decided that his salary was such an inadequate reward for his talents that he would save as much of it each week as he could until he had enough to pay his fare to New York? No? Well he did it because he'd heard that character actors from the Abbey and the Gate were well thought of in New York and that the critics praised their technique. Mind you, this surprised him because, as far as he was concerned, the technique of these people was simply fumbling for the words. When he got to New York he found it was all true and for about twelve years he went from one play to the next, earning a great deal of money. He set himself up in a luxury suite in a fine hotel not far from Central Park. Unfortunately, the inevitable operation of the law of averages eventually kicked him in the teeth and the success melted away like snow off a dyke. He was forced to give up his suite and rent a single room in a much cheaper hotel next door. By an irony of fate the window of this room overlooked the bedroom of his former suite and on summer evenings, for he was now, as we euphemistically say, restin', he would sit lookin' across and grudgin' the new occupants every livin' minute of the time they were there.

'Well, one evenin' a couple entered the bedroom, who were, he was sure, not joined in holy wedlock. So enthusiastic and preoccupied were they that they neglected the elementary precaution of pullin' down the blind. He waited until he adjudged that the psychological moment had arrived and then he lifted his telephone and asked to be connected with the hotel room, the number of which he knew so well. As he watched, a naked arm disentangled itself and trembling fingers took the bedside phone off the hook.

'"Is that room 437?"' he enquired. "Yeah," a breathless voice replied.

' "Well, this is God speakin' and you ought to be ashamed of yourselves!"'

When Liam left the cast to go, of all places, to New York, I put in for his part and got it. Alastair directed me and was kind enough to tell me I had considerable prospects as an actor. When the play folded, we did it on television, as a result of which I got further TV jobs including Tweedledum in *Alice Through The Looking Glass* and Morton Mitchum in *The Good Companions*. A small point of T.V. history was connected with this television production of Priestley's famous play. It was directed by the late Fred O'Donovan, a former Irish actor and radio producer, who only used one camera instead of the three or four, or more normally in use for any TV production. As all TV was live in those days, I could only see odd snatches of the play on a studio monitor screen when I was out of shot, and it wasn't possible to judge the overall effect, but apparently this view from one pair of eyes made a refreshing change from complex camera angles.

I also did a bizarrely unlikely job in the spring of 1949— Scottish technical adviser to the production of the American musical *Brigadoon* by Lerner and Loewe. I had to take the Americanisms out of the dialogue and teach the English members of the cast to speak with a Scots accent. I wasn't, however, allowed to touch Lerner's lyrics, even when eighteenth-century Scots-villagers sang about being 'Down on MacConnachy Square'.

It was an education to watch the director, Robert Lewis, at work—a short, stubby, bald-headed man with horn-rimmed glasses, he taught his cast something that was quite new in the technique of performing a musical. As the musical numbers approached, the dialogue had to be spoken louder and a little faster, so that when the song came, it was an extension of the dialogue, avoiding the impression of a cue for song. After a song the first spoken words had to be as loud as the singing, then gradually checked down to the level of conversation. It was extremely effective.

After he had read the fairly spectacular notice in *The Times* he said,

'I'll take out an annual subscription for that great noospaper provided they promise to print that notice every day for a year.' After the first night party he bade goodbye to the cast with the words,

'So long, kids—I'll be back in a month to take out all the "improvements".' Actors well know the temptation to embellish their role here and there with extra touches, which get a laugh or a reaction, but don't match the style of the show or the producer's intentions. He was as good as his word!

The two Americans in the cast of *Brigadoon*, who discover the highland village that appears once every hundred years were Phil Hanna and Hiram Sherman, always known as Chubby. Phil, who died a few years later, was a fine tennis player. During the run of the show he played in the Queen's Club indoor tournament and gave Jean Borotra a run for his money. Chubby, a firm friend ever since, enchanted London audiences a few years ago with his performance in *Anne of Green Gables*.

While I was working on *Brigadoon* my father died after a brief illness. He was in his eighty-first year and had been gradually failing since his retirement. It's sometimes said that show business folk are obsessed with the necessity to carry on whatever may be happening in their private life. Perhaps so, but often we have no alternative.

He was ill for twelve days with a cerebral thrombosis about which he mercifully knew little. When the end came in the early afternoon, I helped the nurse to lay him out, made the funeral arrangements, rang the newspapers, and then left my mother with Pat in order to be at a rehearsal at five o'clock. I was deeply attached to him, but no one could pretend that he had enjoyed the last year or two, or that he wouldn't have gratefully accepted such a comparatively easy way out if he'd had the choice. For my mother, over twenty years his junior, there was the sad prospect of a long period on her own—but for the moment I had a job to do, and I felt sure that my father would have wanted me to go and do it.

*   *   *

My opera career got under way again very soon. Pomeroy, despite losing his case and being declared a bankrupt, managed to mount a six-week season in May at the Stoll Theatre, to be followed by a fortnight at the Davis Theatre, Croydon. I can't recall how he was described on the billing, but it complied with regulations governing the business activities of undischarged bankrupts. In other words he was not our boss, though the Italians referred cynically to 'the bankrupt with the money in the hip pocket'.

We did the Cambridge repertoire with the exception of *Don Giovanni*, but there were a few major cast changes. Paolo Silveri and Luigi Infantino came into *The Barber* as Figaro and Almaviva, while Daria Bayan replaced Alda Noni in *Don Pasquale*.

The Stoll Theatre, now no more, was a vast ornate barn at the foot of Kingsway where the GKN building now stands. I embarked on the season with added confidence born of the fact that my new singing teacher, Rodolfo Mele, had already helped me enormously, not only vocally, but with Italian pronunciation as well. His aim in life was to make singing easy, and take out of it the technical jargon and meaningless expressions that often inhibit pupils. At my first lesson he said,

'When I listened to you at the Cambridge I used to saya to myself, thees boy, 'as to get rid of the furniture in 'ees throat and letta the sound come out.' He showed me how the voice could carry better by altering the vowel sounds, and he concentrated on getting me to relax, and to stop reaching for the high notes. The improvement was rapid.

'I'm a fool,' he used to say, 'I showa somebody whatta to do. They getta eet it right in a few lessons and then eet'sa good bye. Eef I 'ad any sense I'd make it last longer. But then I don't like to teacha the stupidi. Eef a reech old woman comea for lessons with a voice like a seagull, I say go away, I don'ta likea your face!'

For a quarter of a century he guided me in vocal matters with perfect judgement. A native of Naples, he had lived in London since the 1930s and had been a fellow student with the famous bass Ezio Pinza. He died a year ago within a few days of his eightieth birthday.

Rodolfo was a tenor, who with more luck could have had a big career as a singer. I don't think he regretted that things hadn't turned out as well as they might in this respect, because he once told me that he had wanted to teach singing from the age of sixteen. Before long, singer friends were coming to me and saying,

'We don't want to be rude, but who did it?'

Certainly in this big theatre I felt just as able to hold my own with Mongelli, Silveri, and the rest as I had in the Cambridge Theatre or the King's in Edinburgh, which were about half the size.

The end of Pom's opera dream came abruptly at Croydon. I arrived one evening for *Tosca* conducted by Clemens Krauss to find that the Davis Theatre had closed its doors to the public. We had not been doing good business in this huge cinema and the money to pay us wasn't available. Several of the singers had long-term contracts which could not be honoured. He only owed me £40—one week's salary, and as far as I was concerned, he was very welcome to it. What he had given me in the way of opportunities was beyond price. Many of us felt the same. About a year later Ljuba Welitsch was appearing at the Royal Opera House and Pom went to see her in her crowded dressing room after the first night.

'Darling Pom!' she cried. 'I love you—even if you do owe me £400!'

My luck held. Glyndebourne invited me back to Edinburgh to play one of the conspirators in Verdi's *Un Ballo in Maschera* which was conducted by Vittorio Gui, a distinguished and scholarly Italian, who had made his Glyndebourne and Edinburgh debut with *Cosi* the previous year, and was now rapidly forming the sort of partnership with Ebert that had existed between Ebert and Busch before the war. There were stormy scenes when Gui felt that the music was endangered by an over ambitious manoeuvre on the stage and vice versa. There is a no-man's land in every opera production where good directors and conductors fight tenaciously for artistic concessions, knowing that in the end a compromise will have to emerge. Watching two heavyweights like Gui and Ebert at work in this area was stimulating and at times amusing. Walk-outs would occasionally happen, though, with so much to do in a short time, they were usually over in about five minutes; neither was tactless enough to see the other coming back in. Busch was to return to Glyndebourne in 1950 and '51, but the resumption of the pre-war partnership was short-lived. He was a sick man, who couldn't recapture the ebullience of earlier years. The strain of the '51 season proved too much and he collapsed and died shortly afterwards in his London hotel.

In those days the Royal Philharmonic Orchestra played for all Glyndebourne performances. They were a wonderful collection of musicians, some of whom had abandoned the idea of a solo career in order to play under their principal conductor, Sir Thomas Beecham. The opera seasons were gruelling hard work but they entered into the spirit of the season and gave us on the stage the support and sympathy of first-class musicians, with the music in front of them, accompanying singers, who have to rely on their memory. The leader was David .McCallum, a slim Scot who had a deceptively ascetic appearance. He possessed a strong sense of humour and, as his son David began to make an outstanding success of his career in films and television, his obvious pride was touching and without any hint of family or professional jealousy. The leader of a great orchestra carries a heavy responsibility without the money or kudos of a successful film career. Frederick Riddle presided over the violas and Anthony Pini was principal cellist. The woodwind principals were all at the top of their profession, people like Jack Brymer, Terence MacDonagh, Geoffrey Gilbert and Gwydion Brooke. We couldn't have wished for better.

Before I left Edinburgh after the *Masked Ball* Moran offered me Dr. Bartolo in *Le Nozze di Figaro*, one of the works in the 1950 festival. This is the same Dr. Bartolo as in *The Barber of Seville*—a few years later. By that time in Beaumarchais' story he is no longer a central figure, but it's a good part, which I gladly accepted, wondering if I'd have any opera to do in the ten months till the first rehearsal, and what would happen if I didn't. All my continental colleagues in the two Glyndebourne productions I'd been in returned afterwards to opera houses in Italy, Germany or America, while my few fellow countrymen resumed their round of concerts and oratorio.

After *Don Giovanni* Alastair Sim, TV and Pomeroy's revival of the New London Opera Company had got me through the year; now poor Pom had finally given up all hopes of presenting opera in London or anywhere else. I could hardly expect to make much headway as an opera singer only singing a few performances of one opera a year!

Another sort of career briefly opened its doors to me between these Glyndebourne seasons at Edinburgh. I became in a minor way a film actor. My debut was in a Scots shipbuilding epic called *Floodtide* in which such eminent Scots as Jimmie Logan and Gordon Jackson appeared. Before I went to Pinewood for my first day's filming, Richard Stone gave me a serious talk about the technique of film acting.

'For God's sake don't overact,' he pleaded with me. 'All this opera you've done is much larger than life—you'll have to tone it all down. Just *think* the emotions, don't try to act them.'

I was playing the director of a shipbuilding company—not a particularly important director at that, and in my first scene I was at a cocktail party the night before the launch. All I had to do was to light a cigarette, look over my shoulder to the window and say, 'The wind seems to be rising'. It was one of those remarks that are put into films to make the audience think that the launch will take place in a force 10 gale with disastrous results. From that point of view it was a red herring, and I think it would have been just as good a film without it. Next day at lunch time I went to see the 'rushes', that's the rough uncut prints of the previous day's filming. When my sequence appeared I was trembling with nerves and wondering if I'd overdone it. There I was lighting the cigarette, looking over my shoulder and then on the sound track could be heard, 'The wind seems to be rising.'

'Who said that?' demanded the director in the darkened viewing room.

'I did,' I meekly replied.

'Well you could have fooled me,' he said—rather curtly I thought. He had a point. So determined was I to avoid exaggeration that my lips never moved. I made a note that in future I could give a little more. I rather enjoyed filming (except the hours of waiting to work and the hideously early morning start) and enjoyed a moderate success with a B picture called *Assassin For Hire*, which appeared on every TV screen in the world at one time, with no visible profit to those of us who made it, and a hardy annual called *Tom Thumb*, which has a habit of teaming up at Christmas on double bills with *The Wizard of Oz*.

Nevertheless my opera future looked bleak when, out of the blue, the B.B.C. offered me the part of the Constable in Vaughan William's opera *Hugh the Drover*. The conductor was Stanford Robinson and there were to be two live performances on the Third Programme in October 1949 with three days rehearsal beforehand. It was financially unexciting, but a breakthrough, which had come without any prompting from my agents.

These studio performances of opera took place in the Camden Theatre in north London, an old music hall, which the B.B.C. had renovated and adapted without disturbing the elegant dress circle with its gilded cherubs. It was an excellent place for singing and many artists were sad when the lease fell in, forcing the B.B.C. to leave and perform similar benevolent surgery on Golders Green Hippodrome.

When the score of *Hugh The Drover* arrived I thought the music looked fairly straightforward as I picked it out with one finger on the piano. Being a broadcast I knew I would have the music in front of me. The only acting would be with the voice. All in all I considered it an easy task, which, in retrospect, I know I didn't prepare for as thoroughly as I should. I simply hadn't realized that all the coaching and rehearsal I'd had for the operas at the Cambridge Theatre and Glyndebourne had given me, not only a thorough knowledge of my own part, but the structure of the music going on round me as well. My ear had taken all this in unconsciously during the endless repetitions until I could, like Stabile, correct a mistake instinctively.

There were only three days rehearsal for this opera, which meant that unless I knew it backwards or was a first-class sight reader, I was at a fair old disadvantage. Indeed as soon as 'Robbie' pointed his baton in my direction at the first orchestral rehearsal I was, within moments, up to my neck in the mulliga-tawny. Vaughan Williams was a different musical idiom from Puccini, Verdi, Rossini and Mozart, and I found trying to follow the conductor, while simultaneously keeping my eye on the printed words and music, beyond me. I began to beat time with my right hand, my eyes glued to the score and my breast heaving with panic. To make matters worse, for technical reasons connected with the microphones, we were singing behind the large orchestra at least thirty feet from the conductor.

I could not get my first bit of music right. I either came in too early or too late. When at last I managed to begin at the right moment, I soon wandered out of time—ahead or behind, I couldn't have said which.

Robbie flung down his baton.

'You must not conduct with your right hand while you're singing. I don't know whether to follow your beat or my beat. It couldn't matter less to you—you're not following either!'

I was crushed and humiliated. The whole B.B.C. Opera Orchestra and the B.B.C. Chorus had heard Robbie's outburst —I couldn't deny it was justified. The end of my radio opera career was staring me in the face—before I'd even sung one performance.

Standing next to me was the small figure of Jan van der Gucht, an English tenor of Dutch extraction.

'Be fair, Robbie,' he called out, "You can't have a Constable without a beat.'

Not only did this sally get a huge laugh, in which Robbie joined, I believe it gave me a reprieve from the sack and the chance of a precious few hours study before the next day's rehearsal, which just about saved me from disaster. As a result I became a regular in those studio operas until a few years later the B.B.C. decided they were too expensive, turned the Opera Orchestra into the Concert Orchestra, and relied for future opera performances on gramophone records and relays from opera houses both here and abroad. This was very tough on Robbie, a talented and vastly experienced conductor, who had catered for many different operatic tastes. Among those in which I took part were works as diverse as Borodin's *Prince Igor*, *The Perfect Fool* by Holst, Prokofiev's *The Love for Three Oranges*, *Mignon* by Thomas, as well as works by Rameau and Gluck conducted by Roger Désormière in the original French. We also tackled modern works like Arthur Benjamin's *The Tale of Two Cities*. The casts included celebrated names like Heddle Nash, Dennis Noble, Mary Jarred, Elsie Morison and Owen Brannigan. One of the highlights was when Joan Hammond was engaged for Weber's *Der Freischütz*; I played the wicked Caspar and was allowed to speak my own dialogue—a privilege in these productions, where actors were usually brought in to speak the singers' lines on the assumption that we weren't capable of doing it ourselves.

In the end with the lusty, squalling infant television demanding more and more of the B.B.C.'s slender resources, sadly, the economy of cutting operas performed mostly by British singers on the radio was made with barely a murmur of public protest.

It was ironic that Robbie's brother Eric, a less talented musician with greater popular appeal, should have become so much better known presenting the sort of music on television that Robbie could have conducted in his sleep. That comment is not meant to belittle Eric's considerable achievements. I was honoured to be invited to write and speak his obituary on the British Forces Broadcasting network as well as doing a tribute programme to him on Radio 2. Eric was a great communicator as well as a TV pioneer, solving many of the technical problems of conducting an orchestra in one studio accompanying singers and/or dancers in another; he worked in the nervewracking atmosphere of live TV transmissions, conducting something like two thousand shows from opera to variety. He brought middle-brow music to a vast new public and deservedly became a household word in the process. Robbie, on the other hand, was with B.B.C. Radio for forty years, most of the time conducting large orchestras several times a week. He encouraged and was loyal to the artists he used, he employed British soloists in the face of a public snobbery in favour of the foreign singer or musician and he has one rare quality. He can be blunt to the point of rudeness to your face, and say nice things about you behind your back. I think most people prefer it that way round. Both brothers received the O.B.E. from a grateful country. I doubt if many folk realize how much anonymous pleasure they got from Robbie on the radio.

It was about this time that my friend Ted Jackson, who had written to me years earlier advocating an operatic career, fired off another missive in my direction introducing me to a young composer called Donald Swann. As Ted's first letter had been spot on, I decided to take this one seriously and invited Mr. Swann to supper. He came and afterwards sat at the piano, bouncing up and down, a sort of enthusiastic bespectacled schoolboy, his head nodding like a youthful monarch acknowledging a vast cheering crowd on a royal progress. He began playing and singing in his fervent tenor a curious ditty about the keeper of the Eddystone Lighthouse, for which I didn't see much future. Then he embarked on a song about an amorous Hippopotamus, with which I fell in love at first hearing. He spoke warmly about his lyric writer and ex-school friend Michael Flanders, whom, he said, I must meet. Michael lived only a mile or two away in the Hampstead Garden Suburb and it was arranged for later in the week.

I met Donald outside the Flanders' house and we rang the bell. After a pause I heard the squelch of rubber tyres approaching the front door on the inside. I had visions of some eccentric pedalling up to open it on a bicycle.

I hadn't expected a bearded man in a wheelchair, who dexterously opened the door and then reversed so that we could get in. Donald hadn't told me that Michael, formerly a strapping six foot one, had become a victim of polio while serving in the North Sea with the Royal Navy. Ten minutes later I could understand why. Michael made such light of his handicap, and his flashing wit carried none of the bitterness that his predicament could have inspired in a lesser individual.

His deep voice and fruity chuckle made a sharp contrast with Donald's earnest, restless approach to conversation which was punctuated by high piercing guffaws, when something tickled his sense of fun. It was one of the most fortunate encounters of my career. These two dissimilar young men could obviously solve my most pressing problem—finding material that I could perform in the popular field without cooking my goose with Glyndebourne. Before the war, and even after it, an opera singer had only to accept a part in a musical or a revue to find his or her opera contract cancelled. Looking back on some of the things I did in between Glyndebourne seasons, I'll never cease to be grateful to Moran Caplat for taking the view that so long as I came back vocally unimpaired, he wasn't worried about my extra-mural activities.

It had been impossible for me to find songs that would entertain a popular audience and were also suitable for a basso buffo voice. The Hippo was the first I'd come across, and over tea they were talking cheerfully about a whole series of animal songs:

'So long as a species doesn't become extinct,' Michael declared, 'the songs shouldn't date.' Twenty-six years later I can gratefully endorse that opinion.

Not long after that fateful meeting they set up a bachelor establishment in a ground floor studio flat at Scarsdale Villas, to which I would be occasionally summoned to meet a new arrival at the menagerie. These trips were like a visit to a tailor. The first time the song would be in rough, just scribbled out, with possible alternatives which could be discussed. After we'd been through it a few times and got the feel of it, they'd start ripping out the sleeves and putting chalk marks for the button holes. Then I'd come back a fortnight later to find a neat clean manuscript on the piano. At that stage there was rarely any alteration to be made. Not all were animal songs. There was a delicious number, which I still sing, about an Italian Gondolier on the Manchester Ship Canal, and 'The Income Tax Collector', which has to be constantly up-dated as one grisly Finance Bill succeeds another. I avoid singing it in public at the beginning of January.

It was a minor catastrophe when they discovered some years later that they could perform their own material every bit as well as the artists they'd been writing for. The triumph of *At the Drop of a Hat* and its sequel meant that they simply hadn't the time or energy left to write for people like me. Sustaining two complete shows entirely on their own output, taking them to America and Australia after long runs and provincial tours here, as well as making records and fulfilling all the other commitments that come in the wake of such spectacular success, made up a formidable programme for a writer in a wheel-chair and a composer turned singer and accompanist. All their creative efforts were needed for themselves and they discovered, as others have before, that to try and combine composing and performing in the same period is often impossible and at best exhausting. As I was finishing this book news came of Michael's death, a sudden collapse on holiday with his family at the age of fifty-three. For the last few years he and Donald had gone their separate artistic ways, retaining their close friendship and enthusiasm for each other's achievements. Michael, perhaps sensing that time was short, tended to spend more and more of it within his family circle. I'm too close to losing an old friend to say more than that I'm thankful that someone who battled so gallantly with such daunting health problems was at least spared a protracted illness at the end.

I'm thankful that the Hippo, the Rhinoceros, the Elephant, The Warthog, the Gay Gondolier (Gay in the original meaning!) and the Income Tax Collector got clean away from Scarsdale Villas before Flanders and Swann closed the menagerie to the public! Along with Sydney Carter's 'Down Below' (a song about London's sewers) those songs bridged the gap for me between opera and the popular theatre. Of them all 'Mud' remains the one with which I seem to be associated in many people's minds. I'm very lucky to be linked with a song. It helps folk to remember you.

I once, stupidly, tried to give up singing it on the grounds that audiences would either get sick of it or think I didn't know anything else. I soon found out that I was merely causing disappointment. Its enduring popularity is hard to explain. When I first sang it on television I had a rather hippo-like figure, which helped to make it funny, but Michael and Donald have always had great success with it themselves, so that's not the real reason. Once when I was working on the radio with one of the best radio actors ever, Norman Shelley, he pointed an accusing finger at me and declared in his rich dark tones,

'I caught you singing "Mud" on children's telly yesterday afternoon—a disgraceful performance!'

'What was disgraceful about it, Norman?' I asked. I was intrigued.

'I've never seen anything like it,' he went on, bristling with mock indignation.

'You sang it to those innocent little cherubs with sex oozing from your every pore!' Well, perhaps that's it—but I doubt it.

Despite its success on TV and radio—it just about stopped the show on a Henry Hall's Guest Night—I'd been singing it for seven or eight years before any record company could be persuaded to issue a disc. They all said it was 'too clever to be popular'. In the end a tall, pale young man at Parlophone called George Martin decided to round up four of the animals and put them on a type of record hardly seen today—a 45 r.p.m. extended player. Donald accompanied me on the piano and we called it 'Wallace's Private Zoo'—there was never any danger of it becoming a golden disc, but it sold about 50,000 copies and stayed in the catalogue for a decade. It was my first commercial record—George introduced quite a few artists to the record buying public, including Peter Sellers, Flanders and Swann, and the Beatles.

Not for the first time in this story I'm getting ahead of myself. Back then to my empty diary for Christmas 1949. Richard Stone took a hand in my affairs and secured me the part of the Sultan of Morocco in *Dick Whittington* at the Princes' Theatre, London—now renamed the Shaftesbury. My song was written by Phil Park, whom I'd not seen since the Fiddlesticks concert party. The principal boy was the late Hy Hazel and Alice Fitzwarren was Richard's wife Sara Gregory, who'd been Cinderella in *The Glass Slipper*.

The last scene before the interval took place on board the ship bound for Morocco and it ended with a patriotic scena. Never were so many famous evocative phrases so skilfully knitted together. By the time Hy had finished with the audience they would stumble up the aisle to join the ice-cream queue blinded with tears. She was an excellent actress and had some of the best lines in the English language:

'This royal throne of kings, this scepter'd isle,' came close on the heels of,

'Cry "God for Harry! England and Saint George!" ' There was a snatch of 'Jerusalem' and 'Drake's Drum' for good measure. The climax was heralded by a splendid roll on the timpani as the lights faded right down and the darkness was stabbed by two powerful arc-lights—one on Hy's backview as she saluted the quarter deck, the other on the quarter deck itself revealing Nelson, telescope under one arm, returning her salute, while the orchestra and chorus gave a stirring account of the last few bars of 'Rule Britannia'.

One evening I was in my dressing room putting the final touches to my sultan make-up. I could hear the show issuing forth from the Tannoy public address speaker above the door. As the orchestra began 'Rule Britannia' a gale of laughter drowned everything. It went on and on, finally breaking into a storm of applause as the curtain came down.

The explanation was simple. Bert Montague was an experienced and shrewd pantomime producer of many years standing. When it was necessary to spend money he spent it—but he didn't believe in throwing it away.

When Nelson stood on the quarter deck he was only visible from the waist up. The rest of him was concealed by a canvas screen, which blotted out the ship's rail at the edge of the deck. So, while Nelson had a beautiful wig, tied back with black ribbon, a three-cornered hat, and an immaculate pea-jacket, it had not been thought necessary to hire him breeches, stockings, and buckled shoes, which the audience would never see. Furthermore, the artist who played Nelson had other duties in the show apart from this brief appearance.

On this particular evening someone on the stage crew had forgotten to set the canvas screen on the quarter-deck rail, which meant that when the light picked up Nelson, it revealed him from top to toe—and there he was, the hero of Trafalgar, wearing half a uniform and the back legs of the pantomime horse.

The audience laughed more or less right through the interval. Hy got such a shock that she sat down on the stage in full view and had mild hysterics.

There was another moment in *Dick Whittington* that provided the audience with the same explosive mirth they got that night from Nelson. Idle Jack was played by Nat Jackley, whose father George I had seen in a pantomime at the Lyceum Theatre when I was a little boy. All I remember about George was his tramping about in seven league boots that were about half a league too big, and talking in an extremely lugubrious gruff voice. Nat, tall and lithe as a panther, moved eccentrically round the stage as if his bones were made of india-rubber, and the biggest laughs of the evening came when he appeared as an awkward recruit being drilled by an old-fashioned sergeant-major in a squad made up of half a dozen supporting comics who could certainly have been described as the long and the short and the tall. A sure sign of the quality of their routine, with its lightning costume changes and perfectly executed slap-stick, was the number of the cast who used to stand in the wings and watch it at every performance. Ten years later I did a pantomime with Nat in Leeds in which he was the dame. I wondered how he and his male troupe would cope with the change of sex. It was no problem. They were even funnier doing much the same routine as girl guides and brownies.

Just after Christmas I got a letter from Erede inviting me to sing Masetto in *Don Giovanni* in Parma—a small city in northern Italy noted for cheese and violets. There would be two performances towards the end of February. I couldn't believe it—most singers of my age went to Italy to study, not to regale the native paying customers. There was one ghastly snag. It clashed with the last week of the pantomime. Unless Bert Montague was prepared to let my understudy play that one week or get a replacement, I'd have to turn it down. (Fade in the Archers' signature tune.)

Deh, vieni alla finestra

(*Don Giovanni*)

I went to Parma by train (Good old Bert!), I hate flying, and only do it when there's no other way. I took a costume and wig with me, kindly lent by Glyndebourne. The peasant's straw hat, decorated with flowers for Masetto's wedding day, had the customs man at Domodossola giving me very strange looks until I tossed my head and said, 'Sauce box!' at which he shrugged and put a strange chalk mark on my suitcase. (That's not quite what happened, but at the beginning of a new chapter, particularly number 13, I thought we could do with some light relief.)

I don't mind confessing I felt very proud as the train rumbled through those alpine tunnels. Today British opera singers appear all over the world as a matter of course, but in 1950 I was the only one in Italy and that, I said to myself, was quite something.

When the train arrived at Parma I was the only person to get off. I'd half expected a reception committee, but there wasn't a living soul to be seen. In my halting Italian I asked the one elderly porter if he could find me a taxi.

'Momento,' he growled and disappeared. Twenty-five minutes later he returned with one of the oldest bicycles I've ever seen. It had been slightly modernized. It had a luggage grid on the back mud-guard. Together we strapped on my case, then he wheeled the bicycle through the streets while I walked beside him. He kept pointing me out to his friends, who seemed to comprise the entire male population, shouting, 'Basso Inglese'.

I soon got fed up with this and tapped him on the shoulder. Pointing to my chest I said,

'Basso *Scozese*.'

The first person I met when we got to the opera house—a dignified neo-classical building near the main square—was Antonio Lazzari, a tenor I'd sung with at the Cambridge Theatre.

'Val*a*chay!' he cried (that's the way Italians pronounce my surname).

'Val*a*chay, why you come 'ere?—Why you come 'ere? Issa terrible place witha terrible people. They givea da bird once a week. I gotta come—issa my country—I gotta wife and bambini—but you! Go home before issa too late!'

He wasn't kidding. The Parmesan opera-goers have a formidable reputation and are responsible for the shortest operatic performance on record. One night a baritone came in front of the curtain to sing the Prologue to Leoncavallo's opera *I Pagliacci*, which begins, 'Si Puo?—May I?' The whole house yelled 'NO!'—and that was that.

A couple of days before we were due to open—and this was one of those cases where there were only three or four days rehearsal anyway—one of the sopranos was taken ill and an SOS for a replacement was sent to Milan. The lady who came was admittedly no longer young, but she'd obviously been a fine singer and still sounded pretty good to me. Maybe she was in a little bit of trouble in some of the very high and difficult passages of her aria on the first night, but that couldn't possibly justify the behaviour of the audience. They began by shouting, 'Via! Via!—Off! Off!' and then they whistled and jeered. It was horrible. At least she was spared the ultimate in Italian 'birds' when they join in the aria with you. Luckily for her *Don Giovanni* hadn't been given in Parma for over seventy years, so they didn't know it.

You can imagine how I felt standing there in the wings waiting to make my first entrance. If they can do that to one of their own, I thought, what will they do to the basso Scozese? I noticed a strong smell of burning rubber. When I asked the stage director what it was he pointed to the switchboard and the dimmers which were shimmering with heat.

'They are not old,' he whispered with a broad grin, 'they are antique.'

It seemed that I was in imminent danger of being roasted one way or the other.

Masetto and his bride, Zerlina, make their first entrance with a chorus of peasants. They dance on singing a rapid and joyous duet about how happy they are to be married—it's their wedding day. As our cue approached I realized that all the shouting and jeering had really scared me. I began to tremble, and when I got onto the stage my happy smile froze solid and I couldn't switch it off. When something like that happens as a result of nerves it makes singing almost impossible. Alberto was conducting with one hand and cupping his ear with the other. Emma Tegani, the Zerlina, bore the brunt of that duet, but the audience remained quiet. Perhaps even the citizens of Parma could occasionally feel pity. It took me a few minutes to get a hold on myself, but I felt calmer as we started on the recitative before my aria. Recitatives are those sections where the orchestra stops playing and the singers have a rapid musical conversation which takes care of a large slice of the plot accompanied on the piano or harpsichord.

Almost as soon as I started I was horrified to hear laughter from the audience. Now one of three possibilities occurs to an actor or singer when an audience laughs unexpectedly. One, the bird is winging its way towards you and they are giggling in anticipation; two, a cat or dog has wandered onto the stage; three, your fly buttons are undone. A furtive look round, and down, revealed nothing untoward. Yet every time I opened my mouth they roared with laughter. Any minute now, I thought, thankful that my humiliation was going to happen far from home.

However, I'd forgotten something. All the previous performances of *Don Giovanni* I'd sung had been in Italian to British audiences, who didn't understand a word of it, but would come out afterwards saying how much better opera sounds in Italian. After playing this scene to dead silence about sixty times I'd forgotten that, in a cruel sort of way, Masetto's first confrontation with the Don is amusing. This audience thought so too and were enjoying it. I almost fainted with relief.

This was not the only time I have realized what audiences

and artists mutually miss from one another when the work is in a beautiful but unfamiliar language. The arguments in favour of presenting operas in the original language are overwhelming, especially if the alternative is a poor English translation. But where comedy is concerned, a great deal of enjoyment is lost. Even in Ebert productions at Glyndebourne, which were highly praised, we tended to use a good deal of sign language to put the comedy across to those members of the audience whose Italian was a little rusty.

In the interval Alberto looked haggard and depressed.

'We cutta everything she do in the second act—she don'ta sing again tonight—at all.'

'Everything, Maestro?' I asked unbelievingly. Donna Anna is a very big part. He shrugged.

'Maybe we leava the recitatives, otherwise the public will be confused abouta the plot, but eet would be dangerous to expose her anywhere else.'

'Maestro, cuts like that will wreck the opera!' He smiled grimly,

'You are very right; but eet's a simple choice. We makea the cuts we wrecka the opera. We don't makea the cuts, we getta the tomatoes.'

We madea the cuts.

Near the end of the opera one of the cuts, which had had to be hastily made and given to the orchestra, went hideously wrong. In the supper scene, the orchestra made a sixteen bar cut in the wrong place and the singers on the stage never even noticed. I wasn't one of them. Although this was Italy the others had mostly learnt the opera specially for this performance and, astonishingly, were not so familiar with it as I was. I listened in the wings as they blundered on for several pages, powerless to help. It was an awful cacophony of music and vocal lines that didn't match, and Alberto didn't dare to stop them and put it right. That would have been an invitation to the audience to hoot the whole thing off the stage. By some miracle it got straight when Elvira came on to warn the Don of the Statue's approach, but during the finale worse was to come. When we reached the point where that cut should have been made, the orchestra played straight on. The previous fourteen bars were the beginning of a beautiful duet between Donna

Anna and Don Ottavio, the rest of which would have taken the lady into the high part of her voice, which had caused trouble with the audience in the first act. Both she and the tenor firmly shut their mouths and let the band play on alone. This was an embarrassing place to leave them because no instrument had the melody. All that could be heard was a quiet series of oom-pah-pahs while six singers stood uneasily facing the public, none of us able to utter a cheep.

The prompter, his head peeping out of his little cubby hole down at the level of the footlights centre stage, but invisible to the audience, was obviously feeling the strain and suddenly lost his head. Stabbing his finger in the direction of Donna Elvira, a rather plump young lady with prominent front teeth, he barked.

'Io men vado!' which would have been her next line if the orchestra had made the cut. As it was, there were a good many oom-pah-pahs before it was safe for her to tell us she was heading for a nunnery, but one ignores the prompter at one's peril, and she opened her mouth to draw breath and start.

'Taci!—shut up!' I hissed at her. She started violently and put her hand up to her mouth as if she had nearly blurted out some indiscretion. Meanwhile Alberto was getting through the sixteen bars as quick as he could. Mozart marked them larghetto, which is pretty slow, but the maestro was giving a good imitation of Toscanini conducting a presto, his baton whirling round in circles. Considering that Toscanini was born in Parma that was a dangerous gesture. We had been standing there for about five years, and were still only half way through when the prompter tried again.

'Io men vado!'

'Taci!'

He tried a third time. I walked towards his box, pretended to pick something up, and out of the side of my mouth addressed him, 'Taci,' I whispered. He looked very surprised indeed. Then I turned to Elvira, who was looking both nervous and nonplussed. I smiled at her. I may have had no formal musical education, I may be one of the poorest sight readers in the profession, but I do know with absolute certainty when Elvira comes in in the finale of *Don Giovanni*.

'Io men vado,' I said. At that the prompter slammed his book shut and disappeared. We got through the last five minutes without further incident. When the curtain fell there was no applause at all—none, just a sort of muttering from the audience. Two members of the stage crew, dressed as periwigged eighteenth-century footman with stockings and breeches, came forward to open the curtain. The Zerlina rushed up to them, barring their way.

'No, no, per l'amor di Dio, no!' she gasped. I agreed with her, though I was almost in tears. This wasn't at all how I'd imagined my Italian debut. Then, almost as if they were recovering from a whiff of nerve gas, they began to clap—it couldn't be described as enthusiastic, but they kept it up long enough for us to take four embarrassing curtain calls.

I had one great compensation. The local critic gave me an excellent write up, for which I could thank the solid grounding I had had in the part before I left England. The only other souvenir of the occasion is a photograph of the first night audience! When the photographer appeared at the interval, I wrongly thought that he had come to take pictures of the cast. Instead he brusquely ordered us off the stage so that the curtain could be raised for a picture of the audience. They look a very decent crowd of folk, and they're all in evening dress, but I'll never forget what they did to poor Donna Anna in the first act.

After the second performance, which didn't finish till after midnight, there was a party at a nearby restaurant, where, at two in the morning I was called upon to make a speech, which had to be in Italian, and was loudly applauded. All the limited Italian I know I've picked up from working in opera and consulting a pocket dictionary. Thus I know a good few nouns, a smaller collection of verbs, a cluster of adjectives, one or two adverbs and no grammar whatsoever. An English singer once summed up my command of Italian by saying,

'You know, when the Italians speak their own language I find it very difficult to understand, but when Ian speaks it, I understand it perfectly.'

I had one day in Milan before going home. Alberto arranged for me to see over the famous Scala. I stood on the stage from where, it is said, a whisper carries to the back of the gods. I self-consciously sang a scale to the dark, empty auditorium. I thought it sounded pretty good—but that's another place to which I've never been back.

This haunting refrain

(*Hippopotamus Song*)

'We start with a round of musical identification—Ian, for two marks can you tell me the name of the piece and the composer?' Steve Race, bearded like the pard, starts yet another *My Music* recording. Sitting beside me, Denis Norden is beginning one of his lattice-work doodles, which will cover most of a piece of foolscap paper by the time we've finished; Frank Muir is taking off his jacket and loosening his bow tie, while John Amis, bedecked in one of the more flamboyant examples of his wardrobe's seemingly endless resources, gives me a friendly, benevolent smile, like a bishop welcoming a shy candidate for confirmation. The invited audience sit up and concentrate as if they were going to be asked to supply the answers. Sometimes they are!

In the mobile control box outside the Commonwealth Institute in Kensington, where the above scene regularly takes place, sit, surrounded by a battery of technicians, Tony Shryane, our producer, whom we share with *The Archers* and *My Word*, and Stan Stancliffe of the Transcription Service, which sells B.B.C. recorded programmes all over the world. By the time these two have finished with the tape, skilfully excising our worst indiscretions and the jokes that died, there should remain two reasonably entertaining half hours to be played at home and away. With the exception of John Amis, who joined us two years ago after the death of Bill Franklin, we've been turning up there for this purpose between seven and thirteen times a year for the best part of a decade.

My Music began in 1967 as a flash of inspiration in the fertile mind of Edward J. Mason, the originator of *The Archers* and *My Word* as well as many other successful B.B.C. programmes. The first *My Music* was a 'one off' pilot, recorded at the Paris Studio, a converted underground cinema in Lower Regent Street, which anyone who's been involved with B.B.C. light entertainment during the last thirty years knows well. The formula was—and is—a simple one: get two professional humorists and team each with a musical expert under a chairman who asks the questions about music for half an hour. Don't make the questions too hard, accept witty answers as well as correct ones, allow everyone to gag and reminisce to their hearts' content, and realize that the least important aspect of the whole thing is who wins or loses.

Ted Mason and Tony Shryane made one great mistake—they cast me as one of the musical experts, an error into which readers of this book would not have fallen. Fortunately for me, when they discovered, too late, that I had only a law degree and was, musically, a self-educated man with that education hopelessly overbalanced in the direction of Puccini, Rossini and Mozart, they decided to make the best of it, and ask me questions that tactfully avoided the vast areas of musical knowledge where my showing would be about as impressive as if I were asked to decipher the Dead Sea Scrolls. Since we began, I have managed to plug a few of the gaps in my knowledge by studying various musical dictionaries and trying to memorize the titles of the many pieces of music I've introduced in endless concerts for both the B.B.C. and the British Forces Broadcasting Service.

In the final round of the quiz, in which we all have to sing, I'm expected to make up for my other deficiencies and round off the show by giving a fairly accurate account of a verse from some well-known song or ballad. I freely admit that in recent years I've had prior knowledge of the song; though in the first few series I had no idea what was coming, and often knew none of the words. On one or two embarrassing occasions I didn't even know the song and had to get myself out of trouble by singing something else. Apparently the producer got letters from listeners. The gist of them was 'don't embarrass him, give him songs he knows'. The advice was taken and I'm grateful to the kindly folk who wrote in. Nevertheless, it's not the easiest thing in the world to sit for about forty-five ninutes talking and laughing, and then suddenly burst into song, often unaccompanied, praying that out will come a string of phlegm-free notes; also, whether the song is in my repertoire or learnt specially, I'm expected to sing it from memory, and Steve and I never rehearse it.

My Music is heard in virtually every English speaking country in the world; I get listeners' letters of appreciation from New Zealand, Australia, Canada, South Africa, and many other places. The success of the programme is due, I firmly believe, to two things: the soundness of Ted Mason's original concept, and the fact that we all enjoy doing it. Frank Muir once said that it was a marvellous excuse for table talk. We enjoy one another's company and are usually mildly disappointed when it's over, yet we rarely meet anywhere else. Steve Race must take a lion's share of the credit. Not only does he hold the ring with urbanity as chairman and contributes his share of inspired ad libbing, he also tailors the questions to elicit the maximum response from each of us.

The beginning of *My Music* coincided with one of the many changes of direction in my career, which means that often I have a long journey to get to the recording. In the last eight or nine years I've become an itinerant musician, driving about 20,000 miles a year and clocking up nearly as much again in trains and the occasional flying machine. The assignments vary enormously. There are three different versions of my one man show—*An Evening with Ian Wallace*—with, of course, my faithful accompanist David Money—three versions because people are sometimes plucky enough to ask us back a couple of times. Then, for the last three years, since I parted amicably with Richard Stone and threw in my lot with a young concert promoter called Raymond Gubbay, I've appeared in a great variety of concerts. I've sung Gilbert and Sullivan at the Albert and Royal Festival Halls, I've introduced Viennese evenings in many of the major concert halls in Britain, as well as taking part in a host of smaller Gilbert and Sullivan, opera and operetta concerts, involving two or three other singers in places as far apart as Shetland and Bournemouth. Sometimes my kilt is packed in the boot for a Scots concert at St. Albans or Eastbourne, and once recently I had to drive in one day the 499 miles from Oban to London

211

after a performance of *The Barber of Seville* for Scottish Opera.

One thing nearly all these concerts have in common. I present them to the audience having written the linking script. This is quite a heavy responsibility when one is doing a good deal of the singing as well, but in these days when both TV and radio provide such expert presentation of programmes, I believe that audiences who are prepared to come to a light music or operatic concert are entitled to something more lively than a few notes on the programme.

Isn't it extraordinary that an opera singer, who in 1950 had secured a toehold in Italy and was a member of the Glyndebourne family, should be remembered a quarter of a century later, not for his operatic roles, but for a steam radio quiz and a song about a hippopotamus wallowing in mud? One day I hope to make the sequence of events that brought this about the subject of another book, but I feel that those of you who have struggled thus far with this one are due some sort of explanation.

Let's get one thing clear right away. This is no apologia or admission of failure. Neither of my broad shoulders is adorned with anything remotely resembling a chip. What has happened has mostly been for the best and has had a kind of classic inevitability about it. It does, however, need a little patient understanding.

When I returned to England in the spring of 1950 after that somewhat unusual Italian debut at Parma, my future was gloriously uncertain—as it still is—with one difference. Nowadays I know, God willing, what I shall be doing for approximately the next year, but no further. In 1950, apart from *The Marriage of Figaro* at Edinburgh Festival which was six months ahead, I had very little on the book. Soon I was to become aware for the first time of a problem that was to pose itself repeatedly throughout the next twenty years. Very simply it was this. Managements who present plays, films or musicals book artists at very short notice—a few days ahead—at most, a few weeks (except, of course, for the main stars). The same applies to light entertainment on radio and television. Concert promoters and opera managements, on the other hand, find they have to book singers many months, even a year or two ahead. It's to some extent a question of supply and demand. There are always plenty of good actors and actresses about, but not too many top-class singers. More than that, a big part in an opera may take several months to study and perfect. My problem was that I enjoyed working in many different fields and was reluctant to give any of them up. That reluctance wasn't just an immature lack of judgement. I am something of a specialized singer as far as opera is concerned and there didn't seem to be enough scope for a buffo like me to risk giving up other things even if I'd wanted to. To reinforce my feelings, the door of the Royal Opera House was closed to me, and in those days Sadlers Wells made no move in my direction.

So far as concerts were concerned, I didn't feel too confident of my chances there either. Even though for a short while the B.B.C. had me on a list of singers, who could be entrusted with modern twelve-tone music, because I had managed to cope with it in one or two radio operas, I found it a great strain. When in the middle 1950s I suffered for a few months from severe nervous tension and could only continue working with the aid of mild sedation, I believe that one of the causes was the fear of making musical mistakes, live, on the air in this, for me, fiendishly difficult music. I am a bad sight reader and do not possess perfect pitch, two drawbacks which would have made life very difficult for me if I had tried to tackle the varied repertoire of the concert singer working as a recitalist or with orchestras and choral societies. In my own defence, I have a good ear, a good sense of rhythm, a quick memory, and a reputation for singing in tune—but I like plenty of time to prepare my work and this is not always granted to the busy concert singer.

In consequence, though I never turned down an opera engagement, I did not, for many years, try to build up a concert career. When I was offered concerts months ahead, I would only accept on condition that I could withdraw should a major stage or film commitment arise. Not many concert agents or promoters were prepared to accept that sort of condition, but this didn't worry me, as the work seemed to come in quite happily from other sources.

In the spring of 1950 I sang the Khan Kontchak in *Prince Igor* on the radio, as well as the baritone solos in the St. Matthew Passion at Glyndebourne with Kathleen Ferrier and Eric Greene (the one and only Matthew Passion of my life), yet only a week or two later I was on the telly in a comedy show with

Bobby Howes. After Edinburgh Festival I had an operatic autumn singing Caspar in Weber's *Der Freischutz* and appearing in an unusual double bill for the London Opera Club, Milhaud's *Le Pauvre Matelot* and a charming one acter by Donizetti called *The Night Bell* about an elderly chemist on his wedding night, with a superb English libretto by Christopher Hassall, Ivor Novello's lyric writer. On a shoestring budget we played them at the Fortune Theatre and then at the Chester Festival. But at Christmas time it was back to the Princes' Theatre for me, to appear as the King of Gooseland in *Mother Goose* with Ethel Revnell, in which, to keep the cultural flag flying, my solo spot was Mussorgsky's 'Song of the Flea'.

Possibly if I'd taken time out that Christmas to think, I'd have realized that things couldn't go on as they were—that I'd have to make up my mind to be either an opera singer, a character actor, a musical comedy artist or a comedian. I would have seen that to continue to be all four was out of the question. As it was, I was never out of work long enough to indulge in that important exercise in self analysis, and if I had been unemployed that long, I would doubtless have seized on the first work that was offered, irrespective of its source. I am as haunted as the next artist with a perpetual sense of insecurity, and an impression that the phone has rung for the last time. I also have a superstitious fear that to turn down work, just because something better might come along, is somehow tempting providence. I am enormously lucky to be able to turn my hand to many different tasks in the theatre and music, indeed I relish some of the challenges that extend from Bach to Richard Rodgers and from pantomime to Shakespeare, but to be a freelance, under no long term contract to anyone, and dependent on one thing following another requires steady nerves and an inexhaustible supply of optimism. I have the second and for long stretches of time it has been justified. One stroke of luck has succeeded another to prevent important dates in these various departments clashing, and at one time Richard Stone christened me Lail, which stood for luckiest actor in London.

1951 rolled on in much the same way. It will always be associated by my generation with the Festival of Britain, a faltering step away from post-war austerity. The Glasgow Grand Opera Society celebrated it with three performances of

Above: As *Mefistofele* for Glasgow Grand Opera Society, 1951. You can tell the devil isn't really me—look at the wrinkled tights! *Below:* As a blind harper in *The King of Scots*, Dunfermline Abbey, 1951.

Sesto Bruscantini as *Dandini* and Ian as *Don Magnifico* in *La Cenerentola*, Glyndebourne, 1952.

Boito's opera *Mefistofele*, conducted by Walter Susskind, in which I played the devil for the only time in my life. I enjoyed it, but it's not really my cup of tea. My tights would wrinkle, and I felt that my characterization wasn't just as suave as it might have been. I was far happier as the rollicking sailor in *The Four Men*, a dramatization by Lord Bessborough of Hilaire Belloc's book in praise of Sussex, and one of the happiest engagements I ever took part in. It was presented by the county of Sussex to mark the Festival, and for six weeks we played it in barns, village halls, schools and convents all over that green and pleasant downland area. The other three men were Robert Speaight, who also directed it, John Leather and the late W. E. Holloway, a fine Shakespearean actor, who sat beside me in the car for all the many journeys with fresh reminiscences of his long career to enliven every day. One afternoon we lunched with Belloc at his house beside a windmill, and watched him drink his wine from a silver tankard. After that lunch I got a phone message offering me one of the very few serious parts ever to come my way, the Blind Harper in Robert Kemp's play *The King of Scots* in Dunfermline Abbey as part of the Edinburgh Festival of that year. How serious it was you can judge from the photograph. Once I realized that I wasn't going to get any laughs and that all my songs were stirring or sad, it was a welcome change.

For once there was no pantomime that Christmas—unless you call *Let's Make an Opera* at the Lyric Theatre, Hammersmith by Benjamin Britten and Eric Crozier, a sophisticated form of panto for discriminating kids. I loved working with the children in the first part, and being the villainous Black Bob in the second. Recently I was sharply reminded of the passage of time by a man who asked if he could bring his wife and children to see me in my dressing room at Sheffield's Crucible Theatre where I was appearing with Scottish Opera. He told me that he had been one of the children when I had done *Let's Make an Opera* at the Taw and Torridge Festival in the early 50s. That really does bring it home that the years are passing.

Undoubtedly the biggest break of my career came in 1952 when I was engaged to sing the major buffo role of Don Magnifico in Rossini's opera *La Cenerentola—Cinderella* at Glyndebourne. This was the happy outcome of a friendly difference of opinion I'd had with the management the previous year, when I had turned down their offer of a part in *La Forza del Destino* at Edinburgh, which I felt was too small to do my career any good. Now, a year later, they had come back with the biggest role I'd ever been offered. Don Magnifico is the pompous, wicked stepfather of Cinderella, and he gets his comeuppance in a hilariously funny duet with Dandini in the second act. The cast included Marina de Gabarain, Sesto Bruscantini, Juan Oncina, Alda Noni, who had made·such a success in *Don Pasquale* at the Cambridge Theatre and Fernanda Cadoni. The conductor, of course, was Vittorio Gui. Bruscantini, who, like me, is still on the British operatic scene when he can spare time from his engagements all over the world, displayed a wonderful combination of vocal and histrionic talents as Dandini. The decor was by Oliver Messell and the all-round success of the production encouraged Glyndebourne to follow Gui's advice and make this the first of a series of Rossini revivals, which were to be a feature of the opera house during the 1950s. I certainly had my fair share in it, renewing acquaintance with Dr. Bartolo in *The Barber of Seville* and being introduced to a new and exacting role, the Tutor in *Le Comte Ory*; in the second act most of the male characters, myself included, appeared disguised as nuns! In all these three Rossini operas the tenor was Oncina and the baritone was Bruscantini. We were a sort of Rossini advance guard, knowing each other's way of playing the parts and able, after two or three years, to put up something of a team performance, which gave us almost as much pleasure as I hope we were giving to the audience. But the first night of *La Cenerentola* was my first at Glyndebourne itself, and it was an odd quirk of fate that the year I finally sang at Glyndebourne, the company wasn't invited to Edinburgh. Hamburg Opera went instead, and there was a public outcry, which resulted in Glyndebourne returning the following year. Maybe they were coming back anyway, but it's tidier to make them come back in response to public demand!

Glyndebourne weren't at the 1952 Festival, but I was. I played an English sergeant in a ballad opera *The Highland Fair* by Robert Kemp with music by Cedric Thorpe Davie, whom I'd first met when he'd done the music for *The Forrigan Reel*. The name on the programme that dwarfed all the others was that of

Tyrone Guthrie. This tall, slim Irishman with the quizzical expression on a face that might have belonged to a colonel, and who always rehearsed in carpet slippers, made as deep an impression on me as Carl Ebert. His place in theatrical history is impregnably secure. He could string together paragraphs of the most lucid and perfect prose completely off the cuff, which left the company speechless with admiration. He could use four letter words unexpectedly and without rancour in order to shock a tired cast into working hard for the last half hour of the day, and he could ensure, by the most crushing couple of sentences, that a late comer to rehearsal would never repeat the offence. He also had the knack of getting the best out of everyone and used different methods according to the temperament with which he was dealing. At the first rehearsal when I had finished singing my first song he clapped his huge hands together, making a sound like rapid pistol shots.

'Right,' he declared. 'That's the first encore number of the show, and you'd better get it as I'm not going to take off the chorus until you've sung it the second time.'

This was a daunting prospect for me, but I was determined not to let him down. I think the thought of letting Tony Guthrie down haunted many people over the years from Olivier downwards. He had a shrewd eye for talent. At one rehearsal a very young man was given the job of rushing across the stage of the Assembly Hall bearing a flag. Most of us privately thought that he overdid it. Tony watched entranced.

'We'll hear more of that one,' he announced with satisfaction. We did. His name was John Cairney.

I didn't have the chance to work with him again for twenty years, though we met from time to time. Then he produced *The Barber* for Phoenix Opera at the Brighton Festival. He was far from well, and a week after the final performance he was dead. I simply couldn't believe it, and could only be thankful that during the rehearsal period of three weeks we had lunched together most days on a pie and a pint in the corner of a quiet pub, and talked of everything from his unsuccessful jam factory to the relative strengths of the leading actors he'd worked with. He didn't feel well enough to be surrounded by his cast at the lunch break, which would have normally delighted him. I'm also thankful for many things he taught me.

The most important one, which he tried to convey to everyone, was to believe in oneself as an artist and make the audience aware of that belief.

I became a Glyndebourne regular and in 1954 we were invited to take *La Cenerentola* to the Berlin Festival, where we had the sort of reception one dreams of—thirty-seven curtain calls on the first night, news of which failed to make the London papers; they were on strike that day! Something went wrong on the second night, we only got thirty-six. Maestro Gui invited me to sing the same role at the Rome Opera House in 1955 with Giulietta Simionato in the title role. I was tremendously excited, and relieved to know that my two stalwart companions Oncina and Bruscantini would be in the cast and that the opera would be produced by Carl Ebert's son Peter, who has successfully followed in his father's footsteps. Pat came with me to Rome and so did Rodolfo Mele and his wife. Rodolfo was very superstitious and used to be out early in the morning looking for hunchbacks. If he had spotted one before breakfast then I would do well that night—he always found one, or said he did.

About an hour before the curtain rose on the first performance (the time when you are asking yourself why on earth you chose such a nervewracking way of earning a living), I had my first experience of the claque.* The head of this influential body, looking like a senior politician in a dove grey suit, grey homburg, and carrying a cane with a silver knob, knocked on my dressing-room door. We did no more than exchange pleasantries. This was repeated every night until the last, when he came obviously expecting the pay-off. I gave him what my Italian colleagues had suggested, which seemed very little, yet, to my surprise, he was quite delighted and thanked me profusely. You may wonder why I knew how to deal with this situation and keep him, as it were, at arms' length till the last night. I owed it to Rodolfo who poked his head round the dressing room door a few moments before 'Signor Bravo's' first visit and whispered, 'Ian, the 'ead of the claque 'eesa comin'. Don'ta geev 'eem anything now butta look as eef you're goin' to.' In other words pay by results. I thought the results were excellent. On the first night I was called in front of the curtain three times

---

* Professional applauders in Italian and German opera houses; many are retired singers. They can turn success into triumph, but can't and won't prop up failure.

after the drunk scene in the wine cellar, while Signorina Simionato pretended to be very angry at being kept waiting for the next scene, but when I ducked behind the curtain for the last time she chucked me under the chin and with a broad smile uttered the one word 'Villano!' According to my dictionary that didn't make me a villain, but an uncouth peasant! I'm only sorry that I've never had the chance to work with her again.

One day Pat and I were lunching in a Roman cafe when a party of English schoolgirls on an educational holiday came in for ice creams and orange squash. Eventually after much nudging and giggling the youngest and shyest was pushed forward, blushing and head down.

'Excuse me,' she murmured. 'But aren't you the man who sings "Mud" on the telly at home?' See what I mean? So much for my international opera career! Well not quite. I sang *The Barber* in Venice the following year and I've been to the Bregenz Festival in Austria a couple of times in the 1960s, from where the opera was always put out over the Eurovision link by Austrian Television, and I've sung on the Danish radio from Copenhagen, but I soon realized that if I was to follow up these opportunities and try to build a full-time international opera career, it could only be done if I was prepared to live abroad and stop flirting with more popular forms of entertainment. That was too high a price to pay. Pat and I are not the stuff of which exiles are made, and while I've always been thrilled to work abroad, the most exciting moment (apart from the first night) has always been the start of the journey home. I hope I may still work further afield. I'd love to go to Australia, New Zealand and Canada and take the family with me, but I've no regrets about spending the vast majority of my career in Britain nor about my frequent excursions into light entertainment.

During the fifties the running battle between my opera career and the bright lights of the commercial theatre was at its height. A pattern developed of Glyndebourne and the Edinburgh Festival in the summer and pantomime at Christmas, with a great deal of radio of all shapes and sizes thrown in. I was invited to take part in the Royal Variety Performance at the London Palladium in 1952, with a galaxy of stars that included Maurice Chevalier, Gracie Fields and Beniamino Gigli—to say nothing of Jimmy Edwards, Tony Hancock, Max Bygraves, plus a struggling band of young comics who called themselves 'The Crazy Gang'. What did I do? You may well ask. Dressed as a recruiting sergeant in the Brigade of Guards would have looked in 1903, I sang 'Soldiers of the Queen' in the finale with the Band of the Coldstream Guards, then took my call bang in the centre of the stage with Gracie on one side and Gigli on the other. If that's not the full Walter Mitty, I'd like to know what is. It won't have escaped you that this was a romantic occasion —the first Command Performance in the reign of Queen Elizabeth II.

Those excursions into light entertainment I mentioned followed three directions: the theatre, radio and television. Until about ten years ago my opera performances and my handful of straight concerts took place in between appearances in theatres and broadcasting studios, either for sound or vision. Only one straight concert deserves a mention because it was so unlike anything else I ever did. In 1953 the Queen and the Duke of Edinburgh visited Australia and Sir Arthur Bliss, then Master of the Queen's Music, composed an occasional piece—'A Song of Welcome' with words by C. Day Lewis to be broadcast on the evening of her return with the B.B.C. Concert Orchestra and Chorus conducted by Sir Malcolm Sargent. The two soloists were myself and—Joan Sutherland. Later in the year I was invited to repeat it at my first Promenade Concert in the Albert Hall with another Australian soprano, Elsie Morison. It was an impressive work and was well received, but, like many occasional pieces, did not survive the event which inspired it. Bliss was helpful and encouraging—more like a retired Brigadier than a composer. His death in March 1975 drew expressions of regret from all sorts of people in music who might have been expected to remain unmoved at the passing of such an establishment figure.

My theatrical career is sufficiently limited to be given in full. Between Glyndebourne and the Royal Command Performance I appeared in two plays at the old Grand Theatre, Croydon, *Worm's Eye View* by R. F. Delderfield and *The Hasty Heart* by John Patrick. In each I played the comedy lead and managed to get laughs from the public and good notices from the local papers, but, of course, nothing could be done to follow this up because of future opera commitments. Then in 1954, directly

Ian in the Royal Command
Performance 1952.

The Finale of the same at the Palladium. My immediate neighbours are
Gigli and Gracie Fields, but you can pick out a dozen or more famous
stars disappearing virtually into the wings.

Above: *The Sailor* in *The Four Men* by Hilaire Belloc in Sussex, 1951.
Below: Relaxing during the recording of *Kismet* for Decca. With Ian and Adele Leigh and the American baritone Robert Merrill.

after the Berlin Festival, I appeared in a revue starring Elsie and Doris Waters called *Pay the Piper*, devised and produced by Laurier Lister, which was cheered from Southsea to Aberdeen on a twelve-week tour, and then fell flat on its face the week before Christmas at the Saville Theatre. It certainly deserved a better fate. It was a colourful, witty show with a cast that included the fabulous Elisabeth Welch, who stopped the show every night, Desmond Walter Ellis, who had a sketch, which twenty years ago caused raised eyebrows as he stood on tiptoe on the lavatory pan trying to repair the cistern, April Olrich, a dancer with the sort of face that launched a thousand ships and made forty-five-year-old executives feel twenty-one, and a young man with a toothy smile, and slightly equine face and kind eyes for whom I rightly prophesied success as a comedy actor, Julian Orchard. Elsie and Doris were, perhaps, a little out of their element in West End Revue, but they had some memorable moments, and two dearer people cannot be imagined. Flanders and Swann wrote much of the material and gave me the opportunity to introduce two contrasting songs to the public, 'The Income Tax Collector' and 'The Elephant'.

The highlight of my stage career (so far!) came in 1956 when I was engaged to play César in *Fanny* at Drury Lane. This musical had been a great success on Broadway. It was an adaptation of Marcel Pagnol's famous film trilogy in which César had been played by the celebrated French actor Raimu. In the musical it was Ezio Pinza, the great Italian bass, who was following up his triumph in *South Pacific*. The book was by S. N. Behrman and Joshua Logan, the music and lyrics by Harold Rome. For me the great excitement was my co-star Robert Morley, an actor I adored going to see and whose breeches I had worn in *The Man with a Load of Mischief*.

Though the entire action takes place on the Marseilles water front, and both Pinza and Walter Slezak, who played Panisse (Morley's part), had spoken the lines in fractured rather than broken English, Robert made it clear early in rehearsal that, as he couldn't manage any sort of French accent, I was on no account to attempt one either—and nor was anyone else. This was logical and sensible, but it robbed me of a trump card. I had spent so much time in the previous decade with opera singers of many nationalities that I could manage most European accents quite well, and would have much preferred to play my part in that way. Nowadays this is not the fashion, but nearly twenty years ago it was—and I felt handicapped from the start. I was ridiculously inexperienced to be sharing star billing in a musical at Drury Lane with a man like Robert, and the director, a rice young guy from America called Billy Hammerstein (a relative of the great one), could give me little help. In fact it took me several months of the run, working on different parts of my performance, to produce something that measured up to my august surroundings. The one thing that was all right from the start was my principal song, 'Welcome Home', which I sing to this day. The applause it got on the first night gave me a precious link with Pinza, a singer I unashamedly describe as my idol.

Working with Robert was a stimulating experience, though I confidently predict that he is unlikely to commit himself ever again to appearing in a musical. He spoke his songs with a high pitched fervour, going quicker or slower as he felt the urge. Michael Collins, our vast and talented conductor, somehow kept the orchestra in contact, though total synchronization would have been beyond any conductor, Toscanini included. It didn't matter. Robert's performance as the elderly sailmaker who marries the young girl pregnant by César's wayward son Marius, and is so proud of the baby, was a moving performance that captivated the audience every night. If he held them in his thrall, he had me in the grip of something nearer terror. Robert was an incorrigible ad libber. His off-the-cuff lines made it impossible to stick to the script. I had to ad lib as well in order to make sense. After a while I devised a technique to deal with it. The first time he departed from the proper lines, I'd just give back the next line in the script, idiotic or not. Then next day I'd pace the floor or the garden until I'd thought of a suitable rejoinder that would, if possible, turn the tables and make the audience laugh. After all they had paid to be entertained. As the moment approached that night I would feel almost as nervous as on the first night. If my line went well he would give me an approving nod or a gleam of his eye to indicate that honours were even, and that ad lib would never be made again. We never spoke of this off stage; it was a sort of game he played with his cast and it certainly kept us on our toes.

He is a kindly, generous man, who gave wonderful parties to

the company and presents for everyone. If he asked me again to do a play I'd jump at the chance, and I believe that if any of his friends (and I count myself as one) were to ring him up and say that they urgently needed a thousand pounds to get out of trouble, all he'd say would be,

'Will a cheque do, dear? Because it might take a day or two to raise the cash.'

Fanny did moderate business for ten months and gave me enormous experience. The staff of Drury Lane are legendary for their expertise and their courtesy. I couldn't have been made to feel more welcome if I'd been royalty—or Ivor Novello.

If, however, Robert and I were to ask Sander Gorlinsky, who presented *Fanny* to back us again, I think he'd probably remember a pressing engagement in Nicaragua.

Fanny folded in September 1957 and my theatrical career languished apart from a brief appearance as Pontius Pilate in a production of R. F. Delderfield's *Spark of Judea* in a south London church and a production on television of Shaw's *Arms and the Man*. But a lush *Aladdin* at the London Coliseum got things off to a good start for 1960. The music and lyrics were by Cole Porter. I was the Emperor of China, Aladdin was Bob Monkhouse and Ronnie Shiner was the Widow Twankey. My few dance steps were choreographed by none other than Robert Helpmann, the only person ever to succeed in making me trip a measure for reward. I wasn't in the least surprised when not long afterwards he received a knighthood.

A fairly disastrous, though well paid, pantomime co-starring with Nat Jackley at the Leeds Empire was my reward the following Christmas, but in 1961 came the most significant theatre engagement so far—significant because it was to provide me with a meal ticket, which is still valid. It was a four handed revue called *4 to the Bar*. Bryan Blackburn and Peter Reeves made a major contribution, putting hilariously comic words to well-known tunes, and their wit and satire kept up with current events. Rose Hill, a former opera singer and an accomplished revue and character actress, was saved up for the second half when she and I did a double act written by Joseph Horovitz which consisted of a series of Bournvita commercials in the style of Bach, Mozart, Verdi, Stravinsky and Schoenberg, which I originally performed with April Cantelo at one of the famous

Hoffnung Concerts in the Royal Festival Hall. That was the occasion that inspired the late Sir Neville Cardus to write in the *Manchester Guardian*, 'Mr. Ian Wallace, surely a congenitally unfunny man . . .' When next Gerard Hoffnung invited me to appear in one of his concerts I insisted that that quote appeared under my name in the programme. *4 to the Bar* was devised and produced by Charles Ross and we toured it all over southern England, waiting hopefully for a London theatre. We took it to the Olympia Theatre, Dublin, where it was a riotous success; we did a season at the Arts Theatre Club, returned to Dublin with equally ecstatic results and finally secured the Criterion, where we ran for six months while all around us shows were folding after alarmingly brief runs. Had we not picked one of the worst theatrical seasons on record we might have run much longer. Anthony Bowles played the piano and arranged the music, while John Jobson was a stylish double bass rhythm section. Several of my most successful numbers were written and composed by Vivian Ellis and at the risk of sounding nostalgically mawkish, I must chalk this up as a particularly happy engagement. I wrote my linking dialogue and did the first twenty minutes of the show on my own. Noël Coward came one night, and was kind enough to visit my dressing room afterwards. It was the first and only time we met. He went right through the programme giving marks as if it were an oral exam and finished by saying,

'You have a very good command of your audience. Mind you, anyone who has the hardihood to allow the curtain to rise on them at the Criterion Theatre, sitting in a wing chair with a glass of brandy in one hand and a cigar in the other, has bloody well *got* to have command of his audience!'

It was a kind of accolade and made me realize that I only needed a bit of courage to do a one-man show. That conversation was my first step towards *An Evening with Ian Wallace*.

Since *4 to the Bar* there are only three other theatrical ventures to mention. Christmas 1964 saw me join the long line of Toads in *Toad of Toad Hall* at the Queen's Theatre. It's a hell of a strenuous part and requires the sort of bravado necessary to drive at 80 m.p.h. the wrong way down a motorway with headlights undipped and the horn blaring. In 1965 I played Bottom in *Midsummer Night's Dream* at the Yvonne Arnaud Theatre,

Guildford. The notices were good, the laughter for the play within the play fairly resounding, but somehow the opening was never capitalized. There are those who discount a success as Bottom saying that any comedian can play it, and one Bottom doesn't add up to a Shakespearean actor. They're probably right.

The week that England were battling for the World Cup at Wembley in 1966 I was at the Watford Theatre doing another of my serious parts, The Public Executioner in Durrenmatt's one-act play *Conversation at Night*. There are just two parts and the other was played by André Van Gyseghem. On the Saturday when England were playing in the final with West Germany we sat and watched the match, dressed and made up for the five o'clock matinee. Imagine our horror when the match went to extra time and we had to go on stage! I loved doing this absorbing play and was interested to note that when it was presented on B.B.C. TV they entrusted the parts to Sir Ralph Richardson and Sir John Gielgud. I hope that Durrenmatt at Watford was not the end of my theatrical career. I have a feeling that there may be more to come, especially as England won!

I won't attempt to enumerate or classify my radio appearances over the same period. They have been numerous to say the least. The B.B.C., bless them, have always been my most faithful and consistent employers. After the studio operas came to an end in the early 1950s, there were still opera concerts and potted versions of operas produced in London, Manchester, Birmingham and Cardiff, as well as operettas and musical comedies like *Tom Jones* and *Chu Chin Chow*. I also found myself compering long series of variety programmes at the Paris or the Playhouse, in which I would have a singing spot, introduce the items, take part in sketches or playlets and even sometimes feed a comic. I recall one long series, *Follow the Stars* with Tony Fane and David Evans as my fellow residents. Each week we were hosts to a glittering array of stars that ran the full gamut from Jack Hulbert and Cicely Courtneidge to Claudio Arrau.

The most prestigious radio series I ever did, apart from *My Music* was *Monday Night At Home*, which was produced by John Bridges, who sprang from an unlikely reservoir of cultural activity, the Brigade of Guards. He found a wealth of excellent recorded material—some of it on disc, some specially commissioned; it was my job to link it—and my orders from John were to make my links 'As dry as a martini'. There were always a few pieces of music in the programme and these were chosen by Robert Irwin, who had been the singer in an earlier and most popular series, *Country Magazine*. I can say no more than that Robert had a complete sureness of touch. Our contributors included the late Lord Birkett, C. Gordon Glover, Walter Flesher, the modest but wondrously eloquent Yorkshire gamekeeper, who could take you on a morning walk through the Dales and make you smell the woodsmoke and hear the pheasants. There was Patrick Campbell, long before *Call My Bluff*, Cecile Shevreau, Piers Stephens, and Paul McDowell, Ivor Cutler, Peter Bull, Jonathan Miller and René Cutforth—a totally incomplete list. I still recall a wonderful piece René did about transporting pigs in Chinese junks on journeys of several days, which was made possible by giving each porker a plug of opium and stacking them, blissfully unconscious, one on top of the other for the journey. He suggested that this was the answer to boring air travel for nervous humans. Anaesthetize us all in our hotel, engage a lawyer to handle our passports, and let us wake in a hotel bed at our destination. There was a further bonus. The pigs all lost weight—and therefore, without the bore of dieting, so would we. That was the sort of thing that *Monday Night At Home* rejoiced in.

Our fan mail differed a little from the normal run. For instance there was a retired university don in Oxfordshire, who wrote me most weeks giving his marks for the programme. It was usually alpha minus, and when we slipped to beta plus, John Bridges and I felt it was time to look out.

In the 1960s I had two long, happy series of *Pride of the Pacific* produced by Vernon Harris and starring the Australian actor Bill Kerr—one of the funniest men it's ever been my luck to work with. A great tester of the stomach muscles is Bill. It was an adventure series about a trading schooner in the Pacific Islands. The engineer was the late lamented Duncan McIntyre and I played Tanenui, the Tahitian first mate, speaking like a retarded brother of Paul Robeson and singing each week a Tahitian song arranged for guitar accompaniment by James Moodie. Each episode was complete in itself and there was never a bad one. The only female aboard was the owner of the schooner, played by a delightful Scots actress called Christina

Gray, making her radio debut. The writer was Rex Rienits, who had been responsible for one of the most successful adventure series ever, *The Flying Doctor*, which had also featured Bill Kerr. We followed *Pride* with another series called *Charter Pilot*, but you can't hope to do it twice running, and that was that.

I've also introduced all manner of record programmes, as well as compering several series with the B.B.C. Concert Orchestra. I used to crop up on the old *Housewives' Choice* and, at the Radio 3 end of the business, there have been quite a few ballad operas and features in which I've been involved. I've done a couple of Gilbert and Sullivan Proms as well as a number of light music festivals at the Royal Festival Hall, and I also work for the British Forces Broadcasting Service as a light classical disc jockey on a fairly regular basis.

Throughout all this quarter century I've paid regular visits to Scotland for the B.B.C., and until his death four years ago there was one person who kept my name alive in the north both on radio and television. Eddie Fraser brought me up for countless programmes, featuring me as a singer in my own right, or as a guest to Kenneth McKellar, Moira Anderson, or Helen McCarthur in the many series he presented for these splendid Scots artists. Eddie wasn't just concerned with turning out programmes. He had the smell of greasepaint in his nostrils, and was on the lookout for talent that he could direct towards the star dressing-room with the help of radio and television exposure. He could be a close friend and yet not lose his professional detachment about your performance. He was one of the very few B.B.C. producers with whom I exchanged Christmas cards —I knew he didn't think I was angling for a job—and he would have been sympathetic if I had!

Television? Let's take the B.B.C. first. I started at Ally Pally as I've already said with *The Anatomist* and *The Good Companions*. In the early 1950s I often appeared in an afternoon series called *Leisure and Pleasure*, presided over by Jeanne Heal and talked about opera with the odd sung excerpt thrown in for good measure. I wonder what the tired housewives for whom the programme catered made of that. I did many shows for children including *1066 and All That*, *Alice through the Looking Glass*, and I told stories to under fives in *Playschool* years later, stories I wrote myself about donkeys and mice. I must have caught the animal bug from Michael and Donald. I remember a good many variety shows, which used to be called TV Spectaculars. I was twice on Eric Robinson's famous *Music For You*, once disappearing down a manhole singing 'Down Below' and another time perpetrating that Flanders and Swann number about an Italian gondolier on the Manchester Ship Canal. I played Pat Kirkwood's father when she portrayed Marie Lloyd, and I found myself with Ginger Rogers, David Hughes, and Warren Mitchell in an operetta called *Carissima*, in which Eric Maschwitz allowed me to write a second verse to one of his songs I had to sing, which the director, Francis Essex thought was too short.

Then there were the opera relays from Glyndebourne and the Cambridge, yet—and here's an odd thing—it wasn't until last year, 1974, that I appeared in a studio produced opera—*The Marriage of Figaro*—though I had done Pooh Bah in *The Mikado* a few months earlier. That must have been all right because it had approving letters from the Dean of Windsor and my old headmaster, Sir Robert Birley.

In Scotland I worked almost as much on TV as on radio for Eddie, and I was the first compere of a delightful programme called *The Kilt is My Delight*. In the latter days of that programme, with its gracious Scottish Country Dancing and traditional songs, I returned for a long series produced by the late Alan Rees. Every programme included a Harry Lauder medley, and for the only time in my life I had a full size photo on the front page of *The Radio Times* (Scots edition only!)

I think it's true to say that commercial television has, on balance, had a more vital influence on my career. After *Fanny* the first starring engagement I got was a series with Associated Rediffusion called *The Jubilee Show*, produced by Peter Croft, for whom I'd earlier done several revue programmes at the Walham Green studio with Max Adrian and Betty Marsden. *The Jubilee Show* was a fast moving Edwardian music hall, which I chaired, making the odd quick change to contribute vocal items like George Robey's 'In Other Words' and a refined ditty entitled 'I Can't Do My Bally Bottom Button Up'. Round about that time (1958) the list of my recordings in the Classical Record Catalogue began with LPs of *La Cenerentola*, *Le Nozze di Figaro*, Busoni's *Arlecchino* and *Le Comte Ory*, all with

Glyndebourne and *The Mikado* and *Iolanthe* conducted by Sir Malcolm Sargent, *Sosarme* by Handel conducted by Sir Anthony Lewis and—'I Can't Do My Bally Bottom Button Up'.

In the middle 1960s I did a happy series for Southern Television, *Big Sing*—a gladiatorial contest between school choirs with pop singers and county music advisers acting as judges. I sang with these highly competitive young people accompanied by such stalwarts as Robert Docker, William Davies, and Mary Dickie—Bill Dickie's wife.

When Francis Essex left the B.B.C. to become Controller of Programmes at Scottish Television, he gave me two series in quick succession, *Theatre Royal*, a variety show with the emphasis on music and *Man Behind The Star*, which involved me in interviewing at some length a fascinating cross section of the stars of show business including Frankie Vaughan, Roy Castle, Bruce Forsyth, Andy Stewart and Tony Hancock. This was something completely outside my previous experience and I enjoyed it. Unfortunately it never penetrated beyond Scotland because one of the English companies came up with a similar series called, I think, *The Laughtermakers*, so ours never had a hope in hell of being networked. But by far the most important television assignment to come my way was the invitation from Scottish Television to write and present three series of half-hour programmes on opera called *Singing For Your Supper*. In all this involved me in thirty programmes. The original idea came from Murray Dickie with whom I went to see Francis Essex. In the event Murray's Vienna commitments prevented him from following up the idea, but he generously left it to me. Happily, he was able to come over and take part in some of them. Though they were financed by the adult education budget and written to bring opera to the notice of a wider public, Brian Mahoney, the director, and I were determined to make the programmes entertaining in their own right. The second series was networked extensively outside Scotland, but the third, which was in colour and much more ambitiously conceived, came at a time when the Government levy on TV profits put any national networking of the programmes out of the question. Peter Hemmings, the General Administrator of Scottish Opera, publicly stated that *Singing For Your Supper* had had a markedly favourable effect on their box-office receipts.

With all this patchwork of constant activity how did my opera career fare? Well, throughout the 1950s all went well. I returned to Glyndebourne year after year and to Edinburgh as long as Glyndebourne went there. Even after such an aberration as *Fanny* they took me back to do revivals of *La Cenerentola* at Glyndebourne and *Arlecchino* at Edinburgh in 1960 and *The Barber* in 1961. In 1963 we recorded the latter with Victoria de los Angeles and Luigi Alva—a recording which still holds its place in the catalogue more than a decade later. I had had a wonderful run with Glyndebourne, but that was it—apart from doing Dr. Dulcamara in *L'elisir d'amore* in 1968, the first year of the Glyndebourne Touring Opera, with two marvellous young singers Jill Gomez and Ryland Davies—and a motley selection of donkeys which pulled on my caravan in Newcastle, Sheffield, Liverpool, Manchester, and Oxford. Being, as I've said before, optimistic by nature I hope I shall appear again in that fold of the Sussex downs before I hang up my larynx—but if I don't, I can have no complaints. They've given me as much work as any singer could wish for and taught me enough to see me through the rest of my career. After the B.B.C., there's no organization that's given me so much.

For two or three years after my last performance at Glyndebourne itself my opera career was somewhat in the doldrums until Scottish Opera came along and took me under their wing, where—on and off—I've remained ever since, though Phoenix (*The Barber*) and the Welsh National (*Don Pasquale*) have been kind enough to enlist my services from time to time. Scottish Opera allow me to get some of my old warhorses out of the stable, but have given me several opportunities to get my teeth into something new like Leporello in *Don Giovanni*, Pistola in *Falstaff*, and the Duke of Plaza Toro in *The Gondoliers*. But as I look back on my opera career to date I am often reminded of the fact that dear Maestro Gui, now approaching his ninetieth birthday, was prepared to risk a Scots buffo in so many important places when he had all the singers in Europe to choose from.

Have there been any other activities? Well, er, yes. I've done quite a bit of private function cabaret, writing my own material here and there, though this isn't a form of entertainment I feel is really my métier. I'm a little too old and old fashioned for it.

Above: Robert Morley and Ian as *Panisse* and *César* in the last scene of *Fanny*, Drury Lane, 1957.
Below: As *The Cobbler* in the MGM film *Tom Thumb*, directed by George Pal.

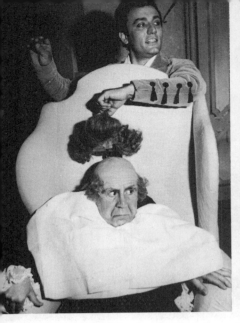

Above left: As *Dr Bartolo* again at the Bregenz Festival.
Above right: Ian and Joanna Peters as *The Duke and Duchess of Plaza Toro* in *The Gondoliers*, produced by Joan Cross for Scottish Opera.
Below: The cast of *Four to the Bar* about to do a show for the prisoners in Wandsworth Gaol, 1961. Left to right: Peter Reeves, Ian, Rose Hill, and Bryan Blackburn.

I lecture a bit when asked, usually on operatic subjects, and now and again I get offered quite healthy sums to speak after dinner, which makes it rather stupid to speak after dinner for nothing, though chums expect it, and sometimes succeed in their expectation.

But, as I've said, in the last decade I've given up waiting for the shadow and gladly accept the substance. In other words, I accept the concert offers months ahead and shrug off the outside chance of the musical or the film that almost certainly won't come anyway. By far the greatest number of the concert offers are for my one man show, *An Evening with Ian Wallace*. This was originally inspired by *4 to the Bar* and it didn't happen overnight. It gradually evolved from a normal recital with spoken introductions between songs into a much more relaxed evening, which draws together all the various strands of my career. I sing songs that vary from operatic arias to comic ditties and talk to the audience in much the same way as I've been talking to you in this book. It's sometimes described as 'a lighthearted look at the pleasures and the hazards of a singer's life'. David Money, my old friend and accompanist has been a great help in compiling the programmes and playing for me all over the country. Not only is he a skilled and sensitive accompanist, he laughs at my stories, which he's heard hundreds of times, and he's the perfect travelling companion, enthusiastically falling in with one's plans for the day, be they energetic or achingly boring. I couldn't have done it without him.

It's only fair to add that the arts centre in Scotland where I've done more versions of my evening than any other—at least four!—belongs to my publisher, John Calder. His house Ledlanet, near Milnathort and Kinross, has become a crucible into which greatly diverse talents have been introduced with exciting consequences for artists as well as stimulating and entertaining results for the public. I hope that by the time these words are published Ledlanet will have overcome its structural problems and be once more catering for an ever increasing public.

Have I had any disappointments? Of course. I've already mentioned one in connection with the Royal Opera House. Another was inevitable. When Glyndebourne first planned to present *Falstaff* they offered it to me before anyone else.

Undeniably it was just a little too high, so I had, with infinite regret, to turn it down. Had I accepted I might have got away with it—but one thing's for sure. I wouldn't have had my voice intact today. As Billy Drew told me all those years ago at Cambridge, singing's like boxing; you've got to do it at your correct weight.

Do I suffer from nerves? Always—and a first performance is agonizing in prospect. Incidentally, it's a complete myth that you are all right once you get started. Most professionals I know are trembling from head to foot while singing a big aria in public for the first time—and the second time as well. This would be a marvellous profession if you could have a written guarantee from the Almighty that your memory would never let you down in public. The snag is that it would take all the tension out of the performance and the public would soon lose interest in such smug, overconfident individuals standing before them.

Am I away from home a great deal? Yes I am, but not usually for more than two or three days at a time, though last winter I had a two month stretch with only four nights in my own bed. When away I usually stay in hotels or with very old friends like the Duffuses in Aberdeen, who understand that someone who does my job needs to relax completely and be treated as one of the family. Sometimes hospitality is offered by the folk who've organized the concert, which is a kind and thoughtful gesture designed to save the artist expense and give him or her a homely feeling, which cannot be experienced in a hotel. The trouble is that one of the great strains of this job is always having to meet new people and get on good terms with them. Therefore, a hotel, where you can disappear into the obscurity of your room has much to commend it. Best of all is when it's possible to get home after the concert. Provided some of the journey is motorway and the weather forecast is not too unpromising, I'll make a bid for home from as far away as 150 miles. Many singers I know will come even further. I'm also a habitué of overnight sleepers, which save time and hotel bills. The itinerary and the way one carries it out has to be influenced by one vital consideration. It's not fair on the public to arrive for an engagement dead beat. To avoid this it's sometimes necessary to refuse an engagement on a day when you're free, because to get there

232

Above: A scene from *Falstaff:* Francis Egerton as *Bardolpho*, Sir Geraint Evans as *Falstaff* and Ian Wallace as *Pistola: Below:* Ian Wallace as *Dr Dulcamara* in *L'Elisir d'amore* by Donizetti, Glyndebourne Touring Opera 1968. Others are Jill Gomez as *Adina*, Ryland Davies as *Nemocino* and Terence Sharp as *Belcore*.

Ian Wallace in his one man show.   (*Photograph by Stuart Robinson*).

would involve the sort of schedule they impose for the Monte Carlo Rally.

Nothing whatsoever that Pat and I did in the 1950s could compare with our decision after ten years of marriage, to adopt two children, both at the age of six weeks, Rosemary in 1958, John in 1960. I won't embarrass them by describing their achievements in detail beyond saying that having them around is the joy of our lives.

What, you may be wondering, do we as a family do in our spare time? Well, Pat is a great gardener and, *not* in her spare time, she's one of those people whose life is dedicated to looking after her family; having seen, and enjoyed, it being done impeccably for twenty-seven years, I rather wonder about those ladies you hear on the telly and radio saying they've done all the chores by nine o'clock in the morning, and must find some other job to fill in the rest of the day; but I'd better pipe down before I'm accused of being a male chauvinist pig. Rosemary is good at tennis and supports Arsenal Football Club through thick and thin, as I do; John is pretty good at any game he sets his mind to, and is learning the tenor saxophone. I enjoy golf, taking photographs and very rudimentary sailing in a ten-foot fibreglass dinghy in light winds. We have a little holiday house on the north Norfolk coast at West Runton that we don't get to nearly as often as we'd like—and that's about it.

This book has taken me five years of odd moments. Some of it has been written in trains, some in hotel bedrooms—but, like a pavement artist, I can boast that it's all my own work. I don't believe in ghosts. I've squashed twenty-five years into this last chapter because so many showbiz autobiographies seem to lose their fascination when you get to the montage of playbills, name dropping, and anecdotage, which seems to set in once the career gets under way. On the other hand, if you'd like the name dropping and anecdotage of the twenty-five years in rather greater detail, I'm quite prepared, after a rest, to have a go at Vol. 2. There's the pilot film with Buster Keaton, the T.U.C. Centenary, starring Vic Feather, to say nothing of the Stage Golfing Society dinners with Bob Hope and Edward Heath, which might amuse you for a paragraph or two. But I'm warning you, I shan't bother to take the cover off the typewriter unless at least six people buy a copy of this one!

233

At my age all sorts of interesting things could still happen to me as a member of such an unpredictable profession. I'm only sure of one thing. So long as I'm singing in public, there will always be somebody who'll come up to me before the concert—it's even happened before the opera—and say,

'Promise me you'll sing, "Mud".'

FINIS

Index

Money, David: 211, 231.
Mongelli, Andrea: 168, 174.
Monkhouse, Bob: 223.
Montague, Bert: 201.
Moodie, James: 226.
Morison, Elsie: 196, 220.
Morley, Robert: 125, 221–3, *230*.
Mother Goose: 214.
Mozart, Wolfgang Amadeus: 174, 185, 193, 203–8, 212, 228, 230.
Muir, Frank: 209.
Murdoch, Bryden: 125.
Music for You: 228.
Mussorgsky, Modest: 152–3, 214.
My Music: 209–11.

N

Nash, Heddle: 196.
New London Opera Company, The: 147, 152–3.
New Theatre (now Albery): 131.
Nicholls, Anthony: 79.
Night Bell, The: 214.
Night in Venice, A: 152–3.
Nilsson, Birgit: 176.
Noble, Dennis: 196.
Noni, Alda: *153*, 160, 163, 216.
Norden, Dennis: 209.
Nowakowski, Marian: 164
Nozze di Figaro, Le: 193, 212, 228.

O

O'Donnell, Josephine: 144.
O'Donovan, Fred: 188.
Old Vic Theatre Company: 131.
Olivier, Laurence: 131–3.
Olrich, April: 221.
Olympia Theatre, Dublin: 224.
Oncina, Juan: 216.
One Damn Thing After Another: 16.
Orchard, Julian: 221.
Ord, Boris (Bernhard): 41.

P

Park, Phil: 91, 200.
Park Theatre: 123–4.
Partridge, John: 112.
Patrick, John: 220.
Pauvre Matelot: 214.
Pay the Piper: 221.
Perfect Fool, The: 196.
Perry, Ronald: 163, 184.

Peters, Joanna: *231*.
Phoenix Opera: 217, 230.
Picchi, Mirto: 173.
Pini, Anthony: 193.
Pinza, Ezio: 221.
Players' Theatre, The: 137.
Playschool: 227.
Polman, Professor: 167.
Pomeroy, Jay: 151–9, 166, 190.
Pope, Stanley: 155, 165–6.
Porter, Cole: 223.
Priestley, J. B.: 188.
Pride of the Pacific: 226.
Prince Igor: 196, 213.
Princes' Theatre, London (now The Shaftesbury): 200, 214.
Prokofiev, Sergei: 196.
Promenade Concerts, Henry Wood: 220, 227.
Puccini, Giacomo: 147, 148, 155, 160–1.

Q

Queen's Theatre: 224.

R

Race, Steve: 209.
Rameau, Jean-Philippe: 196.
Rankl, Karl: 145.
Ravina, Rachele: 173.
Redmond, Liam: 187.
Rees, Alan: 228.
Reeves, Peter: *221*, 223.
Renton, Edward: 173.
Revnell, Ethel: 214.
Ribbentrop, J. von: 35.
Richardson, Sir Ralph: 131–3, 225.
Rienits, Rex: 227.
Riddle, Frederick: 193.
Rigoletto: 169, 173.
Robey, George: 161.
Robinson, Eric: 196, 228.
Robinson, Stanford: 142, 194–7.
Rogers, Ginger: 228.
Rome, Harold: 221.
Rome Opera House: 218.
Ross, Charles: 224.
Rossini, Gioacchino: 166–70, 215, 216, 230.
Rothmuller, Marko: 172.
Royal Command Performance: 219–20.
Royal Festival Hall: 224, 227.

239